Capitalism and Dependence

Agrarian Politics in Western Uttar Pradesh 1951 – 1991

Capitalism and Dependence

Agrarian Politics in Western Uttar Pradesh 1951 – 1991

JAGPAL SINGH

MANOHAR

1992

ISBN: 81-7304-026-5

First Published 1992

Published by
Ajay Kumar Jain
Manohar Publishers & Distributors
2/6 Ansari Road, Daryaganj
New Delhi - 110 002

Lasertypeset by
Ankit Computers Inc.
Flat No.56, Plot No.85
Trilokya Adarsh Kunj
Patparganj, Delhi

Printed at
Elegant Printers
A-38/2 Maya Puri Phase-I
New Delhi-110 064

To the memory of

my father who gave me the first insight into village dynamics

Preface

This book is an attempt to analyse the relationships between the changing agrarian relations and politics in Meerut district of western Uttar Pradesh from 1951 to 1991. The book is a thoroughly revised version of my Ph.D. thesis submitted at Jawaharlal Nehru University (JNU), New Delhi, in 1988. The period following the field-work for Ph.D. in 1984-85 was marked by certain significant developments in western Uttar Pradesh. The Bharatiya Kisan Union (BKU) emerged as a force in 1986/87 and it drew nation-wide attention. Almost at the same time, the Bharatiya Mazdoor Union (BMU), Dalit Sena and Shoshit Mukti Vahini also emerged. In 1990-91, the Bharatiya Janata Party (BJP) emerged as a force to reckon with in the villages of western Uttar Pradesh. The BKU mobilised the market-oriented peasantry and the BMU/the Dalit Sena/the Shoshit Mukti Vahini mobilised the rural poor, mainly belonging to the Chamar caste. Their activities became more intense from 1988 onwards. The BJP mobilised almost all agrarian classes belonging to the Hindus on the issues pertaining to the Ayodhya dispute in the 1991 general election. The BKU, the BMU/the Dalit Sena/the Shoshit Mukti Vahini and their activities and post-Ayodhya developments could not form part of the Ph.D. thesis. The book is an improvement in that it is updated to include these recent developments and the conclusion has been written afresh. In addition, changes to varying degrees have been made in all chapters. The postscript has been written to cover the post-Ayodhya developments.

The book does not make any comprehensive and conclusive statement about these developments as they are still unfolding themselves. It, however, captures those aspects of the developments about which it is feasible to make a relatively more conclusive and authentic statement.

Many persons have contributed to the completion of this book. I am thankful to all of them. I am particularly grateful to Premi brothers of Meerut – late Mr. Rattan Kumar Premi and Mr. Virendra Kumar Premi – who showed me the back volumes of Panchayati Raj with hospitality, my respondents in the villages and Mr Yogesh Sharma, Dr G. R. Malik, Com. Musaddilal, late Master Pitam Singh Rathi, Mr Tejpal Singh, Chaudhary Mahendra Singh Tikait, President of the BKU and Mr Jai Pal Singh Mitharia, President of the BMU, who helped me during my field work. I am also thankful to late Chaudhary Charan Singh, ex-Prime Minister of India, for allowing me to consult his private papers and his P.A. Mr. Ram Atur, for his help. I thank the staff of different government offices in Meerut, the JNU Library, the Nehru Memorial Museum and Library, New Delhi, for providing constant co-operation.

I am thankful to my Ph.D. Supervisor, Dr Zoya Hasan, and Prof. C.P. Bhambhri who has always been a source of fatherly encouragement to me, and Professors S.N. Jha and Kuldeep Mathur, Centre for Political Studies, JNU, New Delhi; I am also thankful to Professors G. S. Bhalla, M. H. Qureshi, Centre for the Studies of Regional Development, JNU, New Delhi; Professor Utsa Patnaik, Centre for Economic Studies and Planning, JNU, New Delhi, and Professors Pandav Nayak and Kapil Kumar, Indira Gandhi National Open University, New Delhi. I thank Pratap, Onkar, Baskaran and Nandini, who helped me in various ways. Finally, I am also thankful to the anonymous reader of the publisher for insightful suggestions.

I need not mention the help and co-operation given to me by my family members, especially my mama.

Department of Political Science, JAGPAL SINGH
Indira Gandhi National Open University,
New Delhi
January 1992

Contents

List of Tables

Abbreviations

AIKCC	All India Kisan Co-ordination Committee
BDO	Block Development Officer
BJP	Bharatiya Janata Party
BKD	Bharatiya Kranti Dal
BLD	Bharatiya Lok Dal
BSP	Bahujan Samaj Party
CLRC	Central Land Reforms Committee
CPI	Communist Party of India
DMKP	Dalit Mazdoor Kisan Party
HYV	High Yielding Variety
IADP	Intensive Agriculture District Programme
IRDP	Integrated Rural Development Programme
Janata (S)	Janata (Secular)
Janata (SC)	Janata (Secular, Charan Singh)
JD	Janata Dal
KMPP	Kisan Mazdoor Praja Party
LD	Lok Dal
MP	Mazdoor Party
NCO	Indian National Congress (Organisation)
OBCs	Other Backward Castes/Classes
PSP	Praja Socialist Party
RPI	Republican Party of India
SCs	Scheduled Castes
SP	Socialist Party
SSP	Samyukta Socialist Party
UPCC	Uttar Pradesh Congress Committee
UPZACR	Report of the Zamindari Abolition Committee, U.P.
VLW	Village Level Worker

Glossary

Bhaichara : An agrarian system marked by the absence of an intermediary between independent peasant proprietors and the state
Bhainsia : Buffalo-keeper
Begar : Unpaid labour
Benami : Fictitious
Bitoda : Heap of dung-cakes
Chaudhary : Chief
Dangwara : Co-operation
Dola : Boundary of a field
Dudhia : Milkman
Fatwa : Religious decree
Gaon Samaj : Village Community
Halsot : A pair of bulls and a plough
Hissa : Share
Hissedar : A person who works for a share
Imam : Religious head among Muslims
Kacha : House or well built of unbaked bricks or mud
Karinda : A person who collected land rent for the landlord
Kar Seva : Religious Service
Kar Sevak : A person who renders religious service
Kamin : A person belonging to lower social and economic order
Khap : Clan Council
Lai : Practice of harvesting wheat for wages in kind
Lava : A person who practises lai
Moodha : A field with left over roots of sugarcane plants
Nazrana : Allowance
Patwari : Village record keeper
Peshagi : Advance
Pooly : Sheaf
Pradhan : Head of the village elected body
Pukka : House or well built of baked bricks
Riaya : Subjects
Sarva Khap : An institution consisting of all Khaps

Shamlat	:	Common land
Sila	:	Practice of collecting left over wheat plants after harvest on a share basis.
Stridhan	:	The property of a woman or wife over which, under ordinary circumstance, she has independent control.
Wazir	:	Secretary.

Chapter I

Introduction

The political economy of India has witnessed two significant developments during the post-independence period. First, the introduction of universal adult franchise and democratic institutions broadened the base of politics to all classes of society. Second, the state intervened in the agrarian economy through different measures: land reforms, Community Development Programme, Agricultural Extension Scheme, Green Revolution, Integrated Rural Development Programme (IRDP), the 20-point programme, etc. The state intervention accelerated the process of various developments in agrarian economy, which had begun during the colonial period.

The introduction of capitalist tendencies and the institutions of democracy have generated both class and non-class issues and fora for the mobilisation and politicisation of agrarian classes. The classes belonging to the rural rich can articulate their interests, dictate terms to the political leaders and parties, get votes cast or prevent votes from being cast through booth capturing and other undemocratic means and play a decisive and domineering role in the agrarian society. On the other hand, classes belonging to the rural poor, despite the formal availability of the institutions of democracy - courts, police, adult franchise (formal option to cast votes), *etc.*, are the victims of the rural rich. Such problems of undemocratic nature remain unabated. Phenomena of rural tension, caste conflict, rural unrest, forcible occupation of land, violence, booth capturing and atrocities against the rural poor, mainly the scheduled castes and lower OBCs (including women) are recurrent in the agrarian society of India. Atrocities against the rural poor are not confined to the "feudal" and "backward" states like Bihar. They are prevalent even in the areas where capitalism has developed to a significant extent. In fact, "most sustained anti-dalit campaigns and mass riots have taken place" in "semi-capitalist regions" and "capitalist states" of western Uttar Pradesh, Punjab, Haryana, Marathwada and Gujarat.[1] In Meerut, like in many other districts of western Uttar Pradesh, the conflict between the rural rich and the rural poor, harassment, oppression and exploitation of the rural poor are not mainly related to the issue of wages of agricultural labourers. That is so despite the development of capitalist tendencies in agriculture. The most important reasons for the prevalence of such problems can be found in the nature of relationships of dependence between the rural rich and the rural poor. But unlike the patron-client relationships these relationships are not based on the "paternalistic" and "moralistic" principles. They affect the social, economic and political life of village society. The mode of production debate was the most important one which discussed the agrarian system in the Indian context.[2] But this debate overlooked certain social and political dimensions of the agrarian society in India. The nature of changes in the agrarian relations affect politics and vice-versa. Therefore, the study of the relationships between agrarian relations and politics becomes necessary in a society dominated by agrarian economy. Western Uttar Pradesh provides an interesting universe for studying the relationships between agrarian relations and politics. With developed means of production and commercialisation of crops, Meerut district presents a particularly important case to be studied.

This book is an attempt to analyse the major issues related to the agrarian economy and politics at two levels, *i.e.*, district and village. At the district level, it focuses on the changes which have taken place in the agrarian society of Meerut and the mobilisation of agrarian classes by political parties, pressure groups and some individuals. At the village level, it attempts to analyse the changes which reflect the district level agrarian economy and their impact on the non-electoral politics. It also attempts to identify and analyse the social bases of political parties. It focuses upon the followings aspects :

(1) The changes which have taken place in the agrarian economy of Meerut district as a result of the state intervention through the Acts related to the zamindari abolition, consolidation of and ceiling on landholdings, Community Development Programme, Agricultural Extension Scheme, Green Revolution, IRDP, the 20-point programme and other package deals in terms of -
   (i) the forces of production: instruments of cultivation, transportation, irrigation, the use of seeds and fertilizers, and the human labour;
   (ii) developments in the conditions of production: expansion and commercialisation of agriculture and
   (iii) pattern of the ownership of land and general socio-economic relations, and the processes of exploitation and differentiation of the peasantry.

(2) Differentiation within the agrarian society of Meerut district at the village level: distribution of the means of production amongst classes, classwise cropping pattern, market relations of the classes and their material conditions including indebtedness, etc.

(3) Social and economic relationships among the agrarian classes, and their implications for non-electoral politics at the village level (dependence, resistance and sanctions).

(4) The issues of the agrarian classes which emerged as a result of changes in the political economy, mobilisation of classes on their respective issues by the Socialists (SP, PSP, SSP), the Communist Party of India, the BKD/Lok Dal, RPI, BKU, BMU/Dalit Sena/ Shoshit Mukti Vahini, some independent leaders and activists and finally the role of the Congress.

(5) Social bases of the political parties: Congress/Congress (I) and Lok Dal.

Meerut district lies in the centre of Meerut division. It is surrounded by Bijnor and Moradabad in the east, Punjab and Delhi in the west, Muzaffarnagar in the north and Ghaziabad in the south. It has an area of 3,911 sq. kms. It consists of 4 tahsils, *viz*. Meerut, Mawana, Baghpat and Sardhana. Meerut district assumed its present shape on 14 November 1976, when Ghaziabad was created as a separate district. Pre-1976 Meerut consisted of 6 tahsils, namely Ghaziabad, Hapur, Meerut, Mawana, Baghpat and Sardhana. The importance of Meerut lies in the fact that it has witnessed the introduction of the Green Revolution, and it has provided a very strong social base to the Lok Dal. Moreover, historically Meerut's agrarian economy was distinct as it was dominated by the bhaiachara.[3]

The period from 1951 to 1991 is significant for our study because during this period, unlike the colonial period, measures in the agrarian sector were introduced by the state government which is a part of the sovereign republic. It is also significant because universal adult franchise made every section of agrarian society an inalienable part of the political processes. Such a long period provides enough space for a proper understanding of the social, economic and political processes. The late 1980s are of a special significance because during this period the BKU has emerged as a strong force which has placed Meerut in the category of regions, like Punjab, Maharashtra, Gujarat, Karnataka and Tamil Nadu, which have witnessed the assertion by the rich and middle peasants for their demands during the late 1970s and 1980s.

Apart from getting information on agrarian and political aspects at the district level from the government publications; gazetteers, settlement reports, district statistical handbooks and census reports, local and national newspapers, information has also been gathered from the pamphlets and demand charters of the BKU and the BMU, Charan Singh's private papers, interviews and field work. The field work was conducted in three phases - first, in 1984-85 in eight villages of Meerut district for my Ph.D., second between January 1988 and December 1990, and third in September 1991.

In 1984-85, two villages were selected from each of the four tahsils of Meerut district. Jalalabad Urf Jalalpur and Jafarnagar Begamabad villages from Sardhana tahsil, Nagla Tashi Qasimpur and Chobla villages from Meerut tahsil, Ahera and Tilwara Sakin villages from Baghpat tahsil and Behzadka and Jaisinghpur villages from Mawana tahsil were selected for the field survey. From each tahsil, one village represented the average number of agricultural labourers of that tahsil and another village represented the average number of cultivators of that tahsil. Average number of agricultural labourers and cultivators of a tahsil was the criterion of selection of the villages because of our perspective. We believe that a correct understanding and identification of classes and relationships among them will help us explain the politics of agrarian society. The 1971 Census has been the source for the selection of villages. The 1981 Census was not available on the eve of the field work. The 1971 Census gives data on two main agrarian classes, *i.e.*, agricultural labourers and cultivators. Hence our selection was on the basis of average number of agricultural labourers and cultivators.

Five of these villages are Jat-dominated, two are Gujar-dominated and one is Meena and Tyagi-dominated. As we will see in the subsequent chapters, the agrarian relations in the villages are an off-shoot of their history. There were mainly two types of agrarian systems before the zamindari abolition in Meerut: the bhaiachara and the zamindari. They are discussed in Chapter II. Five villages of the sample have the bhaiachara background, and three of them have the zamindari background. The class relations within these two sets of villages showed differences in the past. The vicinity of a village to the main city and the availability of an alternative means of livelihood to the rural poor affect the relations in the villages. The villages which were marked by these factors showed difference in the relationships between classes from those in the villages which lacked them. Two of the villages are in the vicinity of Meerut city, in the range of 5-10 kms. Six of them are situated at far-off distance from the Meerut city, in the range of 20-75 kms. In two of the villages, the rural poor have alternative means of livelihood; in one, tanneries as the cottage industries, in another brick-kiln.

In order to make the survey representative of the trends in the whole district, a stratified sampling of the 20 per cent households in every village, covering each and every caste and class of both Muslims and Hindus, was carried out. In case the number of the households of a particular caste was so minimal that it could not form 20 per cent of the total households (the number of households of such castes being less than 5, since of the 5 households 1 would make 20 per cent), it was adjusted with the percentage of the households which were akin to it socially and economically. In total 455 households have been covered in this survey.

A house to house survey was conducted to collect the data. The person interviewed was either the head of the household or any other responsible person who knew everything about his/her family. The data on the agrarian relations were collected in the questionnaires.[4] But information on political aspects was collected through informal discussions, after having interviewed the respondents on the socio-economic aspects.[5] Besides, almost 50 leaders were interviewed. The leaders included those who contested Lok Sabha and assembly elections between 1952 and 1985, both the defeated and the elected, the leaders of various political parties and the independent candidates.

The second phase of the field work was conducted in two villages, one each from Meerut and Moradabad districts in June 1988 (in the village of Moradabad district we conducted survey even in March 1988); the village Bhagwanpur under Mawana tahsil of Meerut district and village Jagua Khurd under Amroha tahsil of Moradabad district. Stratified sample survey of 15 per cent households of each village including every caste and class was carried out. In both villages 57 households were surveyed. The village in Meerut district has the bhaiachara background and is dominated by Jats and Sainis and the village in Moradabad district has the zamindari background and is dominated by Jats. Both of these villages are located near the sites where the BKU movement/agitation turned violent in 1988. This phase of the field work covered the post-1985 developments. During this phase, we started field work in Meerut, Muzafarnagar and Moradabad districts of western UP in January 1988. We made frequent visits to the villages of these districts, to the very sites of BKU activities (dharna, stay put) during January-February 1988 at Meerut and again during October-November 1988 and on October 2, 1989 in Delhi, held frequent discussions with the people belonging to market-oriented peasantry and the landless proletariat; with the participants and opponents of the agitations and with those who were indifferent to them, conducted interviews with leaders of different factions of the BKU, and the leaders of the BMU and the Dalit Sena.

The third phase of the field work was conducted in order to study the trends which have emerged following the Ayodhya developments (30 October - 2 November 1990) and the factors leading to the rise of the BJP during 1991 general election as a strong political force in the villages. This phase of the field work was conducted in September 1991 in three villages - Jalalpur and Khanauda of Meerut district and Barawala of Muzaffarnagar district. In Jalalpur we had conducted the field work even before; this is one of the 8 villages where we conducted field work for the Ph.D in 1984-85. We held dialogues with 83 respondents during this phase.

This book has been divided into seven chapters, apart from the post-script. Chapters II and III deal with the agrarian (socio-economic) aspects. Chapters IV, V and VI deal with the political aspects.

Notes

1. See Gail Omvedt (ed.), *Land, Caste and Politics in Indian States,* Delhi, Authors Guild Publications, 1982, pp. 9, 35.
2. See Utsa Patnaik (ed.), *Agrarian Relations and Accumulation: The 'Mode of Production, Debate in India,* Bombay, Oxford University Press, 1990; Alice Thorner, "Semi-Feudalism or Capitalism? Contemporary Debate on Classes and Modes of Production in India", *Economic and Political Weekly,* vol, XVII, No.50, 4, 11 and 18 December 1982.
3. See Chapter II, Section I.
4. Bias of a researcher cannot be overlooked on the *modus operandi* of the field work. Generally researchers tend to begin their field works with the rural rich and then they go down to the rural poor. Their field works begin from top to bottom. This, in fact, affects the validity of data. The *modus operandi* of our field work saw a departure from the traditional way. We began our field work from below, from the poorest of the poor, in all villages. We moved from the bottom to the top in an order. We did it because we felt that the lower the rung in the villages, safer it would be to get information on some delicate aspects, *i.e.*, indebtedness and other social and economic aspects. It has been observed that the rural poor know about the rural rich very well, as they are related to them in several ways. Moreover, in case there would have arisen any problem in a village in the process of data collection from the rural rich, the rural poor by then would have furnished most of the relevant information to us. But we did not face any such situation. For advantages of conducting field work from below, see Joan Mencher, "Viewing Hierarchy from the bottom up", in Andre Beteille and T. N. Madan (ed.), *Encounter and Experience : Personal Account of Field work,* Delhi, Vikas, 1975.
5. The Field work is generally full of strange and interesting experiences which in certain respects are detrimental and in certain others a booster to the research. I had to make hard efforts in winning over the confidence of the respondents and removing from their minds the suspicion and doubt about my identity as "a thief looking for the prosperous families in the village with an intention to rob them at night", "CID", "Khupia", "a bearded sardar with dressed hair with the bomb in the bag" and a "sarkari aadmi". I could remove the suspicion from their minds about my identity to a great extent. I could not, however, succeed in using the questionnaires for eliciting political information. But I could extract all the relevant political information from the respondents in my notebooks through informal talks with them.

Chapter II

Agrarian Relations: 1830s–1980s

The agrarian economy of Uttar Pradesh has undergone significant transformation since the introduction of the first land settlements (1793-1856). Development of conditions and forces of production, commercialisation and expansion of agriculture, differentiation and expropriation of the peasantry and such other capitalist tendencies which were introduced in agriculture continued to grow till the 1980s.[1] The laws relating to the abolition of zamindari remained redundant in most parts of Meerut and wherever they were implemented, they consolidated the position of the newly emergent peasant-proprietors *vis-a-vis* the landless classes. And the laws relating to consolidation and ceiling of landholdings benefited the better-off sections of the peasantry. The nature of the agrarian system during the colonial period and changes brought about in the nature of relationships between the land-owning and the landless classes have a bearing on the agrarian politics in the post-independence period.

I

Most parts of Meerut came under British rule in 1803, but it was only after the death of Begum Samru, the owner of Sardhana estate, in 1836, that the whole of Meerut became a part of British India.[2]

There were basically three types of agrarian systems in Uttar Pradesh in the colonial period, *i.e.*, taluqdari, zamindari and bhaiachara. Taluqdari prevailed in the Awadh region,[3] and the most numerous taluqdari lands, outside the Awadh districts, were in Aligarh, Mainpuri, Allahabad and Gorakhpur districts.[4] In the rest of Uttar Pradesh, zamindari estates and the bhaiachara existed together almost everywhere.[5] But the proportion of land under either type varied from one district to another: the Jat-dominated regions of western Uttar Pradesh were marked by the predominance of the bhaiachara[6] and Bareilly had the maximum number of absentee landlords.[7] In Meerut, there were basically two types of agrarian systems, *i.e.*, bhaiachara and zamindari.[8] Generally, these two types of systems existed in different sets of villages, but sometimes both could exist in the same village.

In 1940, almost 83 per cent land in Meerut came under bhaiachara,[9] and 8 per cent under zamindari, and the rest of the land fell under revenue free shamlat, resumed maufi and government property.[10] There were only 26 zamindars in the entire Meerut district responsible for payment of annual revenue between Rs. 5,000 and Rs.37,600, and a majority of them belonged to the Bania castes and Jats.[11] The UPZACR II shows that the smaller and medium "zamindars" (proprietors)[12] who paid a revenue of up to Rs.250 annually in Meerut contributed 72 per cent of the annual revenue, which was the largest in western Uttar Pradesh. It was quite unlike the situation in other districts of western Uttar Pradesh, *i.e.*, Dehradun, Bulandshahar, Aligarh, Agra, Mainpuri, Etah, Bijnor, Moradabad, Shahajahanpur and Pilibhit, where more than 50 per cent of the revenue was paid by the bigger "zamindars", who paid an annual revenue as Rs.250 and above.[13]

The domination of the smaller and medium "zamindars" or that of the bigger "zamindars" corresponded to the bhaiachara and the zamindari respectively. Even in those districts of western Uttar Pradesh which were dominated by the zamindari system, the areas belonging to the peasant communities like Jats were dominated by the bhaiachara.[14]

Legacy of the bhaiachara rendered the need for land reforms much less important in Meerut compared to the zamindari and taluqdari districts of Uttar Pradesh.[15] The present relative predominance of the middle peasants in Meerut owes a lot to the bhaiachara background of the district.[16] Several explanations have been offered for the predominance of bhaiachara in the Upper Doab region. Metcalf argued that scanty and uncertain rainfall and proneness to drought and famine were unfavourable to the growth of a class of zamindars.[17] M. H. Elliot, the first settlement officer of Meerut, pointed out that "during the misrule and organisation of the former governments (pre-British), it was necessary for brotherhood to continue for the purposes of resisting the unlawful encroachments of their neighbours and the attacks of predatory hordes".[18] Moreover, the peasant-proprietors found it more prudent to maintain family farming as a result of the "new prosperity" promised by the introduction of railways and irrigation.[19] Explaining the social origin of the bhaiachara, M. C. Pradhan observes that "this system of land tenure is a Jat idea because Jats did not acknowledge the rights of their chiefs to the sole proprietorship of land conquered and colonized by them".[20] But it spread to other communities as well. At the same time it should be noted that the bhaiachara was more specific to Jats, Gujars and Tyagis, and the zamindari and the taluqdari were more common among Rajputs, Pathans and Saiyids.[21]

The term bhaiachara refers to a system where customs (chara) were observed by a community (bhaia) for the management and distribution of land.[22] The bhaiachara communities settled in an area after occupying and colonising it. They divided this area into groups of 84 villages, 42 villages, or 24 or even 12 or 8. All village affairs were managed by "clan councils" or khaps which had jurisdiction over a group of villages. The headship of the clan was hereditary, and the head was known as chaudhari. Some Jat clans had a hereditary secretary known as wazir.[23]

All clan councils or khaps of all castes formed a sarva khap in the entire Meerut Division.[24] The khaps and sarva khaps were originally Jat affairs, but they became a feature of other castes also.[25] The other castes - Gujars, Rajputs, Tyagis and Pathans (Muslims),[26] carpenters, blacksmiths, potters, barbers, oil pressers, water carriers, jogis and sweepers[27] - also had the khap system. Unlike the khap, the sarva khap council had no hereditary chaudhary nor did it have a hereditary wazir. The wazir of the Baliyan khap had taken interest in the affairs of the sarva khap councils and in organising and summoning of its meetings.[28] The khaps of all the castes were autonomous in relation to the intra-caste affairs. But in case of dispute within the lower castes or important issues concerning them, wazirs and chaudharis of the dominant caste were invited for consultation. The khap councils of Jats or any dominant caste functioned as a political institution, and also as an institution of social control over the non-peasant castes.[29]

Each village was divided for the purpose of revenue collection into pattis and thoks. Pattis were formed on the basis of residential and agricultural land in possession of original colonisers. Each patti was named after an influential person and was inhabited by the descendants of the same lineage group known as thok. More than one thok could inhabit a patti, and sometimes one thok could be spread to more than one patti. Thok was the maximal lineage group in a village, and was divided into sub-thoks which were further divided into the khandans or minimal lineage groups.[30]

A village under the bhaiachara was dominated by the "peasant-proprietors", who descended from the same ancestry, and shared the same fraternity or brotherhood. All peasants in such villages belonged to the same caste.[31] However, even peasants belonging to more than one caste could exist in a village under the bhaiachara. Villages could be distinguished according to peasant castes, *i.e.*, Thakurs, Jats, Ahirs, Gujars and other peasant castes in central Doab.[32] Besides peasant-proprietors, there were other classes in these villages which were categorised as riaya. They generally belonged to non-peasant castes, *i.e.*, service castes, artisans and chamars. The classes that worked on the land and in the households of peasant-proprietors were called kamins.

It should be noted that land was not owned communally in the bhaiachara villages. Under this system the peasant-proprietors had individual and hereditary rights on the land. And the peasant was not free to alienate his land.[33] However, M. C. Pradhan holds the view that the land could be alienated in a patti or thok; but he concedes that the right to alienation did not exist outside the patti or thok.[34] The peasants in the bhaiachara villages controlled land from the time they settled down in a particular area. The area conquered or colonised was equally divided amongst the members of bhaiachara community, and for the distribution of land, they used artificial land measures like "bhaiachara bighas". But the increase in the numbers of descendants and cessation of colonisation in the villages led to the division of the bhaiachara villages into thoks (maximal lineage). Likewise, land was equally divided into thoks and within the thok it was further divided into equal shares among peasants inhabiting a thok.[35] Production was carried out by family members of peasant-proprietors, though sometimes

Jats cultivated land as tenants in one plot and proprietors in another.[36] They are called peasant-proprietors by virtue of their proprietorship over land and the family's participation in production process. It must be noted that though peasant-proprietors carried out production themselves, they were assisted in this process by their riaya, belonging to the castes of chamars, koris, kumhars and malis.[37] But the village community carried out several functions collectively, *i.e.*, paying of land revenue, meeting external challenges to the village community and the employment of patwari during the Mughal period. But the British made a patwari the government servant at the time of first settlement, who till then was a servant of village community.[38]

There is evidence that there were peasant-proprietors in eastern Uttar Pradesh as well, but they differed from the bhaiachara in western Uttar Pradesh and Bundelkhand. While the bhaiachara amongst the Jats of western Uttar Pradesh originated from their tribal character, the peasant-proprietorship among the non-Jat communities of eastern Uttar Pradesh, *i.e.*, Brahmans, Bhumihars and Rajputs resulted from the continuous division of land among heirs in successive generations. This process of generational division of territory reduced the high caste landowners into peasant-proprietors, who would not participate in all agricultural activities.[39] In western Uttar Pradesh, peasant-proprietors belonging to Jats, Gujars, Tyagis did not consider any agricultural activity as a taboo and cultivated the land themselves, unlike the high caste Brahmans, Bhumihars and Rajputs of eastern Uttar Pradesh, whose land was tilled by sub-tenants drawn from "lower castes" of Yadavs, Kurmis, Lodhas and Kachis.[40] This system was marked by the absence of intermediaries between the state and the peasant-proprietors, as a revenue collecting body.[41] Instead, they paid their rent to the state through their representative known as muqaddam or lambardar, who "was at best first among the equals".[42] He "was merely a spokesman of the community always acting according to its will".[43] However, sometimes the muqaddam became a very powerful man achieving the status of a zamindar.[44]

In the bhaiachara system, the peasants were independent-proprietors free from the control of an intermediary between them and the state. This independence gave them the strength to exercise direct social and economic control over the riaya. And the relationship between them and the riaya was like that of the jajmans (masters) to the subjects.[45]

The peasant-proprietors of one patti would generally not intervene in the relationships between the riaya and the jajman of another patti or mahal. The riaya of a patti, the chamars and bhangis in particular, were not allowed to serve the jajman peasant-proprietors of another patti.[46]The riaya did not have the right to own the houses; the ownership of the houses belonged to the jajmans.[47] Our fieldwork shows that they could not avail of the fruits grown on their trees, the vegetables grown by them, or bitoda (heap of dung cakes) without the permission of their jajmans. It should be noted that the riaya did not have proprietary rights on the land. It was the prerogative only of the peasant castes. The riaya in the bhaiachara villages could "never aspire to the status of peasants".[48] The riaya had to render compulsory begar to their jajmans. The terms and conditions for the wages of the riaya who worked in the land were determined by the peasant-proprietors. Refusal to oblige their masters was treated with severe punishment. They were subjected to intimidation and non-economic coercion and were even forcibly evicted from their dwelling places.[49] Thus the riaya lived in a "semi-servile" condition,[50] trapped in bondage to a particular community of peasant-proprietors.

By contrast, the peasants in the zamindari system were tenants, who did not have proprietorship of land. The zamindar enjoyed the right to collect revenue from the tenants. A zamindar's right to collect rent extended over several villages, though in the case of a small zamindar it was confined to a few villages and sometimes even to a part of a village.[51] An important difference between the bhaiachara and the zamindari lay in the fact that even the lower castes could become tenants. In zamindari, although the tenants belonged mostly to the dominant castes, Jats, Gujars, Rajputs and Brahmans, peasants of all castes, artisans and chamars, had to oblige the zamindars either by doing begar or by paying nazranas (gifts) or by both. Chamars had to render compulsory labour in the land under personal cultivation of the zamindars which was known as sir and khudkast in every village.[52] The failure to oblige the zamindars resulted in their eviction or physical intimidation. Neither cultivators nor non-cultivators had proprietary rights over their residential places, could cut trees and use fruits grown on the trees without the permission of the zamindars.

A comparison between the bhaiachara and the zamindari reveals the existence of different kinds of relations within them. In the bhaiachara the dominant caste peasant-proprietors were independent of any intermediary above them, and exercised direct control over their riaya. But in the zamindari, peasants/tenants of high castes like those of the low castes and non-peasant classes, *i.e.*, artisans and service castes, were subjects of the zamindars. They could not exercise control over low caste tenants, artisans and service castes. In case of complaints of harassment of low caste peasants and artisans by the high caste tenants, the landlords could intervene, and make the high castes' domination almost non-existent. There were more than 60 castes in Meerut in 1931. Chamars constituted the majority followed by Jats (see Table 1).

Table 1

Percentage of Castes in Relation to the Population of Hindus (Brahminic and Arya Smajists) and Muslims in Meerut

Castes	*Religions*				
	Brahminic Hindus (A)	*Arya Smajists (B)*	*Hindus (A+B)*	*Muslims (C)*	*Total (A+B+C)*
Total No. of persons	11,42,104.00	46,810.00	1,18,8914.00	46,810.00	18,89,424.00
Brahmans	9.68	7.42	9.59	-	6.08
Kayasthas	0.35	8.49	0.36	-	0.24
Tagas (Tyagis)	4.13	2.69	4.07	4.45	3.44
Vaishyas	5.19	9.25	5.35	-	6.66
Jats	14.84	44.80	16.02	12.70	12.13
Rajputs	7.16	8.81	7.23	8.49	7.09
Gujars	6.97	4.97	6.97	5.29	4.39
Ahirs	1.60	0.16	1.54	0.16	0.97
Saiyids	-	-	-	3.34	0.66
Pathans	-	-	-	6.05	1.19
Chamars	20.67	5.57	23.11	-	12.67
Others*	29.41	7.84	25.75	59.52	55.22
Total	100.00	100.00	100.00	100.00	100.00

* Others include more than 30 low castes of Hindus and Muslims.

Source : A. C. Turner, *The United Provinces of Agra and Oudh*, Vol. XVIII, Part II, *Census of India*, 1931, Allahabad, The Superintendent Printing and Stationery, United Provinces, 1933, pp; 500-45.

At the time of the last settlement (1940), Jats, Hindu Gujars, Hindu Tyagis, Hindu Rajputs, Muslims, Brahmans, Ahirs including Rawas and others cultivated 30.70, 11.0, 11.8, 10.1, 7.8, 7.1, 2.7 and 19.8 per cent of the land in the district respectively.[53]

Geographical distribution of castes suggests that each dominant caste was concentrated and controlled land in a specific area.[53] The prevalence and dominance of a dominant caste in an area of Meerut district existed in a relative sense. Even though a particular dominant caste dominated a particular area, other dominant castes could also be found in the same area. Lower castes were found everywhere in the district. Though Jats were found almost in all tahsils, in Baghpat tahsil they formed the majority and outnumbered the Chamars.[54] The north-western part of Meerut - Chhaprauli, Kautana and Baghpat - which was monopolised by Hele Jats is called "desh". Deh Jats were found in the north-east of Meerut. In Baghpat alone Jats controlled 40 per cent of the land, and in "desh" they controlled around 81 per cent of the cultivable land.[55] Gujars were found near Ganga, Jamuna and Hindon rivers, as the culturable land offered them wasteland for grazing cattle, their traditional occupation being "cattle herding with agriculture and cattle lifting as subsidiary professions". The areas inhabited by them included the parganas of Garhmukteshwar, Hastinapur and Puth and, in Mawana tahsil, they controlled about one-eighth of the area. Tyagis were found mainly in the south of Hapur and Ghaziabad tahsils. Some villages were inhabited by them in Baghpat, Mawana and Sardhana tahsils also. In Hapur tahsil they owned from 17 per cent to 25 per cent of the land and in Ghaziabad tahsil around 10 per cent of the land.[56] Their majority was found in Hapur tahsil. The area under the Brahmans who cultivated their land as small proprietors was "unevenly distributed throughout the district". Banias controlled villages in Baghpat tahsil but they had larger possessions in Meerut and Mawana tahsils. They controlled the second largest area as a single caste.

II

Expansion of railways and the construction of metalled roads between 1901 and 1940 and the bridge over Kali river near Parikshatgarh and the tramways linking the villages with sugar mills at Daurala and Mawana provided better transportation conditions for agricultural produce to reach the market. The granaries (mandis) in Kesarganj in Meerut, Muzaffarnagar, Bulandshahr and Hapur were linked to each other and to the villages through the improved means of transportation. The rails and roads provided the district a direct contact with Delhi, Punjab, Rohilkhand, Calcutta and Bombay.[57]

The means of irrigation in Meerut, which were "scanty" and "backward" till the 50s of the 19th century developed and the area under irrigation increased over the period of next 100 years. Unlike the case of permanently settled districts of eastern Uttar Pradesh, the government took exceptional steps in introducing canal irrigation in western Uttar Pradesh, Punjab and in some parts of Madras Presidency. The Ganga Canal was opened in 1855, and it was redesigned in 1888. The East Jamuna Canal was repaired and made functional in 1870. These canals and rivers which flow through Meerut district, *i.e.*, the Ganges in the east, and the Jamuna, the Hindon and Kali in the west were linked through innumerable tributaries with the agricultural land almost all over Meerut district. The quality of the means of irrigation saw significant improvement ; the number of kacha wells declined by 64.10 per cent and that of the pukka wells increased by 20 per cent between 1874 and 1901 in the entire district. The improvement in the irrigation system brought more land under irrigation. Upto 1940 around 60 per cent area had come under irrigation. It should be noted that the area irrigated under the improved means, *i.e.*, pukka wells, canals and tube-wells increased, while the area under the traditional means, *i.e.*, kacha wells, tanks, streams, lakes and Persian wheels declined.[58]

The improved conditions of production resulted in the expansion of agriculture in Meerut district. Maximum area had come under cultivation during the late 19th century and first half of the 20th century.[59]

The development of the conditions and forces of production, and the access to market gave a fillip to the commercialisation of crops. While the area under double crops (do-fasli) and cash crops increased, it declined under non-cash crops. The double-cropped area increased by five times between 1874 and 1940. The area under cash crops increased from 4.5 to 28 per cent of the cultivated area during the same period. Sugarcane and wheat became the main crops in the district. Sugarcane became the most important commercial crop from which "tenant pays (aid), his rent and zamindar his revenue". In 1809, the whole area under sugarcane was only 22,000 acres in Saharanpur district, of which Meerut and Muzaffarnagar were a part at that time. Before the 1930s sugarcane was mainly used for "gur (jaggery)" and "very little indeed is (was) manufactured into sugar". Most inferior quality of sugarcane was grown in Meerut. In 1902, the area under sugarcane was only 11 per cent of the cultivated land. It was only after the passage of the Indian Sugar (Protection) Bill 1932, that Meerut became one of the most important sugarcane growing districts. Sugar factories in India enjoyed protective discrimination over a period of 18 years (1932-33 to 1949-50).[60] The area under sugarcane increased from 22 to 36 per cent of the cropped area between 1938-39 and 1950-51.[61] The establishment of major sugar mills at Mawana, Daurala and Modinagar from the 1930s in Meerut developed a market for sugarcane. Western Uttar Pradesh, however, was the last entrant into the sugarcane growing area compared to Gorakhpur and eastern Uttar Pradesh.[62] The variety of wheat improved and the area sown under it showed a great increase. Wheat covered 26 per cent of the cultivated area in 1860. It increased up to 51 per cent in 1358 fasli (1950-51). The area under maize, barley, jawar, bajra, gram, peas and zaid crops declined considerably. Cotton and indigo which were grown quite extensively became almost "extinct".[63]

The expropriation and differentiation of the peasantry during the pre-colonial period were expressed through the transfer of land from the cultivating communities to the non-cultivating communities and fragmentation of the mahals and landholdings. The transfer of land, perhaps, occurred not because of the development of forces and conditions of production but because of indebtedness and population growth. It is interesting to note that indebtedness of the peasantry was not caused due to the increase of revenue. Despite the increase of revenue by 61.62 per cent between the first and last settlements in Meerut,[64] only 5 per cent of loan was taken for payment of rent and revenue.[65] Growing indebtedness of the peasantry led to the inter-caste transfer of land between 1901 and 1933-37.[66] The maximum gainers of the transfer were Banias, who by virtue of moneylending mortgaged land of the cultivating castes[67] (See Table 2).

Several tenants and self-cultivators lost their land due to indebtedness and were reduced to the status of hired labourers.[68] The process of transfer of land resulted in the increase of the number of co-sharers by 139 per cent between 1874 and 1940 and, in the fragmentation of mahals.[69] This process further led to the fragmentation of landholdings. According to the UPZACR II, around 79 per cent of the landholdings were below 5 acres and they covered around 30 per cent of the area.[70] Growth of population had been an additional factor for the fragmentation of mahals and landholdings. Population of Meerut surpassed all districts of UP except Gorakhpur and Basti during the late 19th century.[71]

Table 2

Area Owned by Different Castes : 1904 - 1939-40

Caste	*Percentage of area held*		*Percentage change (±)*
	1901	*1939-40*	*(1901 – 1939-40)*
Jat	26.1	24.7	– 7.25
Vaish	9.8	14.7	+ 33.46
Hindu Tyagi	13.6	11.8	– 15.59
Hindu Rajput	9.4	7.5	– 25.17
Hindu Gujar	5.0	6.0	+ 16.77
Brahman	3.8	4.7	+ 17.71
Muslims	18.0	15.2	– 18.60
Others	14.0	15.4	+ 9.31

Source : C. H. Cooke, *op. cit.*, p.13.

III

The UP Zamindari Abolition and Land Reforms Act, 1951 became effective from July 1952. The most significant provision of this Act was for the abolition of intermediaries between the state and the peasants, besides the provisions for the tenurial reforms, voluntary co-operatives and Goan Sabhas. The intermediaries lost their right to collect rent, and the existing more than 22 tenures were converted into the four - bhumidhars, sirdhars, asami and adhivasi. The bhumidhars had permanent heritable and transferable rights over the land. They could use land for agricultural and non-agricultural purposes. Their revenue had been reduced to half. The sirdhars were given permanent and heritable rights but they were denied transferable right over the land and they were not entitled to use it for non-agricultural purposes. Their rent would not be reduced; it would remain intact. However, sirdhars were entitled to become bhumidhars after paying 10 times of their rent to the State. In 1954, all sirdhars were granted bhumidhari rights without paying 10 times of the rent. Asamis had only heritable, but not the transferable right. They were liable to eviction in case they were the tenants of students, mentally or physically handicapped persons, persons serving in defence and the convicts. Adhivasis were the tenants in sir and khudkast land which came under "personal cultivation". They were entitled to become sirdhars or bhumidhars after 5 years of commencement of the Act on payment of 15 times of the rent, failing which they were liable to ejectment.[72] Daniel Thorner observed that Uttar Pradesh was an area where the zamindari abolition had introduced "perceptible change".[73] Kripa Shankar holds the view that the zamindari abolition in fact reduced the number of tenures into 4 and it "was more in the nature of revenue reform than land reform as such."[74]

The UPZAL Act 1951, had varied impact on the caste and class relations in the bhaiachara and the zamindari. In majority of the villages of Meerut district, the zamindari abolition virtually had no impact, because as noted earlier, nearly 83 per cent of land was under the bhaiachara. In the bhaiachara, the aim of the UPZAL Act 1951, to remove the intermediaries and introduce peasant-proprietorship was virtually redundant, as there were no intermediaries, since they were already enjoying the ownership right over the land. And most of the peasants became bhumidhars directly without paying 10 times of their rent.

A study conducted in the late 1950s shows that the percentage of the peasant households which received direct bhumidhari without paying 10 times of rent was higher in western Uttar Pradesh than in central and eastern Uttar Pradesh. It was still higher in Meerut than in other districts of Uttar Pradesh. They formed around 52 per cent of households in western Uttar Pradesh, 31 per cent in central and eastern Uttar Pradesh and 70 per cent of the households in Meerut.[75] In 4 of the 5 bhaiachara villages it was observed that the peasant-proprietors became bhumidhars directly.[73] The zamindari abolition did not change the relationships of the peasant-proprietors with the non-peasant classes in these villages. Nor did it change the pattern of ownership of land. It affected the peasant-proprietors adversely and the riaya positively. The riaya were supposed to become free from the control of the peasant-proprietors as henceforth they would be owners of their dwelling places, and would be free to cut their trees, use their vegetables, dung-cakes (bitoda), *etc.*[77] But in practice the peasant-proprietors still continued to exercise domination over them. The zamindari abolition did not provide the ex-riaya with land or any other alternative means of livelihood which could free them from the dependence on the peasant-proprietors. The ex-riaya in villages with the bhaiachara background still depend on the peasant-proprietors in more than one ways, *i.e.*, defecation in the fields, cutting grass from the fields, receiving loan and getting daily work in the fields. Such dependence exists even in the villages with the zamindari background, but the intensity of its implications vary from that of the villages with the bhaiachara background.[78]

However, the zamindari abolition did provide proprietorship to the tenants in the villages which fell under the zamindari.[79] It must be noted that the UP Tenancy Act of 1939, had already provided hereditary rights to the tenants and deprived the zamindars of their rights to resume land for making improvement in it. It had provided them security, at least theoretically.[80] The UPZALR Act, 1951 made an additional contribution by removing the zamindars' right to collect rents from the tenants. As noted earlier there was not much land under the zamindari. It formed only 8 per cent of the area with 26 zamindars paying revenue of more than Rs.5,000 annually. In three of the eight villages surveyed, which have the zamindari background, the zamindari abolition provided proprietorship to the tenants, who mostly belonged to the castes of Gujars, Sainis and Jats. The Act did not provide any right of ownership over the land to the non-tenants, mostly from the lower castes. The zamindari abolition in fact, benefited the "middle castes" in Uttar Pradesh.[81] It consolidated their position against the harijans.[82] But regarding this "consolidation" of the "middle peasants" there was a basic difference between the Meerut district and the districts of central and eastern Uttar Pradesh. The peasants of the "middle castes", *i.e.*, Jats, Gujars and high caste Tyagis along with the peasants of some other castes in Meerut were already in a consolidated position in the bhaiachara, even before the zamindari abolition. But position of peasants of the "middle castes" of central and eastern Uttar Pradesh, *i.e.*, Yadavs, Kurmis, Kachis and Lodhas was consolidated only after the zamindari abolition. However, in the zamindari areas of the Meerut district, the position of the "middle caste" tenants and the tenants of the other castes was consolidated only after the zamindari abolition. These tenants acquired domineering positions *vis-a-vis* the agricultural labourers, artisans and serving castes after the"consolidation".

Consolidation of landholdings in Meerut covered only two of the six tahsils, Sardhana and Bhagpat between April 1955 and April 1960.[83]

The fieldwork reveals that in many villages, particularly in Sardhana tahsil, the programme remained unimplemented. The influential landholders bribed the consolidation staff and took the best land at the location of their choice. The poor peasants, on the other hand, were given land of poor quality.

The programme of land ceiling remained redundant and unimplemented till the 1960s in Uttar Pradesh.[84] The defective nature of the legislation, high ceiling limit, non-availability of surplus land, lack of interest on the part of the Congress politicians, connivance of the bureaucrats with the rural rich, varying definitions of the family, the reluctance and resistance on the part of the landowners, influence of dominant classes over the Gaon Sabhas, exemption of several kinds of land from ceiling, and benami transactions were among the chief reasons for the failure of land ceiling programme.[85] The subsequent amendments to this Act also failed to rectify these defects.

Fresh efforts were made from the early 1970s to impose ceiling on the landholdings. This fresh move was prompted by the "land grab" movement launched by the CPI in 1969-71. In response, the Central Land Reforms Committee (CLRC) was set up under the chairmanship of Union Agricultural Minister, Fakhruddin Ali Ahmad. On the recommendation of this Committee, the definition of family was changed. But the exclusion of Stridhan from the ceiling gave enough room for fictitious transfer of land.[86]

Under the New Ceiling Plan of the 1970s and 1980s[87], the Government was supposed to take possession of 1,907.47 acres of land which involved 367 cases. But it could take possession of only 1,701.46 acres involving 351 cases between August 1973-74 and August 1985. The possession of 205.81 acres land involving 15 cases was stayed by the court orders, and that of 10.10 acres was due to be taken over. Of the land taken under possession, 1,309.07 acres was allotted to the "poorer classes", 97.21 acres to the Gaon Samaj, 267.27 acres was further stayed by the court order and 6.06 acres of land was taken over under the cases of "correction". A total of 23.85 acres of this area was transferred to the government departments - 6.60 acres to Meerut Development Authority, 6.25 acres to Forest Department and 11 acres to Madhya Ganga. Since the data on how many persons or families were allotted the land could not be made available, it is difficult to ascertain the average size of landholding allotted to each individual or household.

The landowners moved the court to prevent the implementation of the ceiling. There were 1,198 cases in the court, of which 1,188 were settled and 10 cases were left unsettled during the period between 1973-74 and 1985. The Government paid compensation to those land-holders whose land was taken over. In all, 309 cases were to be compensated with Rs. 325,502. In fact, 273 cases were paid Rs. 281,332 and the balance of Rs. 44,181 was left unpaid. On an average every single case received Rs. 1,030.52 as compensation.

The data seem to suggest that there was some success in the implementation of land ceiling programme in Meerut district. The field-work, however, shows that the programme in the district was a virtual failure. In fact, the plots of land which were allotted to the landless or poor sections were too small and uneconomic. They were not fit for cultivation. Moreover, in the absence of the resources: means of irrigation, transportation, cultivation, *etc.*, the land allotted irrespective of its size, proved to be useless. Instead of benefiting the rural poor, it proved to be disadvantageous to them, particularly harijans. On the one hand, it kept them under the illusion of owning a piece of land which distanced them from going in search of work, on the other hand, the land allotment resulted in their harassment and intimidation by the landowning classes. In majority of the cases, the rural rich did not allow them to take possession of the allotted land and imposed sanctions against them. The landowners, in collusion with the administration, took advantage of the loopholes in the legislation. They even planted branches of trees overnight in their fields and bribed Government officers to register them as 'gardens' which were exempted from the Ceiling Act. In many cases, the allottees were evicted from the land by violent means. For instance, in some villages of Meerut district, the allottees were evicted forcibly during the Janata rule from the plots which were allotted to them during the emergency period.[88] Moreover, it divided the poor classes between those who benefited, and those who did not benefit from this programme. This division affected the village level politics and, more importantly weakened the unity of the rural poor in relation to the rural rich.

IV

The Agricultural Extension Scheme and Community Development Programme provided incentives to agrarian sector during the 1950s.

But it was only after the introduction of Green Revolution that more intensive and substantive impact of these incentives was felt. The Green Revolution accelerated the development of capitalist tendencies, mainly mechanisation of agriculture and use of modern inputs, *i.e.*, chemical fertilizers and HYV, commercialisation of agriculture and expropriation and differentiation of the peasantry,[89] which were introduced during the colonial period.

There has been an improvement in the agricultural implements and machinery in Meerut district. Significant changes have taken place in the implements and machinery between 1956 and 1987-88. The number of modern (improved) implements, *i.e.*, tractors, iron ploughs in comparison with wooden ploughs, harrows and cultivators have increased, while the traditional implements have become almost extinct especially during the Green Revolution in the 1970s and 1980s (See Table 3).

The distribution of improved seeds (HYV) showed a seven-fold increase and area under them increased five-fold between 1961 and 1971.[90] The area under the main commercial crops of the region, *i.e.*, wheat and sugarcane increased, while the area under other crops declined considerably (See Table 4).

Though the area under the tube-well irrigation increased and the area under the other sources of irrigation including canals declined before 1951, the canals, wells and Persian wheels still remained as the significant source of irrigation till 1960-61.[91] But in the 1970s and 1980s, the private tube-wells and pump-sets became the main sources of irrigation (See Table 5).

The use of chemical fertilizers in the district increased between 1969-70 and 1987-88 (See Table 6). This almost led to the demise of the traditional compost manure. The yield rates of crops such as maize, wheat and sugarcane rose from 8.36, 14.49 and 440.54 quintals per hectare to 13.63, 22.89 and 541.12 quintals per hectare respectively between 1974-75 and 1980-81.[92]

Table 3

Changes in the Number of Agricultural Implements and Machinery: 1956-1987-88*

Item	*1956 (a)*	*1971 (b)*	*Variation Percentage of imple-ments (a±b)*	*1976-77 (c)*	*1979-80 (d)*	*1987-88 (e)*	*Variation percentage of imple-ments (c±e)*
1. Ploughs	140,422	165,215	+17.66	-	30,675	-	-
i) Wooden	-	126,196	-	-	23,111	87,331	+277.88
ii) Iron/Western	-	39,019	-	963	7,564	66,534	+6809.03
2. Tractors	403	3,716	+822.08	4,069	7,590	13,100	+221.95
3. Seed Drill	-	40,011	-	512	110	-	-
4. Hand Plough	-	-	-	-	1,100	-	-
5. Dibler	-	-	-		572	-	-
6. Harrow		-	-	-3,483	966	14,918	+1444.31** (Harrow & cultivator)
7. Chaff Cutters	-	-	-	-	-	-	-
i) Manually operated		160,316	-	-	-	-	-
ii) Power operated		2,957	-	-	-	-	-
8. Sugarcane crushers		-	-	-	-	-	-
i) Power operated		8,162	-	-	-	-	-
ii) Bullock operated		3,948	-	-	-	-	-
9. Persian wheels	-	4,870			-	-	-
10. Crop cutting machines	-	74	-		-	-	-
11. Bullock carts	86,699	93,101	+7.38	-	-	-	-
12. Oilseed crusher		1,564	-	-	-	-	-

* Figures between 1956 and 1971 are related to the pre-1976 Meerut which included Ghaziabad and Hapur tahsils, besides four other tahsils; and figures between 1976-77 and 1987-88 cover post-1976 Meerut excluding Ghaziabad and Hapur tahsils which became part of Ghaziabad district, which was created as a separate district in 1976.

** Between 1979-80 and 1987-88.

Sources: E.B. Joshi. *op.cit.*, p.102; District Census Handbook 1971, Allahabad, Superintendent Printing and Stationery 1972; *District Statistical Handbook*, Meerut 1977-78, 1979-80, 1983 and 1989, Economic and Statistics Officer, State Planning Institute, Economic and Statistics Division, Lucknow, U.P.

Table 4

Percentage of Area Sown under Different Crops: 1950-51 - 1987-88

Crops	1950-51	1955-56	1960-61	1975-76	1979-80	1985-86	1987-88
1. Wheat	22.30	25.12	25.21	40.79	43.76	33.17	31.84
2. Wheat mixed (gram and wheat)	3.30	3.60	3.04	-	-	-	-
3. Barley	3.01	2.35	1.97	-	-	0.13	0.08
4. Jowar	4.81	3.63	2.52	0.22	0.12	0.11	0.04
5. Bajra	5.01	4.20	4.62	1.77	1.07	0.47	0.24
6. Maize	12.35	7.98	8.08	11.88	9.30	5.97	5.07
7. Paddy	1.89	1.10	1.75	3.95	6.30	3.77	2.63
8. Potato	0.11	0.13	0.19	0.78	-	1.21	1.50
9. Pulses	12.02	11.55	9.36	3.86	2.73	2.54	2.10
10. Sugar-cane	18.08	20.14	23.14	35.00	35.25	29.91	34.72
11. Cotton	0.10	0.11	0.12	0.74	0.99	0.49	0.32
12. Others	17.12	19.98	20.00	0.52	0.15	22.23	21.46
Total	100.00	100.00	100.00	100.00	100.00	100.00	100.00

Sources: Data for 1950-51, 1955-56 and 1960-61 are compiled from E.B. Joshi, *op.cit.*, p. 379; for 1975-76 from *District Statistical Handbook*, Meerut, 1977; for 1979-80, 1985-86 and 1987-88 from *District Statistical Handbook*, Meerut, 1981 and 1989.

Although maximum area had come under the agricultural utilization in Meerut District by 1951, the expansion of agriculture continued even after independence. While the uncultivated area shrank, the çultivated area expanded between 1951 and 1971 (See Table 7).

There has been a trend of expropriation and differentiation of the peasantry in the post-independence period. Between 1961 and 1981 there has been a decrease in the number of cultivators and an increase in the number of agricultural labourers[93] (See Table 8).

Table 5

Percentage Distribution of Irrigated Area by Source of Irrigation: 1950-51 - 1979-80

Source	1950-51	1956-57	1960-61	1970-71	1975-76	1979-80	1985-86	1987-88
1. Canal	58.97	54.13	53.36	35.96	32.26	34.69	30.38	26.43
2. Govt. tube-well	-	-	-	35.84	8.77	7.52	{	{
3. Private tube-wells	-	-	-	15.68	39.69	56.34	{68.83{	72.66
4. Pumping sets	-	-	-	1.45	11.51	-	{	{
5. Wells	40.36	45.37	46.13	8.08	3.28	0.98	0.42	0.68
6. Persian wheels and other sources+	-	-	0.50	2.39	4.21	-		
7. Ponds and others	0.67	0.50	-	0.58	0.28	0.46	0.37	0.23
8. Percentage of theirrigated area by all sources	60	62	100.00	100.00	100.00	100.00	100.00	100.00

\+ Other sources for 1950-51, 1956-57 and 1960-61 include tube-wells, tanks, etc.

Sources: Data for 1950-51, 1956-57 and 1960-61 have been compiled from E.B. Joshi, *op.cit.*, pp. 91-94. Data for 1970-71, 1975-76 and 1979-80 have been compiled from *District Statistical Handbook*, Meerut, 1974, 1977, 1981 and 1989.

Table 6

Use of Chemical Fertilizers in Meerut District: 1969-70 - 1979-80

Item	1969-70		1975		1979-80		1985-86		1987-88	
	Quantity Metric Tonnes	Percentage	Quantity Metric Tonnes	Percentage	Quantity Metric Tonnes	Percentage	Quantity Metric Tonnes	Percentage	Quantity Metric Tonnes	Percentage
Nitrogen	14,088	64.10	19,220	80.61	34,087	78.05	48,104	81.00	39,566	83.78
Phosphorus	5,571	25.34	3,131	13.13	7,244	16.59	8,807	14.83	6,519	13.80
Potash	2,320	10.56	1,490	6.25	2,343	5.36	2,478	4.17	1,139	2.41
Total	21,979	100.00	23,841	100.00	43,673	100.00	59,389	100.00	47,224	100.00

Source: *District Statistical Handbook*, Meerut, 1974, 1975, 1981 and 1989.

Table 7

Decadal Variation in Land-use Pattern: 1951 - 1979-80

(Fig. in percentage)

Classification of Area	*1951*	*1961*	*1971*	*1979-80**
1. Area under Forest	- 96.45	+ 99.89	- 0.13	- 27.92
2. Uncultivated land	- 14.93	- 14.08	- 22.02	- 61.08
3. Land under cultivation				
i) Total cropped area	+ 1.95	+ 13.03	+ 5.42	- 27.49
ii) Area sown more than once	- 11.23	+ 58.67	+ 18.59	- 15.83
iii) Net cropped area	+ 6.03	+ 1.09	+ 0.15	- 33.10

* Decadal variation in land-use pattern in 1981 over 1971 declined in all types of land because of reduction in size of Meerut district as two of its tahsils, Hapur and Ghaziabad, were separated from it to form Ghaziabad district in 1976.

Source: Compiled from *District Census Handbook, Meerut District*, 1961, *op.cit.*, p. 164; and 1971, p. 633; *District Statistical Handbook* Meerut, 1981.

Table 8

Variation in Percentage Distribution of Agrarian Classes: 1951-81

Agrarian Classes	*1951*	*1961*	*1971*	*1981*
1. Cultivators	86.49	40.4	37.7	36.00
2. Lessees and agricultural labourers*/ agricultural labourers	12.31	4.8	15.2	18.51
3. Others/ landlords*	1.18	54.8	47.1	45.49
Total	100.00	100.00	100.00	100.00

* Used for the Census year 1951.

Sources: *District Census Handbooks*, 1951, 1961 and 1971, *op. cit.*; *District Statistical Handbook*, Meerut, 1982.

Table 9

Percentage Distribution of Landholdings and Area under Landholdings: 1974 - 1980-81

Size of the land - holdings (acres)	1974		1975-76		1977		1980-81	
	% of land-holdings	% of area under land-holdings	% of land-holdings	% of area under land-holdings	% of land-holdings	% of area under land-holdings	% of land-holdings	% of area under land holdings
Up to 2.5	56.43	14.66	66.81	16.61	57	17.94	58.78	15.34
2.5 to 7.5	13.99	34.85	20.14	43.68	29.69	42.31	29.02	38.14
Above 7.5	29.50	50.50	12.07	39.70	13.34	39.73	12.20	46.51
Total	100.00	100.00	100.00	100.00	100.00	100.00	100.00	100.00

***Source:** District Statistical Handbook*, Meerut, 1975, 1975-76 and 1982.

The increase in number of "agricultural labourers", and the corresponding decrease in the number of cultivators have been mainly for two reasons. First, as a result of the introduction of modern technology, many of the cultivators working in their own fields with small landholdings have been expropriated from the land and have thus become wage laboureres. Second, with the decline in the jajmani system, those who were attached to the traditional occupations, *i.e.*, artisans: carpenters, blacksmiths, weavers, oilmen, *etc.;* and serving classes: barbers, washermen, sweepers have also gradually become "agricultural labourers". The expropriation of peasantry was accompanied by the fragmentation of landholdings. The number of smaller landholdings increased, while that of the bigger landholdings declined between 1974 and 1980-81[94] (See Table 9). Even the number of persons owning small landholdings increased and that of owning bigger landholdings declined between 1951 and 1971.[95]

Notes

1 The "introduction" of capitalist tendencies is used in the relative sense. There had existed the "potentialities" of capitalism even during the Mughal period. See Irfan Habib, "Potentialities of Capitalist Development in Economy of the Mughal India", *Equiry,* New Series, Vol. III, no. 3, winter 1971, pp. 1-56

2 E.B. Joshi *(ed.), Uttar Pradesh District Gazetteer, Meerut*, Lucknow Department of Uttar Pradesh District Gazetteers, 1965, p. 49; E.T. Atkinson, *Statistical, Descriptive and Historical Account of Meerut District*, Allahabad, North-Western Provinces, Government Press, 1876, p. 100.

3 The term taluqdari came to be used in the latter part of the seventeenth century, and it denoted the simultaneous presence of two classes, *i.e.*, taluqdar and zamindar. For details, see Irfan Habib, *The Agrarian System of Mughal India* (1556-1707), Bombay, Asia Publication House, 1963, p. 147, fn. 40, pp. 171-72.

4 Thomas R. Metcalf, *Land, Landlords and the British Raj: Northern India in the Nineteenth Century*, Delhi, Oxford University Press, 1979, p. 54, fn. 18. See also Zoya Hasan, "Power and Mobilization: Pattern of Resilience and Change in Uttar Pradesh Politics", in Francine R. Frankel and M.S.A. Rao *(eds.), Dominance and State Power in Modern India: Decline of Social Order*, Vol. I, Delhi, Oxford University Press, 1989, p. 146, fn. 21.

5 See Asiya Siddiqui, *Agrarian Change in a North Indian State: Uttar Pradesh, 1819-1833*, London, Oxford University Press, 1973, p.25.

6 Although the bhaiachara was more prevalent in western Uttar Pradesh, there was no uniformity in the extent of the area covered by it in all districts of western Uttar Pradesh. While the bhaiachara could exist even in the non-Jat dominated areas, it was not so always necessarily.

7 N.C. Saxena, "Caste and Zamindari Abolition in U.P.", *Mainstream*, Vol. XXIII, no. 42, 15 June 1985, p. 16.

8 Pattidari, bhaiachara, mahalwari and zamindari are the terms often used "indiscriminately" to describe the agrarian system of Meerut in the colonial period. "In the absence of any authorised definition", the settlement officer was "left to use the discretion...to class them as he thinks *(ed)* proper", and "it matters *(ed)* little what name is (was) given to it"See M.H. Elliot, *Report on the Settlement of the District of Meerut: 1835-40* (publication details not available), pp. 186-89. About the indiscriminate use of categories, Baden-Powell observed that if a peasant was asked in North India about his profession, he would reply "I am a poor man, a zamindar". See B.H. Baden-Powell, *The Land System of the British India*, Vol. 1, London, Oxford University Press, 1972, p. 7. However, authentic works, *i.e.*, Irfan Habib, *op.cit.*, M.C. Pradhan, *The Political System of the Jats in North India*, London, Oxford University Press, 1966, and our fieldwork provide enough help to understand the agrarian system of Meerut in the colonial period. If a village or a group of villages dominated by a single community was divided into shares, each share was known as a mahal. B.H. Baden-Powell, *ibid.*, p. 170. And this system was known as mahalwari. It does not seem to be different from pattidari, because in pattidari a village was divided into pattis and each patti was named after an influential person. M.C. Pradhan, *ibid.*, p. 24. Similarly, in a mahalwari village a mahal was named after an influential person. Sometimes pattidari was used in the same sense as bhaiachara. See Asiya Siddiqui, *op.cit.*, pp.16-18; M.H. Elliot, *ibid.*, p. 188. See also Eric Stokes, *The Peasants and the Raj: Studies in the Agrarian Peasant Rebellion in Colonial India*, Delhi, Vikas Publishing House, 1973, p. 241, fn. 36.

9 We have included the joint zamindari in the category of the bhaiachara because it generally represented very small proprietors *differing hardly at all from bhaiachara and pattidari* (emphasis added), C.H. Cooke, *op.cit.*, p. 12.

10 Of the 83 per cent, 70 per cent of land fell under bhaiachara and 13 per cent under joint zamindari. See *ibid.*

11 See *ibid.*, p.156. As for how the zamindari rights were acquired by certain families of Jats, Gujars, Muslims, Banias and Tyagis in Meerut and adjoining districts, see E.T. Atkinsons, *op.cit.*, pp. 96-98, 100-01, 151-68; *The Imperial Gazetteer of India*, Vol. XVII, new edition, London, Oxford, Clarendon Press, 1908, pp. 255-56; Kunwar Lachman Singh,

Historical and Statistical Memoir: Zila Bulandshahar, Allahabad, North-Western Provinces Government Press, 1876, pp. 151-68; H.R. Nevill, *Meerut - A Gazetteer Being, Vol. IV of Agra and Oudh*, Government Branch Press, Lucknow, 1922, p. 190.

12 It should be noted that most of these "zamindars" were not big estate owners; they were the peasant-proprietors of the bhaiachara.

13 Based on the calculations from *Report of the United Provinces Zamindari Abolition Committee,* Vol. II, Allahabad, Superintendent Printing and Stationery, 1948, pp. 12-17.

14 See for details Zoya Hasan, *Dominance and Mobilisation: Rural Politics in Western Uttar Pradesh*, New Delhi, Sage Publication, 1989, Chapter 2.

15 See this Chapter, pp. 18-20.

16 See Chapter III, p. 43.

17 Thomas R. Metcalf, *op.cit.*, p. 48.

18 M.H. Elliot, *op.cit.*, p. 189.

19 See Eric Stokes, *op.cit.*, p. 238.

20. M.C. Pradhan, *op,cit.*, p. 34.

21 M.H. Elliot, *op.cit.*, p. 190.

22 B.H. Baden-Powell, *op.cit.*, p. 162.

23 M.C. Pradhan, *op.cit.*, pp. 1-6, 35; M.H. Elliot, *op.cit.*, p. 191; H.R. Nevill, *op.cit.*, p. 108.

24 M.C. Pradhan, *ibid.*, p. 131. Formal meetings of the sarva khap are held only for the resolution of major disputes. Council meetings of four or five khaps of the neighbouring areas are more common. Activities of the sarva khap were revived in 1950. See M.C. Pradhan, *ibid.*, p. 132.

25 *Ibid.*, p. 44, fn. 1,p.58. Khaps still play a decisive role in settling social issues in the village society. The khaps played a significant role in mobilising farmers during the agitation of the western Uttar Pradesh farmers, which began in 1986-1987 and which was led by Mahendra Singh Tikait, chief of the Bharatiya Kisan Union (BKU) (see Chapter V, p.100). The BKU movement started as a class-based agitation involving farmers of different castes, therefore the khaps of Jats, Gujars and Rajputs were involved in the mobilisation of farmers. The authority of the khap/sarva khap chaudhary was recognised even by the Mughal emperors, who did not intervene in its affairs. M.C. Pradhan, *ibid.*, pp. 97-99, 106-07. For the role of khap in pre-Mughal, Mughal periods and during 1857 revolt, see M.C. Pradhan, *ibid.*, pp. 252-59. See also Girish Chandra Dwivedi, *The Jats: Their Role in the Mughal Empire*, Bangalore, Arnold Publishers, 1989, pp. 16-18.

26 For important khaps of these castes, see M.C. Pradhan, *ibid.*, Appendix I, p. 249, and for Gujar khap, see p. 115.

27 *Ibid.*, p. 190, fn. 1.

28 *Ibid.*, p. 132.

29 *Ibid.*, p. 130.

30 See M.C. Pradhan, *ibid.*, pp. 23-24. Even in village Rampur (fictitious) near Delhi, a bhaiachara village was divided into groups or panas, which were further divided into tholas. Panas and tholas like pattis, were named after influential persons. See Oscar Lewis, *Group Dynamics in a North Indian Village: A Study of Factions*, New Delhi, Programme Evaluation Organization of Planning Commission, 1954, p. 8. Pradhan bases his observations on his study of the Baliyan khap in Muzaffarnagar district of Meerut Division. Although his observations are based on his research in a village of the district, they have been made in the context of the khap/sarva khap system in the entire Meerut Division. Thus the generalisation can be made from his findings. In fact, Pradhan suggests that "Baliyan khap... study, will also be generally true for other clans of areas of Meerut Division" (p. 7). We will, therefore, be using his observations about the bhaiachara and khaps/sarva khap system as generalisations applicable to the bhaiachara, unless otherwise distinguished in relation to our work.

31 Irfan Habib, *op.cit.*, pp. 122-33.

32 *Ibid.*

33 See *ibid.*, pp. 115-16, 123

34 See M.C. Pradhan, *op.cit*, pp. 35-36.

35 *Ibid.*, pp. 34-35; B.H. Baden-Powell, *op.cit.*, p. 162.

36 H.R. Nevill, *op.cit.*, p. 89.

37 E.T. Atkinson, *op.cit.*, p. 104.

38 See Irfan Habib, *op.cit.*, p. 125.

39 For a discussion on this point see Eric Stakes, *op.cit.*, pp. 76-89.

40 In Banaras Province, which was marked by the presence of peasant-proprietorship, the settlement was made with the representatives of villages. The rights of others were ignored, and they were generally relegated to the status of tenants. See *UPZACR*, Vol. 1, 1948, p. 94. However, Rajputs abhorred manual labour even in some villages of Meerut. See, Kunwar Bahadur in *Report of the United Provinces Provincial Bank Committee, 1929-30*, II, Allahabad, Superintendent Printing and Stationery, 1930, p. 228. For castes and their relative role in the process of production in agriculture in western and eastern Uttar Pradesh, see also Asiya Siddiqui, *op.cit.*, pp. 49-50.

41 It is not appropriate to call the cultivators in the bhaiachara system as tenants, since they were not obliged to any intermediary between them and the State. They had permanent and hereditary rights in the land. The peasant-proprietors in the bhaiachara villages were known khud-

zamindars and in local parlance the system was known as kucha zamindara. This was in contrast to zamindari which was known as pukka zamindara.

42 Thomas R. Metcalf, *op. cit.*, p. 55.

43 Irfan Habib, *op. cit.*, p. 128.

44 See Asiya Siddiqi, *op. cit.*, p. 29.

45 For a discussion on the patron-client relations, see M. C. Pradhan, *op. cit.*, pp. 40-51.

46 *Ibid.*, p.25.

47 *Ibid.*

48 Irfan Habib, *op. cit.*, p.122. That is why in a majority of the villages which belonged to the bhaiachara the ex-riaya do not hold land even today. However, in some of the ex-bhaiachara villages riaya worked as tenants of peasant-proprietors. For example, in Jaisinghpur village, the ex-riaya who got the proprietorship of land after zamindari abolition, were the tenants of Jat proprietors.

49 H.R. Nevill, *op. cit.*, p. 88. There are even examples of riaya fleeing their villages overnight due to coercion and intimidation at the hands of dominant caste peasant-proprietors. Interview: An 80-year old man of Gadaria caste (OBC) in village Jaisinghpur, substantiated by another 82-year old man of Jat caste, 25 March 1985.

50 Irfan Habib, *op. cit.*, p. 122.

51 Big zamindars, generally absentees, had their revenue staff which was headed by a karinda (agent). The revenue staff moved from village to village for collection of rent from the peasants. Besides, patwari (record keeper), and other intermediaries, *i.e.*, muquddam, lambardar and mukhia existed in the villages. They generally belonged to the dominant castes. Small zamindars, however, did not have the revenue staff, though the village level intermediaries existed in their zamindaris as well.

52 Chamars were divided into two groups, for carrying out their duty - mitar and hali. Mitar, heading a team of 10-12 persons, was assigned the duty of arranging chamars, for working in sir and khudrast land, and for serving the revenue staff of zamindar. Hali worked in the sir land and was not paid for whatever service he rendered to zamindar.

53 C.H. Cooke, *op. cit.*, Statement 5, p. 15.

54 Jats can be divided into two sects: Heles and Dehs. Heles who came to Meerut in 9th century were more numerous in the district. H.R. Nevill, *op. cit.*, p.90. But according to C.H. Cooke , *op. cit.*, p. 14, they came in 1100 A.D. They ousted Tyagis in 1100 A.D. from the north-west of Meerut, which was inhabited by them till the arrival of Jats. Dehs came to Meerut much later than Heles. E.T. Atkinson, *op. cit.*, p. 67.

55 C.H. Cooke, *ibid.*, p. 13. Jats are the most vocal political group in this region, which had provided a strong base to Charan Singh, and after

his death, to Ajit Singh.

56 *Ibid.*, p. 14.

57 See C.H. Cooke, *op. cit.*, pp. 5-6.

58 Based on H.R. Nevill, *op. cit.*, pp. 49-54, 60. E.B. Joshi, *op. cit.*, pp. 89-91; Elizabeth Whitecombe, *Agrarian Conditions in Northern India: The United Provinces under British Rule,* Vol. 1, New Delhi, Thomson Press, 1971, pp. 69-70.

59 See E.B. Joshi, *ibid.*, pp. 87-88; H.R. Nevill, *ibid.*, pp. 36-37. A substantial part of "culturable waste" had been brought under cultivation which however saw six-fold increase between 1902 and 1940. It was, probably, because the landlords showed their surplus land as "waste land", fearing the impact of impending zamindari abolition programme.

60 *Report of the Sugar Inquiry Commission,* The Government of India, 1965, pp. 2-3, 15, 23. For a discussion on the growth of sugar industry in the 1930s in India, see Sanjaya Basu, *The Political Economy of Indian Sugar: The State Intervention and Structural Change,* Delhi, Oxford University Press, 1990, Chapter II.

61 See E.B. Joshi, *op.cit.*, pp. 97, 379-91, Table VI (VI).

62 See Shahid Amin, *Sugarcane and Sugar in Gorakhpur: An Inquiry into Peasant Production for Capitalist Enterprise in Colonial India,* Delhi, Oxford University Press, 1984, p. 107.

63 See E.B. Joshi, *op. cit.*; H.R. Nevill, *op. cit.*, p. 40.

64 Calculated from E.B. Joshi, *op. cit.*, Table III, pp. 292-93. The first thirty years' settlement was made in Meerut in 1835-37, followed by the subsequent settlements in 1856-57, 1901 and 1931-39. In bhaiachara the settlement was made with the village as a unit of mahal. It was made with the zamindars wherever they existed. The most usual method of collecting revenue was to collect it from the entire village or a patti or a mahal by zamindars in the zamidari and by the head of village community in the bhaiachara. Having collected rent from the tenants and the peasant-proprietors, they paid revenue to the State. The settlement officer was free to use his "sound discretion" in the process of revenue collection. See E.B. Joshi, *op. cit.*, pp. 191-97; B.R. Misra, *Land Revenue Policy in the United Provinces under British Rule,* Banaras, Nand Kishore and Brothers, 1942, p. 75; for *modus operandi* of the settlements, see M.H. Elliot, *op. cit.*, p. 185.

65 In Meerut, almost every agrarian class was indebted. Marriage was the main purpose of the two-thirds of loan in contrast to Gorakhpur where money was evidently borrowed as advances by the sugarcane cultivators. Despite the availability of branches of banks, moneylenders mostly from Bania caste were the main source of loan. C.H. Cooke, *op. cit.*, pp. 17-18, Kunwar Bahadur, *op. cit.*, pp. 213-37. See on Gorakhpur, Shahid

Amin, *op. cit.*, p.60.

66 The differential of alienation of land in the bhaiachara and the zamindari is not clear. But since the bhaiachara system was rigid about the transfer of land outside the thok or patti (see this chapter, p.11), it was more likely that the peasants in the zamindari dominated villages would have suffered more from the alienation than the peasants in the bhaiachara. Even the increase in revenue would have affected the peasantry more in the zamindari than in the bhaiachara.

67 Transfer of land in Meerut was more spectacular and effective in the first half of the 20th century. There was "not a single" case of transfer during the first three decades of the 19th century. However, there were a few exceptions of land transfer in the 19th century which "did not affect the cultivators severely". See E.B. Joshi, *op. cit.*, p. 193.

68 See C.H. Cooke, *op. cit.*, *Settlement Commissioner's Note on the Final Settlement Report on Meerut District*, Allahabad, Superintendent Printing and Stationery, 1940, p. 2.

69 See Eric Stokes, *The Peasant and the Raj...*, *op. cit.*, pp. 208-09, 227. See also M.C. Pradhan, *op. cit.*, p.18. Pradhan observes similar kind of inequalities which had developed within the peasant-proprietors of Jats of the nearby district of Muzaffarnagar during the colonial period. This was because of the commercialisation of agriculture and growth of industries.

70 See UPZACR II, pp. 34-38. See also Eric Stokes, *ibid.*, pp. 220-23; C.H. Cooke, *op. cit.*, p. 17.

71 The density of population in Meerut increased from 488 sq. miles to 587.2 sq. miles between 1847 and 1901. The population of the district increased by 52.5 per cent between 1921 and 1951. See H.R. Nevill, *ibid.*, pp. 78-88; E.B. Joshi, *ibid.*, pp. 62-63.

72 See Charan Singh, *Land Reforms in U.P. and the Kulaks*, New Delhi, Vikas Publishing House, 1986, pp. 10-13.

73 Daniel Thorner, *op. cit.*, pp. 46-48.

74 Kripa Shankar, *Concealed Tenancy and Its Implications for Equity and Economic Growth: A Study of Uttar Pradesh*, New Delhi, Concept Publishing House, 1980, p.16.

75 See Baljit Singh, *Next Step in Village India: A Study of Land Reforms and Group Dynamics*, Bombay, Asia Publishing House, 1961, pp. 26, 28, 121-22, Table 3.

76 In the fifth village, Jaisinghpur, which has the bhaiachara background, sub-infeudation had taken place during the colonial period. People of riaya and even some Jats became the tenants of the Jat peasant-proprietors. These tenants got bhumidari only after paying 10 times of the rent, despite the bhaiachara background of the village.

77 Pradhan and Hasan also make similar observation about the impact of zamindari abolition in the bhaiachara dominated areas in Muzaffarnagar and Aligarh districts respectively. See M.C. Pradhan, *op. cit.*, p. 25. Zoya Hasan, *Dominance and Mobilisation, op. cit.*, p. 56.

78 See Chapter IV.

79 In Aligarh, the areas of Hathras, Atrauli, Koil and Sikandra Rao tahsils, which were dominated by the zamindari were affected by the zamindari abolition. See Zoya Hasan, *op. cit.*, p. 53.

80 See Thomas R. Metcalf, *op. cit.*, pp. 70-72; W.C. Neale, *Economic Change in Rural India: Land Tenure and Land Reform in Uttar Pradesh, 1800-1955*, New Haven, Yale University Press, 1962, pp. 291-94; B.R. Mishra, *op.cit.*, pp. 122-48, 167-84.

81 Baljit Singh, *op. cit.*, p.29, Table IV. See also Rajendra Singh, "Caste, Land and Power in Uttar Pradesh", in Gail Omvedt *(ed.), Land, Caste and Politics in Indian States,* Delhi, Authors Guild Publication, 1982, p. 81.

82 W.C. Neale, *op. cit.*

83 For details see E.B. Joshi, *ibid.*, p. 204; *District Census Handbook: Analytical Administrative and Censes Tables,* Meerut District, Part C, Series 21, Allahabad, Superintendent Printing and Stationery, 1971, p. 641. This programme was implemented under the consolidation of Landholdings Act, 1953. This Act was opposed by the socialists, and Congress leaders on the floor of the House. The Act came into force in 1954 and its implementation was suspended on the advice of the revenue minister Thakur Hukum Singh. It was, however, resumed shortly. See Charan Singh, *op. cit.*, pp. 101-04. See also W.C. Neale, *op. cit.*, p. 265.

84 It is noteworthy that the ceiling programme in U.P. came almost after one decade of the zamindari abolition programme. This programme was opposed by Congress MLAs including Charan Singh, Swatantra Party, Jan Sangh, "the leftist parties" and a "section of the bourgeoisie" on different grounds. For details see Charan Singh, *ibid.*, Z.A. Ahmad, *Ceiling on Agricultural Land,* New Delhi, Communist Party of India, 1972, p. 60. Richard S. Newill, "Ideology and Realities: Land Redistribution in U.P.", *Pacific Affairs,* Vol. 45. no.2, summer 1972, pp. 220-390. See also Grigory Kotovsky, *Agrarian Reforms in India,* New Delhi, People's Publishing House, 1964, pp. 90-94.

85 See Richard S. Newill, *ibid.*

86 See Z.A. Ahmad, *op. cit.*, pp. 17-24.

87 Data on the progress of the implementation of ceiling in Meerut in the 1970s and 1980s have been collected from the Ceiling Section, Collectorate, office of the District Magistrate, Meerut.

88 "Land Dispute or War on Harijans?", *National Herald,* 11 July 1977.

89 For a discussion on the contribution of Green Revolution to the growth of these tendencies in India, see Paul R. Brass, "Introduction", "Institutional Transfer of Technology: Land Grant Model and the Agricultural University of Pant Nagar"; T.J. Byres, "Political Economy of Technological Innovation in Indian Agriculture", and Aruna Nayyar Michie, "Agricultural Modernisation and Rural Inequality in the United States and India", in Robert S. Anderson, *et al.*, (ed.), *Science, Politics and Agricultural Revolution in Asia,* Boulder, Westview Press, 1982, pp. 15-124; T.J. Byres, "The Dialectic of India's Green Revolution", *South Asian Review,* Vol.1, no. 2, January 1972, pp. 101-02. T.J. Byres, "India's Green Revolution", *Economic and Political Weekly,* Annual, nos. 6-8, February 1977, pp. 241-60. Francine R. Frankel, *India's Green Revolution: Economic Gains and Political Cost,* Princeton, University Press, 1971, Biplab Dasgupta, *op. cit.*

90 *District Cenus Handbook,* Meerut District, 1961, no.18, Allahabad, Superintendent Printing and Stationery, 1966, Table 3.3, p. 165.

91 E.B. Joshi, *op. cit.*, p. 90.

92 *District Statistical Handbook,* Meerut, 1975, 1983. Even in Bulandshahr district of western UP, the yield of wheat and sugarcane increased as a result of the Green Revolution. See Gilbert Ettinne, *India's Changig Rural Scene, 1963-1979,* Delhi, Oxford University Press, 1982, pp. 22-23. A study of Palanpur village of another district of western Uttar Pradesh, Moradabad, also shows an increase in the yield per acre between 1957-58 and 1974-75, as a result of the Green Revolution. See C.J. Bliss and N.H. Stern, *Palanpur: The Economy of an Indian Village,* Delhi, Oxford University Press, 1982, p.32.

93 The Census of 1951 uses categories for agrarian classes which are different from those of the subsequent censuses. Therefore, it is difficult to compare the variations in the data about the agrarian classes used in the Census of 1951 with those of the subsequent years. According to 1951 Census, there were four agrarian classes, *i.e.,* (1) cultivators of the land wholly or mainly owned and their dependents, (2) cultivators of the land wholly or mainly unowned and their dependents, (3) cultivating labourers and their dependents, and (4) non-cultivating owners of land, rent receivers and their dependents. Each of these classes was further subdivided into three sub-classes, *i.e.,* (1) self-supporting persons, (ii) non-earning dependents, and (iii) earning dependents. However, by categorising these four classes on the basis of the participation in the process of production and ownership of land and clubbing them together we can have three agrarian classes for the purpose of our use. Category (1) can be called cultivators, since they own the land partially or wholly and also they participate in the

process of cultivation. Categories (2) and (3) can be termed as lessees/ agricultural labourers, as they do not own the land but carry out cultivation. Category (4) can be termed as the landlords, since they consist of the non-cultivating owners and rent receivers. See *Meerut District Census Handbook*, 1951, *Uttar Pradesh Census Handbook, 1951*, Meerut, Allahabad, Superintendent Printing and Stationery, 1966.

94 In village Mirpur of Bulandshahr district of western Uttar Pradesh, the landholdings below 5 acres showed on increase between 1963-64 and 1978-79. The landholdings fragmented as a result of the process of partition of land among the members of a family. See Gilbert Ettinne, *op. cit.*, pp. 13-14.

95 Between 1951 and 1971, the percentage of persons owing landholdings up to 5 acres increased from 63.61 to 78.22. The persons owning landholdings between 5 and 15 acres declined from 33.47 to 18.6 per cent. Based on the *District Census Handbook*, Meerut, *op. cit.*, 1951, 1961 and 1971.

Chapter III

Class Differentiation within the Agrarian Society

Expropriation and differentiation of the peasantry form the most significant trends in Meerut's agrarian economy. The socio-economic conditions of the agrarian classes find their reflection in the social, economic and political relationships among them. The identification of classes and the understanding of their material conditions and inter-relationships are necessary to explain the agrarian politics.

For identification of agrarian classes we have followed the "labour-exploitation criterion" devised by Utsa Patnaik.[1] The "labour-exploitation" criterion denotes "the use of outside labour relative to the use of family labour".[2] The numerical value of the labour-exploitation ratio is the basic criterion, and not the only one, which can denote the class position of an individual. Apart from the labour-exploitation ratio, a host of other factors, *i.e.*, the ownership and the nature of means of production, size and nature of families, size of landholdings, cropping pattern, level of indebtedness and market relations can show the level of class differentiation of an agrarian society. Following classes can be identified in the agrarian society of Meerut:[3]

The rural rich : (1) Landlords
(2) Rich peasants
(3) Middle peasants

The rural poor : (4) Small peasants
(5) Poor peasants
(6) Landless proletariat
(i) Agricultural labourers
(ii) Wage labourers in non-agrarian sectors
(iii) Traditional occupation holders
(7) Miscellaneous.

Landlords own the means of production and their families do not participate in the process of production manually. They depend solely on hiring in of labour power. Supervision or operation of machinery is not considered as manual labour. Rich peasants also own the means of production. They are different from the landlords in the sense that their families participate in the process of production, apart from hiring in labour power. But the number of family labour days are much less than the labour days hired in. In principle, the middle peasants own the means of production and participate in the process of production in the absence of hiring in and hiring out of labour power. This is the most important category of the Chayanovian or the "Neo-populist" school of thought.[4] Middle peasants may not exist in an ideal form; they may hire in labour power. But the labour days they hire in are much less than their family labour days. Small peasants and poor peasants also own some of the means of production, and their families participate in the process of production. Their production, however, is not enough for their family needs. Therefore, apart from working in their own fields they hire out their labour power in the agrarian or non-agrarian sectors. The number of labour days hired out by the small peasants are less than their family labour days, and the number of labour days hired out by the poor peasants are more than their family labour days.

The landless proletariat do not own any means of production, and they have to sell out their labour power for subsistence. But all of the landless proletariat do not work on the land; they work in different sectors. On the basis of the sectors in which they work, they can be divided into agricultural labourers, wage laboureres in non-agrarian sectors and traditional occupation holders. Agricultural labourers work exclusively in agrarian sector either throughout the year or for some months in a year. Wage labourers in non-agrarian sectors work exclusively or mainly in the non-agrarian sectors either in a nearby town or in the open labour market or as casual migrants. These non-agrarian sectors include construction work, any work in the open labour market, riksha-pulling, loading of donkeys, tannery, weaving in a factory, working in a brick-kiln, making ropes, running carts for hire, grinding mill and electricity work. As we shall see in the next chapter, varying degrees of dependence on land leaves a different impact on the relationships between the landowning and the non-landowning classes. Traditional occupation holders work neither in agrarian nor in non-agrarian sectors, but perform traditional work assigned to them by the varna system. The following traditional occupations fall in our sample: lifting dung (sweepers), making pots (potters), carpentry, making and repairing things made of iron (blacksmiths), hair-cutting (barbers), basket-making (kahars or dhiwars), beggary; faqirs (Muslims) and jogis and nats (Hindus), and performing rituals (Brahmans).

The miscellaneous category consists of those who are neither related to land nor the traditional occupations. But they reside in the villages. The category includes the following people: tailors, teachers, doctors (Registered Medical Practitioners: RMPs), retired police constables, clerks, bus conductors and drivers, workers in a factory or mill, tannery owners, shopkeepers, cart runners, cycle mechanics,grinding millowners and electricians.

Despite the differentiation of the agrarian society in the above-mentioned classes, on the basis of their social, economic and political characteristics, they can be broadly divided into two groups: first, the rural rich who hire in the labour power - landlords, rich peasants and middle peasants; second, the rural poor, who hire out the labour power - small peasants, poor peasants and landless proletariat. It should be noted that the classes which form the social groups of the rural rich and the rural poor are fraught with intra-class contradictions. We are, therefore, not using the rural rich and the rural poor as analytical categories. They are being used as descriptive categories for the sake of analysis. Table 10 shows the distribution of the classes in agrarian society of Meerut district.[5] Around 67.03 per cent households are related to agriculture either in terms of ownership of means of production or in terms of participation in the process of production or both. Agriculture is their main source of income or livelihood. About 32.97 per cent households are not mainly related to agriculture. But our investigation shows that their domicile in the villages makes them dependent on land in one or the other way. The dependence on agriculture in any form makes a distinct impact on the social, economic and political relationships between classes. The percentage of persons dependent on land is less in the villages which are located in the vicinity of the city, and where the rural poor have some alternative means of livelihood, *i.e.*, factory or cottage industry, than in the remote villages where rural poor do not have any alternative means of livelihood.

Though the rural rich form only a minority of the village households, they control maximum area. Among them the middle peasants constitute the largest single class. The area controlled by them is more or less equal to the area under the landlords. But due to their numerical superiority the middle peasants are politically the most dominant class in their villages (See Table 10).

The numerical superiority of the middle peasants with their control over the maximum area owes a lot to the bhaiachara background of the district. Though the peasants who were the tenants of zamindars also became peasant-proprietors after zamindari abolition, they numbered much less than the peasant-proprietors with the bhaiachara background. Moreover, in the process of differentiation, a majority of them tend to become the small peasants. But on the basis of this relative dominance of middle peasants the agrarian economy of Meerut cannot be described as "middle peasant economy" or the mode of production as the "middle peasant mode of production". Unlike the Chayanovian or the "Neo-populist" category of ideal type middle peasants, they are not non-exploiters. In fact, they exploit the labour power from outside the family, but the proportion of outside labour power is much less than that of the family. Moreover, as we shall see in the course of our discussion in this chapter, they are also subjected to the conditions of capitalist economy producing for the market and undergoing a process of differentiation. Even the fact that landlords, though they constitute only 5.49 per cent of the households, control an area which is almost equal to that controlled by middle peasants shows that the middle peasants are not the only dominant class of agrarian society.[6]

It should be noted that we have divided the landless proletariat into three sub-categories - agricultural labourers, wage labourers in non-agrarian sectors and traditional occupation holders. This is because the wage labourers in non-agrarian sectors do not directly depend on

Table 10

Class Differentiation within the Agrarian Society of Meerut District

Class	No. of households	Perce-ntage	Average no. of labour days hired in (HI) in a year	Average no. of labour days hired out (HO) in a year	Net labour days hired in X=(HI - HO) in a year	Family labour days (F) in a year	Net labour exploitation ratio E = X/F	Perentage of the area owned
The Rural Rich								
1. Landlords	25	5.49	938.25	-	938.25	-	∞	38.84
2. Rich Peasants	10	2.20	528.5	-	528.5	342	1.55	8.69
3. Middle Peasants	93	20.44	93.38	-	93.38	817.83	0.11	39.30
The Rural Poor								
4. Small Peasants	96	21.10	2.66	42.40	-39.74	509.21	-0.08	12.58
5. Poor Peasants	10	2.20	-	1060.2	-1060.4	120.7	-8.78	0.59
6. Landless Proletariat*	181	39.77	-	-	-	-	-	-
(i) Agr. lab.	71	15.60	-	318.91	-318.91	-	∞	-
(ii) Wage lab. in non-agri. sec.	86	18.90	-	303.15	-303.15	-	∞	-
(iii) T.O. Holders	24	5.27	-	-	-	-	-	-
7. Miscellaneous	40	8.79	-	-	-	-	-	-
Total	455	100.00	-	-	-	-	-	100.00

the land of the rural rich for employment and they face relatively less harassment from the rural rich. The agricultural labourers and traditional occupation holders, on other hand, are more prone to domination and harassment of the rural rich. This, however, does not mean that the wage labourers in non-agrarian sectors are not subjected to any kind of domination of the rural rich.

Given the nature of agrarian economy of Meerut, leasing of land is not very common. There are only 4.84 per cent cases of leasing in and 1.32 per cent cases of leasing out. Most of the lessees belong to the rural poor, mainly to the agricultural labourers and small peasants. A few lessees belong to the rural rich who lease in land only for the crop of potato. They employ the agricultural labour to cultivate the leased in land. The lessees belonging to the rural poor have to bear half of the cost of production, besides carrying out the process of production. They are given half of the produce for carrying out the process of production. But the lessees in villages of Tilwara Sakin and Chobla have to render service in lieu of the land leased in by them. All of the lessors belong to the rural rich - landlords and middle peasants. Around half of them do not lease out land for the entire agricultural year; they lease it out only for the crop of potato. They lease out land for some or all of the following reasons: the land leased out is not very fertile, the owner of the land has too much of land to manage by his family, and the plot of land leased out may be far from the rest of the land of the lessor.[7] Majority of the households of the rural rich belong to Hindu dominant castes of Brahmans, Tyagis, Banias, Meena,[8] Jats and Gujars,[9] while the majority of the rural poor belong to the lower castes such as the Scheduled Castes and Other Backward Castes (OBCs) of Hindus and Muslims (See Table 11).

The dominant castes - Brahmans, Tyagis, Banias, Meenas, Jats and Gujars together control maximum area. But among them, the Jats are the most dominant who control a little more than half of the area. This clearly establishes the dominance of Jats in the economy and polity of Meerut. The average size of landholdings of the dominant castes except that of the Brahmans and Gujars, is quite high in relation to the low castes (See Table 12).

The rural rich have mostly joint families with bigger size and the rural poor have predominantly nucleus families with smaller size, (See Table 13). The rural rich retain the joint families in order to prevent

Table 11

Percentage Distribution of Castes in Relation to Classes

Class	No. of H.H.*	Brahmans	Tyagis	Banias	Meenas	Jats	Gujars	OBCs	SCs	Muslims High Castes	Muslims OBCs	Total
The Rural Rich												
Landlords	25	1.56	1.56	1.56	0.78	9.38	2.34	-	0.78	0.78	0.78	19.52
Rich Peasants	10	-	-	-	0.78	6.25	-	0.78	-	-	-	7.81
Middle Peasants	93	3.13	-	0.78	1.56	28.91	21.09	12.5	1.56	1.56	1.56	72.65
Total of the rural rich	128	4.69	1.56	2.34	3.12	44.54	23.43	13.28	2.34	2.34	2.34	100.00
The Rural Poor												
Small Peasants	96	0.70	-	-	-	4.88	8.36	10.10	4.88	1.05	3.48	33.45
Poor Peasants	10	-	-	-	-	0.35	-	1.74	0.70	-	0.70	3.49
Landless Proletariat*												
(i) Agr. Lab.	71	-	-	-	-	1.05	-	6.27	12.89	-	4.53	24.74
(ii) Wage Lab. in non-agr. sec.	86	0.35	-	-	-	-	-	8.36	17.42	-	3.83	29.96
(iii) T.O. Holders	24	0.70	-	-	-	-	-	4.18	1.74	-	1.74	8.36
Total of the rural poor	287	1.75	-	-	-	6.28	8.36	30.65	37.63	1.05	14.28	100.00
Miscellaneous	40	7.5	-	7.5	-	-	12.5	30	30	-	12.5	100.00
Caste-wise percentage of H.H. from the total sample	445	3.08	0.44	1.32	0.88	16.49	12.97	25.72	27.04	1.32	10.78	100.00

* Agr. Lab. = Agricultural Labourers; wage lab. in non agr. sec. = Wage la[illegible] in non agrarian sector;

the division of the family property, particularly land. Division of family, moreover, is not considered good. During the fieldwork, there were instances that some of the respondents tried to hide the information about the division of their families. Remnant of the bhaiachara tradition which had strong inclination for the joint family system is an additional factor for its predominance. The rate of division of the families among the rural rich is much slower. Disputes over domestic matters, and the proportion of labour shared in the family land by different members of family generally are the reasons which lead to division of families. The nature of family system of the rural rich has even certain political implications. For example, the predominance of the joint family system among the rural rich was one of the reasons that the Bharatiya Kisan Union could continue its rallies at Meerut (January-February 1988) and in Delhi (October-November 1988) for more than 20 days on

Table 12

Caste-wise Distribution of Area

Caste	Area in acres	Percentage of the area	Average area per household in acres
1. Brahmans	46.6	3.23	3.33
2. Tyagis	57.0	3.95	28.5*
3. Banias	65.0	4.51	10.83
4. Meenas	57.0	3.95	14.25
5. Jats	739.6	51.27	9.86
6. Gujars	225.05	15.60	3.85
7. OBCs (Hindus)	152.1	10.54	1.3
8. SCs	38.45	2.67	0.31
9. Muslim High Castes	12.6	0.87	2.1
10. OBCs (Muslims)	49.1	3.40	1.00
Total	1442.5	100.00	6.14

* The average size of landholdings for Tyagis in our sample is quite high. It should not be confused with the average size of landholdings for Tyagis of Meerut district as a whole. In fact, of the eight villages in our sample only one, Jafarnagar Begamabad, is inhabited by Tyagis and all of them fall in the landlords' category. This average size is, therefore, for the landlords category of Tyagis.

Table 13

Distribution of Joint Families and Average Size of Families in Relation to Classes

Class	Total no. of families on which information is available	Percentage of joint families	Average size of the family
The Rural Rich			
1. Landlords	21	80.95	11.43
2. Rich Peasants	10	90.0	10.2
3. Middle Peasants	92	76.09	9.46
Percentage of Joint families of the rural rich	123	78.05	
The Rural Poor			
4. Small Peasants	95	56.84	7.66
5. Poor Peasants	10	70.0	7.88
6 Agricultural Labourers	71	32.39	6.04
7. Wage labourers in non-agrarian sectors	86	39.53	6.51
8. Traditional occupation holders	24	58.33	6.00
Percentage of joint families of the rural poor	286	46.15	
9. Miscellaneous	40	45	6.44
Percentage of joint families in the entire sample and average size of the family	449	54.79	7.64

each occasion, with some members of the families participating in the rallies and the rest being left behind to look after the agriculture and families.

The rural poor do not have special inclination towards the joint family system because they lack big size landholdings which need to be preserved from fragmentation. This is more particularly so in the case of the landless proletariat. Generally their sons set up independent families separate from the parental families immediately after marriage. It is interesting to note that like the rural rich, the rural poor also do not consider the division of family as good. But the slightest dispute or protest results in the division of a family.

More than 80 per cent landholdings of the rural rich fall in the range of 3 acres and above. It is noteworthy that only the landlords control the landholdings of 20 acres and above. By contrast around 79 per cent landholdings of the small peasants and poor peasants are below 3 acres.[10] Following examples explain how the households owning above 3 acres landholdings fall in the category of the rural rich and how the households with landholdings below 3 acres fall in the category of the small peasants and poor peasants.

Hriday Ram's is a joint family of 15 members of Jats of Behzadka village. It owns 45 acres of land and controls all the necessary means of production including two tractors. The family members do not participate in the process of production; they only supervise and one member of the household operates a tractor and another manages a brick-kiln owned by the family in Bulandshahr district. They do not hire out labour power. They hire in around 4,740 labour days in a year. The net labour exploitation ratio for the household is positive infinite (∞). This household falls under the category of landlord which is also the biggest in our sample.

Bedi Ram's is also a joint family of 13 members which belongs to the Jats of Nagla Tashi Qasimpur village. It owns 18.6 acres of land and possesses all the necessary means of production. The family members work in their own land for 300 labour days in a year and they hire in labour power for 345 labour days in a year. They do not hire out labour power at all. The net labour exploitation ratio for the household is more than plus one (+1.15). This household falls under the category of rich peasants.

Bed Singh's is a joint family of 22 members and belongs to the

Jats of Tilwara Sakin. It owns 6 acres of land and almost all the necessary means of production, except tractor and troly. The household depends mainly on the family labour putting in 600 labour days in a year. But they hire in labour power for 120 labour days in a year for certain activities, like tying of the sugarcane standing in the fields (Ikh: sugarcane), harvesting of wheat, *etc*. They do not hire out labour power at all. The net labour exploitation ratio for the family is less than plus one (+ 0.2). This household belongs to the category of the middle peasants. But it is not the ideal type of middle peasant family which is not supposed to hire in and/or hire out the labour power.

Sher Singh's is a nucleus family of the Sainis of Jalalpur village. It owns 2 acres of land but does not own all the necessary means of production. It owns only an iron plough, a Dunlop cart and a tube-well (jointly with two small peasants). For all other necessities the household depends on others. The family members work in their own land for 400 labour days in a year and hire out labour power for 240 labour days in a year. They do not hire in labour power at all. The net labour exploitation ratio for the household is more than minus one (-0.06). This household belongs to the category of small peasants.

Rame's is a nucleus family of kumhars of Ahera village. The household owns only 0.4 acre of land but does not own any other means of production. The members of the family work for 360 labour days on their land in a year, while they hire out 540 labour days in a year working in a brick-kiln. They do not hire in labour power at all. Their net labour exploitation is less than minus one (-1.5). The household belongs to the category of poor peasants.

Land and the other means of production - means of cultivation, *i.e.,* ploughs, harrows and cultivators; means of irrigation, *i.e,* tube-wells, pump-sets and diesel engines; means of transportation, *i.e.,* Dunlop carts and trolleys, and tractors; other means such as threshers and agricultural livestock, are concentrated in the hands of the rural rich.

As a result of increasing mechanisation marked by the use of tractors, threshers, tube-wells and pump-sets by all sections of the peasantry, the traditional means of production including the agricultural livestock - he-buffaloes and bulls - have greatly declined.[11] The "ideal" peasant with his "two bulls to plough and one he-buffaloe to drive the cart" has undergone a considerable change. Though the rich peasants and middle peasants have also faced the replacement of their traditional means of production by modern technology, it is the small peasants and poor peasants who have been severely affected by the replacement. The traditional means of a large number of small peasants, and almost all poor peasants have become redundant, as they have to compete in agrarian economy with the owners of modern technology. Eventually, finding themselves unable to compete, they have lost control over the means of production except land. And in certain cases the poor peasants have lost even their land, and have either become the landless proletariat or fallen in the miscellaneous category. The increasing dependence of all segments of the peasantry on modern technology, but more importantly the incompatibility of the traditional means with the modern means, and the unequal access of different classes to the means of production have accelerated the process of expropriation and differentiation of the peasantry.

All those who do not partially or totally own all the necessary means of production depend upon those who own them.[12] They hire in the services of the tractor-owners, cart-owners, thresher-owners, trolley owners, *etc.;* water of the tube-well and pump-set owners, and canal. A large number of small peasants and poor peasants co-operate with each other in exchanging both means and services. This practice of co-operation is called dangwara. It is essential for all types of peasants to use tractors at least on some occasions. For example, the sugarcane growers find it too hard to plough moodha (the field after the cutting of sugarcane) by the wooden or iron ploughs. So, they hire tractors for ploughing. The small peasants and poor peasants find it more expedient to get their small patches of land ploughed by tractors for hire.

More than fifty per cent households of the rural rich and around eighty-four per cent households of the rural poor and the miscellaneous[13] category are indebted. The share of the rural rich is around 12 per cent of the total debt and the rest is borne by the rural poor. The microscopic minority of the moneylenders belong to the rural rich,[14] (See Table 14).

Only 64 per cent of the indebted households could reveal the sources of their debt. The sources of the rural rich and the rural poor are different. The rural rich mostly (90.91 per cent) borrow from modern institutions, *i.e.*, co-operative societies and banks. The rural poor mostly borrow from traditional and non-governmental institutions, *i.e.*, landlords, milkmen and relatives. It should be noted that none of the landlords and rich peasants borrows from the traditional institutions. Those few rural rich who borrow from them belong to the middle peasants. On the contrary, most (74.47 per cent) of the rural poor borrow from the traditional institutions. Only 20.74 per cent of households borrow from the modern institutions. A total of 79.26 per cent households borrow from the traditional institutions such as moneylenders and milkmen and from relatives (4.79 per cent).

Table 14

Percentage Distribution of Indebted Households, Moneylenders and the Amount of Debt in Relation to Classes

Class	No. of households	Indebted households	Moneylenders	Amount indebted Rs.	Average amount indebted Rs.
The Rural Rich					
1. Landlords	23	2.05(30.43)*	40.00 (1.34)*	173,306.00	24,758.00
2. Rich Peasants	10	0.88(30)*	6.67 (0.22)*	38,.000.00	12,666.67
3. Middle Peasants	93	17.65(64.52)*	26.67 (0.89)*	318,850.00	5,314.17
Total	126	20.58(55.55)*	73.34 (2.45)*	530,156.00 (11.93)**	4,207.59
The Rural Poor and Miscellaneous					
4. Small Peasants	90	20.59(77.78)*	6.67(0.22)*	414,640.00	5,923.42
5. Poor Peasants	10	2.94 (100)*	-	23,065.00	2,306.5
6. Agricultural labourers	71	19.12(91.55)*	-	263,450.00	4,053.08
7. Wage Labourers in non-agrarian sectors	86	23.34 (91.86)*	-	3,095,550.00	39,184.18

(Contd.)

8. T.O. Holders	24	5.88(83.33)*	-	46,850.00	2,342.50
9. Miscellaneous	40	7.65(65)*	20.00 (0.67)*	68,700.00	22,900.00
Total	321	79.42(84.11)*	26.67	3,912,255.00 (88.07)**	
Grand Total	447	100.00(76.06)*	100.00 (3.34)*	4,442,411.00	13,065.92

* Percentage of the indebted households of every class in case of indebted households.

** Percentage of amount of total debt.

Like the sources, the purposes of the debt of the rural rich differ from those of the rural poor. Most of the rural rich (62.5 per cent) borrow for agricultural goods, *i.e.*, tractors, instruments, seeds, fertilizers, and a few (1.56 per cent) for brick-kilns. Only 37.5 per cent of them borrow for other purposes, *i.e.*, domestic needs, buffaloes, social obligations, foodgrains, education of children and buying land. All of them belong to the middle peasants. On the contrary, only 4.64 per cent households of the rural poor borrow for agricultural purposes. And 95.36 per cent of them borrow for domestic needs, buffaloes, social obligations, foodgrains, education of children, buying means of self-employment, land and for giving bribe to the village level officials, *i.e.*, village level workers (VLWs) and patwaris. It should be noted that only 4.64 per cent of their households borrow for foodgrains, and 61.07 per cent borrow for buffaloes and social obligations.

The livestock form a very significant aspect of the agrarian economy. The purposes behind keeping the livestock and the sources from which they are available reveal the economic conditions of the households. They also show the nature of relationships between the rural poor and the rural rich. The rural rich own half of the livestock and the rural poor (along with the miscellaneous category) keep the rest (See Table 15).

Buffaloes have become the backbone of the economy of the rural poor in the post-independence period. Milk-selling has become a significant means of livelihood and employment for them with the emergence of local milk market and its linkages with outside markets in Delhi and Bombay. While the rural rich own buffaloes to meet their family milk consumption, the rural poor keep them as a means of subsistence.

Table 15

Percentage Distribution of Livestock in Relation to Classes

Class	No. of cattle owned by each class	Buff-loes	He-buff-aloes	Bulls	Off-spring	Cows	Goats	Pigs	Horses	Donkeys	Percentage of total cattle owned by each class
1. Landlords	189	10.44	10.36	21.60	12.36	13.70	-	-	-	-	12.45
2. Rich Peasants	92	3.75	5.93	16.43	4.72	6.85	-	-	-	-	6.06
3. Middle Peasants	491	28.22	54.07	41.78	26.97	38.36	-	-	42.86	27.78	32.35
percentage of cattle owned by rural rich	772	42.41	70.36	79.81	44.05	85.91	-	-	42.86	27.78	50.86
4. Small Peasants	368	25.12	28.15	19.72	27.42	12.33	25.00	-	14.29	-	24.24
5. Poor Peasants	21	1.31	0.74	0.47	1.80	4.11	-	-	-	-	1.38
6. Agr. Labourers	117	11.75	-	-	9.21	4.11	12.5	-	-	-	7.71
7. Wage Lab. in non-agr. sec.	131	9.79	0.74	-	8.76	9.59	37.5	100.00	28.57	72.22	8.63
8. T.O. Holders	43	4.40	-	-	3.15	2.74	-	-	-	-	2.83
9. Miscellaneous	66	5.22	-	-	5.62	8.22	25.00	-	14.29	-	4.35
Percentage of cattle owned by the rural poor and miscellaneous	746	57.59	29.63	20.19	55.96	41.1	100.00	100.00	57.15	72.22	49.14
Percentage of each cattle out of total livestock	1,518	40.38	8.89	14.03	29.31	4.81	0.53	0.46	0.46	1.19	100.00

Table 16

Percentage of the Households Deprived of the Means of Production

Class	Means of Cultivation				Means of Irrigation		Means of Transportation		Tractors	Threshers
	Iron ploughs	Wooden ploughs	Harrows	Cultivators	Tubewells	Pumpsets	Carts	Trolley		
Rural Rich	33.59	30.47	81.25	57.81	42.19	68.75	21.09	88.2	78.13	71.88
Small Peasants	77.08	58.33	100.00	96.87	87.5	90.62	59.37	100.00	100.00	1.04
Poor Peasants	100.00	100.00	100.00	100.00	100.00	100.00	100.00	100.00	100.00	100.00

More than ninety per cent households of the rural poor keep buffaloes as a means of subsistence.[14] The rural rich generally do not sell milk; milk selling is considered to be below dignity by them. However, under the changing circumstances some of them do sell milk. But the purposes, terms and conditions for which they sell milk are different from those of the rural poor. The rural rich sell milk for commercial purposes or to earn "extra" money. On the contrary, the rural poor sell it as an inevitable aspect of their economic activity for subsistence. Around 71.55 per cent households of the rural poor sell milk. Only a few (6.69 per cent) of them keep buffaloes to meet the family milk consumption. In contrast, only one-third households of the rural rich sell milk. All of them belong to the rich peasants and middle peasants, and none to the landlords.

Even the agencies to which the rural rich and the rural poor sell milk are different. The rural poor sell milk to the village milkmen. None of the rural rich sells milk to milkmen; they sell it to dairies. Milkmen and dairy are two distinct agencies which buy milk from buffalo-keepers. Dairies are of two types- (i) private dairies located in the cities, where the milkmen supply milk after buying it from buffalo-keepers, and (ii) co-operative or Parag dairies, which set up their branches in the villages and to which the villagers sell milk directly. Milkman is a person generally having local background: either hailing from the same village or from a neighbouring village. He buys milk from buffalo-keepers in the villages and sends it to the private dairies in the cities like Meerut, Mawana and Delhi. Economically, selling milk to co-operatives or Parag dairies is more advantageous than selling it to the milkmen. The price of milk offered by these dairies is higher than given by the milkmen.[15] Moreover, the measurement of milk is done in a scientific manner at these dairies which also provide higher rate for better quality of milk. Conversely, selling milk to milkmen is exploitative on many grounds. The measurement of milk by the milkmen is very faulty: the measuring pot is expanded by the milkmen so that it can contain more milk than the exact quantity. Many milkmen still use the ser and not litre as the unit of measurement. The price of the milk paid to the buffalo-keepers by the milkmen is much lower than the market price. The buffalo-keepers are aware of the difference between selling milk to the co-operatives or Parag dairies and to the milkmen. But due to some constraints a majority of them are bound to sell it to the milkmen. There are economic reasons for this. The buffalo-keepers need money for their daily necessities. The milkmen also serve as moneylenders. They lend money to the buffalo-keepers as advance. Apart from this, whenever the buffalo-keepers require money they turn to the milkmen. In many cases, the buffalo-keepers only have to rear the buffaloes which are actually bought by the milkmen. Moreover, they ask the milkmen to buy the khal (a mix made of pulses) for cattle, and things of daily needs in many cases. They charge more than the market price from the buffalo-keepers for these things. Under such circumstances the milkmen make profit by faulty measurement and paying low price for milk to the buffalo-keepers. On the other hand, the co-operative or Parag dairies pay more and their measurement of the milk is also scientific and done in litre, but they cannot pay advance. They make weekly payments, and that too after the buffalo-keepers have sold the milk. Due to these factors, despite being aware of the disadvantages of selling milk to the milkmen, they prefer them rather than dairies. It should be noted that not all the milkmen are alike in their economic conditions, some of them are poor but some of them are very rich. They are landlords, rich peasants, middle peasants and moneylenders. In one of the villages of our sample, Ahera, a milkman is the village pradhan.[16]

Apart from keeping them for selling their milk, the rural poor keep the cattle of others just to rear them up. This practice is called as hissa. In the case of livestock, hissa is a very significant phenomenon practised by the rural poor. Under this process a household which does not have enough resources, called hissedar, enters into an informal contract with another person who owns the cattle and is known as the malik (owner). The malik gives the cattle to the hissedar to rear it up. This contract is made for a specific period. A buffalo is generally given on hissa for a period till she conceives and delivers. As soon as she delivers, the market price of the buffalo is fixed. And a part of this market price is given to the hissedar for having looked after the buffalo. This part of the market price is known as hissa. Hence the practice is called as such. In the case of young cattle the period varies depending on the mutual contract between the malik and the hissedar, and on general custom prevalent in the area. In this case also a hissa of market price is given to the hissedar.

The amount of hissa given to the hissedar varies from case to case.

But generally in the case of young cattle it is half of its market price, and in the case of buffalo it is one-fourth of its market price. The practice of hissa is generally prevalent specifically in the villages which are far from the market, and where the milkmen are not rich enough to buy buffaloes for the buffalo-keepers. Similar practice is prevalent in Muzaffarnagar district of western Uttar Pradesh.[17] Though 73.09 per cent households of the rural poor have buffaloes, all of them do not practically own them. Around 41.42 per cent of them just look after them and they get them either on credit (20.08 per cent) or keep them on hissa (21.34 per cent). Milkmen and "levy" are the main sources, which lend them buffaloes on credit. "Levy" is given to the buffalo-keepers of poor background under the IRDP. Milkman's *modus operandi* of providing buffaloes to the buffalo-keepers is two-fold: (i) providing advance money for buying buffaloes, and (ii) buying buffaloes himself for them.

Wheat and maize are the main food crops of the people of Meerut, while wheat and sugarcane are the main commercial crops. The latter cover 72.22 per cent of the cultivated area : 35.41 per cent of it being under wheat and 36.81 per cent under sugarcane. The rural rich cultivate larger area under wheat (33.72 per cent) and sugarcane (40.52 per cent) than other crops. While no poor peasant grows sugarcane, the small peasants cultivate sugarcane in around 20 per cent of their area. Wheat, maize and fodder are the main crops of the small and poor peasants.

The rural rich and the rural poor are subjected to varying degres of terms and conditions of the market. They are related to the market for selling their produce and buying foodgrains. The rural rich sell their surplus produce in the market for commercial purposes. On the contrary, the small and poor peasants sell their foodgrains under certain compulsions. They sell the foodgrains at a lower rate than the market price immediately after harvesting as they need cash for buying agricultural goods and household goods, for repaying debt, for education of their children and to meet social obligations. Later, they have to buy foodgrains from the market at higher rate than the rate at which they sell out, for family consumption. A majority of the rural rich produce surplus foodgrains for market. None of the households of landlords or rich peasants sells foodgrains under compulsion. However, some of the middle peasants have to sell food grains under certain compulsions.

Majority of the households of the rural rich are self-sufficeint in foodgrains but none of the households of poor peasants is self-sufficient in the foodgrain production. They buy foodgrains from the market for 9 months of the year. It is interesting to note that 47.78 per cent households of the agricultural labourers and wage labourers in non-agrarian sectors, though deprived of the means of production in agriculture, do not depend on market for foodgrains throughout the year. This is because of the prevalence of the system of lai. Harvesting of wheat for wages is called lai. The wage labourers who carry out this process are called lavas and they are paid in kind in terms of sheaves of wheat. They gather foodgrains from the lai which can sustain them for some months in a year.[18] The rate of wage varies from 3 to more than 5 sheaves for 100 sheaves cut by a lava. The differential in the wages depends on the agrarian history of the villages, the vicinity of a village to a city and the demand for increase in wages by the agricultural labourers in howsoever unorganized and unsuccessful way. A new phenomenon has appeared in the last few years in some villages. Under this, the owner of the field makes an informal contract with a family or a group of agricultural labourers to get the wheat harvested, and the agricultural labourers are paid wages on the basis of wheat cut per bigha as per the conditions of the contract. The contract wages vary from 4 dhadi (1 dhadi = 5 kg) to more than 4 dhadi wheat along with 4 dhadi of straw for cutting wheat in one bigha. Another dwindling process is the sila. Under this process women belonging to the rural poor, collect the left-over wheat plants after harvesting is over. They are given some portion (muthi) of the wheat plants which they collect from the fields. However, this process is fast disappearing and is not a common feature now.[19]

Though the rural rich share common characteristics of hiring in the labour power and controlling the maximum resources, they are embedded in internal contradictions, cleavages and rivalries. Not all the rural rich are self-sufficient in the means of production. Table 16 shows the relative deprivation of the means of production of the rural rich, small peasants and poor peasants. Most of these deprived rural rich belong to the middle peasants, and not to the landlords or rich peasants. The deprived rural rich depend for resources on those who control them - landlords, rich peasants and the resourceful middle peasants. The inter-dependence within the rural rich for resources and credit bespeaks of the economic contradictions within the rural rich. Apart from these contradictions, there exist social cleavages on caste basis and rivalry for domination of village and district level politics among them. Moreover, distress sale by some of the middle peasants and purchase of foodgrains by them later at an exorbitant price, unlike the landlords and rich peasants, suggest that the rural rich have unequal ability to deal with the market.

To sum up, the agrarian classes can be broadly divided into two groups - the rural rich and the rural poor. There are intra-class contradictions also within the rural rich as well as the rural poor even as there are inter-class contradictions and dependencies. Middle peasants are the single largest class among the rural rich which control the maximum area in the district. Although the landlords control almost as much area as the middle peasants, numerically they form a minority. But the agrarian economy of Meerut cannot be described as one based on "middle peasant economy" or "middle peasant mode of production". Contrary to the middle peasant thesis, the middle peasants of Meerut are subjected to the conditions of capitalist economy producing for the market, and undergoing the processes of expropriation and differentiation. Moreover, they exploit the labour power of others, albeit to a less extent than the family labour power. They behave almost in the same manner with the rural poor as the landlords and rich peasants. Meerut represents the tendencies of capitalism, which are significant features of the agrarian economy of western Uttar Pradesh.

Notes

1 Utsa Patnaik, "Class Differentiation within the Peasantry : An Approach to the Analysis of Indian Agriculture", *Economic and Political Weekly*, Review of Agriculture, Vol.XI, no. 39, 25 September 1976, pp. A82-A101. Patnaik's model is "a slight formalisation", and "synthesis" of the framework provided by V.I. Lenin, "Preliminary Draft Thesis on the Agrarian Question", *Collected Works,* Vol. 31, Moscow, Progress Publishers, 1966, pp. 152-64; and Mao Tse-tung, "How to Differentiate the Classes in the Rural Areas", *Collected Works,* Vol. 1, Peking, Foreign Language Progress, 1967, pp. 137-39. The former deals exclusively with the capitalist society and the latter with the feudal society: Patnaik's model is meant to be applicable to India, and for that matter to almost all of the Third world countries. Patnaik has made a slight improvement on the labour-exploitation criterion in her book published afterwards. She has included in it even the surplus labour days embodied in the interest payment. Inclusion of the labour days of interest payment,

however, does not alter her original criterion. See Utsa Patnaik, *Peasant Class Differentiation : A Study in Method with Reference to Haryana*, Delhi, Oxford University Press, 1987, pp. 51-59.

2 "The labour-exploitation criterion" has come in use recently. See Ednaldo Araquen da Silva, "Measuring the Incidence of Rural Capitalism: An Analysis of the Survey Data from North East Brazil", *The Journal of Peasant Studies*, Vol.12, no. 1, October 1984, pp.65-75. Barbara Harriss, "Social Classes in Dryland Agriculture", in Barbara Harriss, *et al.*, (*ed.*), *Exchange Relations and Poverty in Dryland Agriculture*, New Delhi, Concept, 1984. Lenin's and Mao's criteria were used by P. Sundarayya, "Class Differentiation within the Peasantry: Results of Rural Surveys in Andhra Pradesh", *Social Scientist*, Vol.5, no.8, March 1977, pp. 51-83, and no.9, April 1977, pp.45-60. Atiur Rahman, *Peasants and Classes: A Study in Differentiation in Bangladesh*, Delhi, Oxford University Press, 1986.

3 Based on Utsa Patnaik, *op. cit.*, 1976 and 1987. In her article on differentiation within the peasantry (1976), Patnaik divided the middle peasant category into upper middle peasant and lower middle peasant. But in her book (1987) she has substituted the upper middle peasant by the "middle peasant" and the lower middle peasant by the "small peasant". Accordingly, we will also use the categories of "middle peasant" and "small peasant" in our analysis. The category 6 has been used as "full time labourer" and "landless labourer" in her article (1976) and in her book (1987) respectively. But they do not include the traditional occupation holders, like carpenters, barbers, blacksmiths, *etc*. Since we are dealing with the class differentiation within the entire agrarian society, not only within the peasantry, we are replacing this category by a much broader category of the "landless proletariat".

4 For a discussion on this school of thought see A.V. Chayanov, *On the Theory of Peasant Economy*, edited and introduced by Daniel Thorner, Basile Karbley and R.E.F. Smith, Homewood, Illinois, 1966, and three articles written by the editors in the same book : Basile Karbley, "Chayanov and the Theory of Peasantry as a Specific Type of Economy", and Daniel Thorner, "Peasant Economy as a Category in Economic History", in Teodor Shanin (*ed.*), *Peasants and Peasant Societies*, Harmondsworth, Penguin, 1971; Mark Harrison, "Chayanov and the Economics of the Russian Peasantry", *The Journal of Peasant Studies*, Vol.2, No. 4, July 1975, pp. 389-417; "Chayanov and the Marxists", *The Journal of Peasant Studies*, Vol.7, No.1, October 1979, pp.86-100; "The Peasant Mode of Production in the Works of A.V. Chayanov", *The Journal of Peasant Studies*, Vol.4, no.4, July 1977, pp. 323-36; Judith Ennew, Paul Hirst and Keith Tribe, "Peasantry as an Economic Category", *The Journal of Peasant Studies*,

Vol. 4, no. 4, July 1977, pp. 295-321; Susan A. Mann and James M. Dickinson. "Obstacles to the Development of a Capitalist Agriculture", *The Journal of Peasant Studies,* Vol.5, no. 4, July 1978, pp. 466-81. Utsa Patnaik, "Neo-populism and Marxism : The Chayanovian view of the Agrarian Question and its Fundamental Fallacy", *The Journal of Peasant Studies,* Vol. 6, no. 4, July 1979, pp. 375-419.

5 We have taken one year (360 days) as the basis for labour days hired in and hired out. For calculating the labour days hired out, we multiplied the number of persons hiring out labour power from families with number of days for which they hired out. And in the same way, we calculated the labour days hired in by multiplying number of persons hired in with the number of days for which they were hired in. In case of the family labour days, we calculated them by multiplying the number of the family members working on the land owned by the family by number of days they worked in a year. Since the traditional occupation holders and miscellaneous categories do not hire in or hire out labour power in the way the other classes do, we did not make any calculations about them.

6 For a critique of the middle peasant thesis see, Utsa Patnaik, "Neo-populism and Marxism...", *op. cit.*

7 A new phenomenon which has taken place in almost the last 10-15 years is that of giving land and getting some work done particularly unveiling of sugarcane on contract. This trend shows a strong tendency towards capitalism in agriculture involving the role of money. We have 2 cases of unveiling of sugarcane on contract. One middle peasant and one small peasant no longer get their sugarcanes unveiled in the traditional way. Rather they make a contract with the agricultural labourers who are paid fixed money to do this work. In one case which did not fall in our sample, one Gujar family has given out the entire land on contract for Rs. 200 per bigha or Rs. 1000 per acre annually. He has given out this land on contract because he does not have any son or resources to look after it.

8 Meenas are generally found in Rajasthan. But four villages in Meerut district, Jafarnagar Begamabad, Maharmati Meena, Sakauti Tanda and Khirwa are also inhabited by them. Since caste is not our criterion of selection of a village, the village Jafarnagar Begamabad of Sardhana tahsil which falls in our sample coincidently is inhabited by Meenas with other castes which are usually found in Meerut. They are included in the category of the Scheduled Tribes in Rajasthan, but in the villages of Meerut inhabited by them, they occupy a dominant position economically and politically. That is why we are putting them in the dominant caste category. However, they are demanding that they should be accorded the status of Scheduled Tribes in Uttar Pradesh also.

9 Gujars are included in the Other Backward Classes in U.P. But due to their numerical and economic position in Meerut we have placed them in the position of a dominant caste.

10 The average size of landholdings of all classes is 6.14 acres. The average size of landholdings of the landlords, rich peasants and middle peasants is 22.41, 12.54 and 6.10 acres respectively and that of the small peasants and poor peasants is 1.89 and 0.85 acres respectively.

11 See also Sanjay Sinha, "Economics vs Stigma: Socio-Economic Dynamics of Rural Leather Worker in UP", *Economic and Political Weekly,* Vol. 21, no. 24, 24 June 1986, p. 1065. Sinha makes a point about the replacement of cattle by tractors while studying the leather work economics of Meerut, Gorakhpur and Kanpur. Besides the decline in their numbers, even the reduction of the pair (Jode) of the agricultural livestock into the single in any household denotes their replacement by modern technology in agriculture. In our sample 50.85 per cent households of the peasantry possess he-buffaloes and 52.14 per cent of them possess bulls; rest of them do not possess them. Only 5.13 per cent households possess he-buffaloes in pairs, while 47.01 per cent of them own he-buffaloes in singles. Around 26.81 per cent of households possess bulls in pairs, while 28.51 per cent of them own bulls in singles.

12 Although the means of production are concentrated in the hands of the rural rich, all of their households do not possess all the necessary means of production. While the small peasants own some of the means of production, the poor peasants do not own any other means except land. Table 16, shows the classwise deprivation of the means of production.

13 Most of the persons falling under the miscellaneous category share several common socio-economic characteristics with the rural poor. Therefore, for the sake of brevity of analysis they will be considered as a part of the rural poor henceforth.

14 A study conducted in a village of the neighbouring state of Haryana presents a contrasting picture to that of most parts of Meerut district in terms of classwise ownership and purposes of buffaloes. While in Meerut the rural poor keep (not always own) buffaloes for the purposes of selling their milk, in Haryana generally the rural poor neither keep buffaloes nor do they own them. The buffaloes are owned by "big landowners", and like the rural rich of Meerut they also do not sell milk. They use milk for family consumption. They distribute butter milk. (This practice, which is now almost extinct, had existed in Meerut till a few years ago). The rural poor in Haryana do not own or keep buffaloes, perhaps because like in some parts of Meerut, they lack the market and sources [such as the milkmen of Meerut), who could give them Peshgi (advance)] or who could buy buffaloes for them. See Surendra Mohan Batra, *The Place*

of Livestock in the Social and Economic Systems of a Village in Haryana, Chapter III, Ph.D. thesis, University of Delhi, 1981.

15 See Chapter IV, p.84, fn.12.

16 See also Sanjib Kumar Baruah, *Getting a Fair Share : Politics and Poor in Rural India,* Ph.D. thesis, Chicago University, 1983, pp. 98-103. Baruah discusses the role of milkmen and milk economy in the economy of village Khanauda of Meerut district.

17 See M.C. Pradhan, *The Political System of the Jats in North India,* London, Oxford University Press, 1966, pp. 47-48, 163, and for Haryana see Surendra Mohan Batra, *ibid.,* pp. 199-206. Harriss finds the existence of leasing of sheep to shepherds in Tamil Nadu. This practice had existed even in Meerut. But this has almost ceased to operate as the shepherds rarely graze the cattle. The expansion of agriculture has made the grazing land scarce. See John Harriss, *Capitalism and Peasant Farming : Agrarian Structure and Ideology in Northern Tamil Nadu,* Bombay, Oxford University Press, 1982, p.90.

18 Half of the households of agricultural labourers and wage labourers in non-agrarian sectors can sustain on foodgrains gathered from lai on an average for 3.62 months in a year. The families of the small and poor peasants can sustain themselves from the wages of lai on an average for 4.33 and 7.22 months in a year respectively. A study of 50 agricultural labourers in 5 villages of Mawana tahsil of Meerut district shows that every household earns approximately 10 to 12 quintals of wheat and 5 to 6 quintals of fodder from lai. This can meet the yearly needs of a family of five. According to the findings of Baruah from village Khanauda of Meerut district the earnings from lai can feed a family for six months. Even some people who live in the cities go to the villages in Meerut district during harvesting in order to do lai. See J.S. Garg and T.R. Singh, "An Enquiry into the Pattern of Unemployment and Level of Earnings of Landless Agricultural Labourers in Western U.P.", in S.M. Pandey *(ed.), Rural Labour in India : Problems and Policy Perspectives,* Delhi, Shri Ram Centre for Industrial Relations, 1976, pp. 58-59.

19 See also Sanjib Kumar Baruah, *op. cit.,* pp. 92-95.

Chapter IV

Dependence, Resistance and Sanctions

There exist relationships of dependence between the rural rich and the rural poor. In the Indian context, these relationships have been perceived as the patron-client relationships, patrons belonging to high/dominant castes and clients to low castes. The patron-client thesis assumes that these relationships are moralistic and obligatory in nature. The patrons adopt "paternalistic" attitude towards clients, guard their interests and show "affection", "generosity" and "intercession" to them. The clients in return pay them "respect", "loyalty" and "support".[1] "It has not generally been recognised that the exchange (of 'goods' and 'service' between the patrons and clients) was founded on exploitation".[2] Moreover, this thesis ignores that the rural poor (clients) do not accept the domination of the rural rich (patrons) willingly. It also ignores the fact that they resist the exploitation/oppression/harassment of the latter through the everyday forms of resistance which may include ordinary weapons of the oppressed groups, "ranging from clandestine arson and sabotage to foot dragging, dissimulation, false compliance, pilfering, slander, flight and so forth".[3] Observations from western Uttar Pradesh show that the rural rich dominate and harass/exploit/oppress the rural poor in various ways which are the consequences of the relationships of dependence. Quite contrary to the patron-client thesis, the rural poor do not accept their harassment/oppression/exploitation willingly. They resist them in different ways. On the other hand, the rural rich retaliate by imposing sanctions against the rural poor.

The relationships of dependence are of two types - one-sided dependence and mutual dependence. The latter can be called contradictions.[4] It is necessary to distinguish the relationships of one-sided dependence from the contradictions, as their solution may lie in different ways and as they have different types of implications. The relationships of one-sided dependence represent only the dependence of the rural poor on the rural rich; the dependence is not two-sided or mutual. The rural poor have no bargaining power in these relationships. They cannot refuse to comply with the rural rich. If they do so, the relationships can be snapped by the rural rich at their will, since they do not depend on the rural poor in the particular processes or phenomena involving those relationships. Thus, this type of dependence makes it possible for the rural rich to force the rural poor to oblige them. Contradictions, on the contrary, involve mutual dependence between the rural poor and the rural rich. Both sides have bargaining power, though it is of unequal nature. The processes or phenomena involving their relationships concern the interests of the both. Unlike the case of one-sided-dependence, relationships between them are based on market rules. This type of relationships cannot be cancelled unilaterally, so long as the phenomena or the processes of these relationships exist.

It should be noted that the rural rich, though share several common characteristics, do not form a homogeneous group. As mentioned in the earlier chapter, they are embedded in internal contradictions, cleavages and rivalries. Moreover, they are also subjected to the fluctuating conditions of terms of trade and have their contradictions with the traders (merchant),[5] the state and the monopoly capital. Neither the rural poor form a homogeneous group. They are also full of contradictions, cleavages and rivalries. In spite of their internal contradictions and cleavages, the categories of the rural rich and the rural poor can be used, for the purpose of analysis, as two groups of classes, with unequal terms of relationships.

Some of the relationships of dependence are the continuation of the past and some of them have emerged after the development of capitalist tendencies in agriculture and milk economy in the villages. A few of the relationships of dependence have witnessed some changes in those villages which are located in the vicinity of a city, and where the rural poor have some alternative means of livelihood, *i.e.*, cottage industries. But if seen in totality, there still exist relationships of one-sided dependence even in those villages. Moreover, the emergence of milk economy in the post-independence period bred new types of relationships of dependence: the relationships between the buffalo-keepers and the milkmen. And the arrival of new technology made many of the peasant households which do not own the new means of production, dependent on those who own them.

I

The relationships of dependence both one-sided and mutual (contradictions) in agrarian society of Meerut can be broadly seen in the following ways :

(i) The one-sided dependence of the rural poor on the rural rich : for cutting grass from the fields, defecation in the fields, passing through the dolas (boundaries) of the fields, carrying the halsot (ploughs and bulls) through the fields, dumping the kuda (garbage) and making the heap of dung-cakes (bitodas).

(ii) The mutual dependence between the rural poor and the rural rich involves the following types of relationships: (a) between the agricultural labourers and lavas (harvesters) and the rural rich: for wages and labour-power, (b) between the rural poor and moneylenders (rural rich) : for borrowing money and earning interests, (c) between the small and poor peasants and the rural rich: for hiring resources and payment, and (d) between the buffalo-keepers and milkmen: for money and milk.

For feeding their livestock which form one of the most significant aspects of their economy,[6] the rural poor need fodder. Since the landless proletariat do not own fields, they have to depend on the fields of the landowning classes for cutting grass. It should be noted that even though the small and poor peasants feed their livestock with the fodder grown in their small patches of land, they too have to depend on the fields of rural rich for cutting grass, as the fodder grown in their own fields runs short quite often.

The rural poor, particularly the landless proletariat defecate in the fields of the rural rich in the absence of public facilities. Moreover, in the absence of proper chak-roads, they walk along the boundaries (dolas) of the fields of the rural rich. The small peasants have to pass through the fields of others with their halsots (ploughs and bulls). Although this is a problem even for the rural rich, they do not face much difficulty because they are very influential people compared to the small peasants.

The landless proletariat do not own the small patches of land, where they can dump their garbage (kuda) and make dung-cakes (bitoda). Even those households of the small and poor peasants whose fields are not in the vicinity of the village face this problem. For this they depend on the sides of kucha roads, and sometimes even on the village graveyards. Though this sort of dependence is not based on the property of the rural rich but on the common village property, this again depends on the mercy of the rural rich.

The relationships of one-sided dependence are more extensive (comprehensive), numerically larger than the relationships of mutual dependence or contradictions.

The relationships of agricultural labourers, lavas (harvesters) and the rural rich show the existence of contradictions between them. These contradictions stem from the fact that the agricultural labourers and lavas are dependent on the land of rural rich for the wages and the rural rich are dependent on the former for the labour-power. In the case of agricultural labourers, the relationships of contradictions exist throughout the year. And in the case of lavas, it is short-lived; it exists during the harvest season only.[7]

The poor and small peasants depend on the rural rich for buying water from their tube-wells or pump-sets, hiring tractors, hiring their means of transportation, and other resources.In reciprocity, the rural rich depend on the small and poor peasants for hiring out the resources. In this mutual dependence, the small and poor peasants are in weaker position. The relationships of contradictions exist even amongst the rural rich. Those rural rich who do not possess all the necessary means of production depend on those who own them.[8]

The moneylenders (the rural rich) lend money to the rural poor. While the latter borrow money, the former get interest in return .[9]

The relationships between the buffalo-keepers and the milkmen are also those of mutual dependence or contradictions. Milkmen belong to a new class which has emerged in the post-independence period with the ever growing market for milk in the cities. Consequent upon the opening of market for milk and the emergence of the milkmen, the buffalo-keepers started selling milk to the milkmen. Before the emergence of milk market, the buffalo-keepers either used the milk for family consumption or made ghee from it to sell in the cities or to the better off people in the villages. After buying milk from the buffalo-keepers, the milkmen in turn (as mentioned in Chapter III) sell it to the private dairies in the cities of Meerut and Mawana to meet the demands of local consumption or export it to Delhi. The richer milkmen belong to the rural rich. They wield very strong influence on the social, economic and political life of some villages.[10]

The buffalo-keepers depend on the milkmen in several ways. In the absence of job avenues and means of livelihood, the rural poor depend on selling of milk. Keeping buffaloes and selling milk provide them self-employment and means of livelihood. But around 41 per cent households of the rural poor keep the buffaloes which they do not own; they just look after them. Milkman is the main source which provides them money for buying buffaloes, besides the moneylenders and the government agencies. Sometimes the milkmen finance partly to buy buffaloes,and the balance cost is managed by the buffalo-keepers mainly by borrowing from moneylenders. Thus, the otherwise unemployed members of households of buffalo-keepers get self-employment and means of livelihood through looking after the buffaloes. The buffalo-keepers belong to the poor classes, they require money for their day to day needs.[11] In the absence of any source, they turn to the milkman who gives advance money, even before buying milk from them. This advance is called peshgi. Even otherwise, as and when they require money, they turn to the milkmen. Despite the availability of dairies as alternative market, which make better payment and measurement, the buffalo-keepers sell milk to the milkmen.[12] They do so because the dairies cannot provide them money whenever they want. They pay only one week after the milk has been sold to them. Moreover, as many of them do not own the buffaloes in reality and are indebted to the buffalo-keepers, they are placed in a sort of bondage which does not let them make free choice of market. Besides, some of them ask the milkmen to buy their daily needs from the market, since they do not have cash with them. These items may include flour, khal (mix of pulses for cattle), stationery for school-going children, and many other things. But the dairies cannot do this.

It is the relationships of one-sided dependence which are more decisive than the contradictions between the rural rich and the rural poor in their day-to-day relationships, though the latter are not less significant. It must be noted that the presence of the contradictions does not subside the one-sided dependence to any significant extent. Though the agricultural labourers have the capacity to bargain with the landowners (the rural rich) in the processes or phenomena in which they depend mutually, there still exists one-sided dependence between them which are common to the other sections of the rural poor. Neither do the lavas (harvesters) become free from other kinds of dependence. They can bargain with the rural rich only in one aspect of dependence, *i.e.*, harvesting of crops and not in other aspects of dependence. In the case of the relationships of contradictions, it is possible sometimes that the rural poor challenge the harassment/oppression/exploitation and domination or demand their dues and enter into a bargain with the rural rich, irrespective of the consequences. But in the cases of the one-sided dependence, it is not possible because the rural rich do not have direct stake in it, notwithstanding its socio-political and economic implications.

II

The dependence of the rural poor on the rural rich finds its expression in the day to day economic, social and political relationships between them. Due to their dependence on the rural rich, the rural poor are made to do begar, their women are harassed and they are not allowed to avail the "help" of the government properly due to the nexus between the lower level bureaucracy and the rural rich (village pradhans). Socially, the rural poor are expected to "behave properly". Politically, they are forced to exercise political choice in accordance with the wishes of the rural rich. The consequences of the dependence has a varying impact at the level of panchayat elections, and the assembly and the Lok Sabha elections. The harassment of the persons belonging to the rural poor sometimes results in their migration from villages.

Begar or unpaid or forced labour is very common in the villages of Meerut district. The rural poor have to do many kinds of begar for the rural rich. Begar is more rampant in the villages of Jafarnagar Begamabad, Chobla, Tilwara Sakin, Jaisinghpur than in the villages of Jalalpur, Nagla Tashi Qasimpur, Ahera and Behzadka. This difference in intensity of begar between the two sets of villages exists due to the following reasons: All the four villages in the first set have the bhaiachara background, their distant location from the city and the absence of any non-agrarian means of livelihood to the people of rural poor make them mainly or solely dependent on the rural rich. Hence their easy susceptibility to do begar. But on the contrary, in the second set of villages, three out of four have the zamindari background. And in the fourth one, Behzadaka, which has the bhaiachara background, the cottage industry of tannery has made the landless chamars relatively free from dependence on the rural rich. In village Ahera, the rural poor work either in the brick-kilns of their own village or in those of neighbouring districts of Muzaffarnagar and Ghaziabad, which makes them free from the dependence. Moreover, three of these villages are situated in the vicinity of the cities.

The rural poor are asked to do begar by the rural rich in several ways. They have to pay half of the gola (leaves of the unveiled sugarcane) to the landowners. This particular type of begar prevails in village Jafarnagar Begamabad. Besides, they have to get their carts and trolleys loaded with the sugarcane. The indebted person either has to employ his son with the moneylender for low wages or has to perform all sorts of works, wherever he is asked to do, without wages. Sometimes the rural poor, however, volunteer to render begar so that they can be allowed to do lai in the fields of the landowners. In many cases the persons belonging to the rural poor have to do all kinds of work either in the households or in the fields as asked for by the rural rich.

Cases of harassment and oppression such as molestation and rape of women belonging to the rural poor of lower castes by the men of rural rich are not uncommon. These women fall prey to the lust of the men of the rural rich while they go to their fields either to defecate or cut grass. But sometimes attempts to molest them are made when they are at their homes. Due to the delicate nature of the issues we could not get many instances of such harassment and oppression from all the villages of our sample, though this problem exists there in one form or the other. However, the data from three villages - Nagla Tashi Qasimpur, Chobla and Jalalpur - substantiate this aspect. In 1967, in village Nagla Tashi Qasimpur, a girl belonging to the agricultural labourers' family of Gadaria caste (OBC) was raped by a rich Jat peasant when she was cutting grass from his field for her cattle. In village Chobla, a chamar women belonging to the family of agricultural labourers was molested by a rich Jat peasant, when she went to defecate in his field. In another case in the same village, a Jat middle peasant entered the house of a chamar agricultural labourer and made an attempt to rape his wife. He was caught by the chamars. The Jats threatened the witnesses and bribed the police. The chamars could not pursue the case. In 1973, in Jalalpur village the son of a middle peasant Gujar molested a chamar woman belonging to the family of a wage labourer in non-agrarian sector, when she went to cut grass from his field. Besides, he snatched her khurpa (hoe) and beat her up. The chamars lodged a complaint with the police but they were forced to withdraw it because the Gujars imposed sanctions against them. In another case in the same village, the son of a middle peasant Gujar molested the wife of a Muslim barber when she went to cut grass from his field. When she complained about this, she was implicated in a false case of crop-theft, and sanctions were imposed against her family.

In the villages where the landless proletariat work as wage labourers in the non-agricultural sectors, the male members are relatively free from harassment of the rural rich.[13] But with the development of milk economy as a very significant phenomenon of the economy of the rural poor, there are women who have become the subject of harassment and oppression of the men of rural rich in such villages. While the male members of these families work in non-agrarian sectors, the women have to go to the fields of the rural rich to cut grass. Three women in village Nagla Tashi Qasimpur, one belonging to the Kumhar (potter) caste, and two belonging to the Gadaria caste, whose husbands do not work on the land but go to work in Meerut city every day, made the following statements, which confirm that it is the women rather than men who become the victims in such villages.[14] A woman, whose husband was denying the existence of any harassment or oppression of women in the village, said :

> *Ladkiyo aur aurto se puchho jo ghas khodti hain. Admiyon ko kya malum? Admi to cycle uthake Meerut chale jate hain. Ghas to aurte khodti hain.* (Ask the women and girls who have to cut grass. What do the men know? Men go to Meerut on their cycles. These are the women who cut grass and as a result have to undergo harassment at the hands of rural rich).

Another woman said :

Khet men to aurten jati hain. Unko kya malum? Musibat to hamari hai. (Women have to go to the fields. What do they (men) know? Only we face the problems).

Third woman said:

Mein pichhle sal chholne gai thee to kaha vahien chholo Kankarkheda jahan tera admi jata hai kam karne (I went for unveiling the sugarcanes last year to fetch fodder. The landowner said unveil the sugarcane in Kankarkheda - a locality in Meerut city - where your husband works).

Moreover, the rural rich expect the rural poor to behave respectfully towards them. They often resent their "defying behaviour".

Some families of the rural poor and even sometimes those of the minority high castes such as Banias, migrate from their respective villages either as a result of harassment by the rural rich or as a result of the lack of employment prospects in the villages. Some families have permanently migrated from five villages of our sample. These villages are Jalalpur, Nagla Tashi Qasimpur, Chobla, Jaisinghpur and Ahera. A family of small peasant of the Jogi caste (OBC) had to sell out its property and migrate from village Jalalpur. This family had a dispute with the family of pradhan, who is middle peasant of Gujar caste and also a moneylender. He got the poor peasant family intimidated with the help of some "goondas" and usurped their land. As a result, the poor peasant family left the village for ever. Five households of the agricultural labourers of Chamar caste from village Chobla and one family of a Bania shopkeeper from village Nagla Tashi Qasimpur and majority of Telis (oilmen), Jullahas (weavers) and some Chamar families of the landless proletariat from village Jaisinghpur have migrated to the cities. The families of Telis and Jullahas have migrated from the village Jaisinghpur partially due to harassment and partially due to lack of employment in the village. The families of Chamars have migrated from this village due to harassment and oppression of their women and their inability to pay the debt. Twenty families of Bhangis have migrated from village Ahera and settled in Ghaziabad city, as they faced unemployment in their village.

Likewise the relationships between the milkmen and buffalo-keepers are exploitative. The buffalo-keepers have to pay a heavy price for their dependence on the milkman. In case a milkmen has bought the buffalo for a buffalo-keeper, the latter cannot sell the milk to anyone else except that particular milkmen. If any buffalo-keeper tries to sell milk to others, he can even be subjected to physical intimidation and coercion. The buffalo-keepers live in some kind of bondage to the milkmen. They pay back the loan which is taken in the form of advance or buffaloes only in the form of milk. The value of the milk taken by the milkmen is more than the market price of the buffaloes and the amount of advance because of the low price paid for the milk and faulty measurement. Ever since the advent of milk economy, the milkmen have been measuring the milk in the traditional unit of ser. As compared to the litre, the ser contains more milk. Moreover, they expand the bottom of ser so that it can contain more milk than its original capacity. The milkmen expand the bottom even of the litre, which they have been forced to introduce because of the agitations of buffalo-keepers. They exploit the buffalo-keepers miserably, and make lot of profit through this business. It should be noted that it is almost the entire family of a buffalo-keeper which undergoes the exploitation at the hands of the milkmen. While women of all age groups contribute in rearing the buffaloes, other members of the family contribute in one way or the other as and when required.

In the context of broad social, economic and political relationship between them, the rural rich and the rool poor function as two opposite social groups.[15] Harassment of a single person or more than one person belonging to the rural poor finds its echo in moulding of the attitudes of the entire rural poor towards the rural rich as a whole in the entire district, and sometimes in the entire western Uttar Pradesh. Likewise, the rural rich demonstrate a dominant position, especially when they are confronted by the resistance of the rural poor. Even a scuffle involving two or more individuals from the two sides on any issue, including trivial ones, in the village is echoed throughout other villages.

III

The rural poor resist the harassment/oppression/exploitation and domination of the rural rich through individual stray actions, litigations and informally organised protests. When asked to do begar they try to resist by avoiding the rural rich who ask them to do it. Sometimes the rural poor take recourse to legal means to resist harassment and oppression. Though court verdict might go in their favour, their harassment does not get subsided, since they still remain dependent on the rural rich.[16]

The demand for higher wages by the agricultural labourers, better price for milk and the demand for correct unit and pot for measuring milk by the buffalo-keepers show the expression of resistance against their exploitation. The agricultural labourers of village Tilwara Sakin and the buffalo-keepers of village Jalalpur attempted to fight for their respective class problems through informally organised ways. The agricultural labourers in village Tilwara Sakin organised a strike for better wages in 1982-83. The buffalo-keepers of village Jalalpur went on a strike demanding better price for milk and introduction of the correct unit and pot for measuring milk in 1973-74 and 1982-83.

The village Tilwara Sakin reveals a clear polarisation of classes : the rural rich on the one hand, and the landless proletariat on the other. The rural rich form 10.73 per cent households in the village. Jats form 90.91 per cent households of the rural rich, and Brahmans form 9.09 per cent of them. Almost entire land of the village is controlled by them. The landless proletariat form 89.27 per cent households in the village, 94.74 per cent of their households belong to the OBCs of Hindus and Muslims.

This village is marked by the near absence of small peasants and poor peasants. The rural poor do not have any alternative means of livelihood, except working on the land of rural rich. The remoteness of the village (around 70 km from Meerut city) further handicaps them from going for daily work in the non-agrarian sectors, unlike their counterparts of villages in the vicinity of the city. A total of 34.14 per cent of households, which supply the monthly rated agricultural labourers get work for 12 months in the fields of their employers. Rest of them get work for 3.4 months on an average in a year. In the remaining months they either sit idle at home, or some of them migrate temporarily in search for jobs. People from almost all households of the rural poor have to do begar for the rural rich. Working conditions of the salaried agricultural labourers are abysmal. They have to work for almost 18 hours a day. They begin working for their employers around 4 a.m. and continue working till 10 p.m. They get barely 6 hours to be with their families. Moreover, they can be called any time from their homes, even at night to work.

The wage rate varies from one kind of agricultural labourer to another.

The wages of the monthly rated agricultural labourers are paid in cash. Their monthly wage varies between Rs. 120 and Rs. 200 without meals. Besides, an agricultural labourer is allotted a small piece of land by his employer. And in some cases, the agricultural labourers are allotted small pieces of land in lieu of which they have to render services to the landowners without getting wages. However, depending on the mercy of landowner an agricultural labourer may be paid some wages in kind or cash.

A daily wage-agricultural labourer gets wages in kind. Till 1982-1983 he was paid one-quarter to two (1.75) ser of foodgrains and breakfast consisting of 2 rotis for the whole day. From 1982-83 his daily wage consists of 2.5 ser of foodgrains and 2 rotis. However, in some cases the wages are paid in cash-Rs. 6 per day. The peak season when the landowners need the labour desperately is the period of harvesting wheat which falls between the first week of April and the mid of May. As explained in Chapter III, the process of harvesting wheat for wages is called lai. The wages for lai were given in sheaves (poolies) up to 1982-83. A lava (a person who does lai) was paid wages of sheaves in the ratio of 3 sheaves for 100 sheaves cut by him/her. But in 1982-83, the payment of wages in sheaves was replaced by a system of paying wages in kind, on the basis of wheat harvested per bigha land. Since then they are paid 4 dhadi (20 ser) of wheat for harvesting wheat in one bigha land. A sharecropper is given 1/4 (chauthai) of the produce, if he does not pay for the resources. He gets half of the produce, if he contributes half for irrigation, seed and fertilizers.

The agricultural labourers were dissatisfied with the low rate of wages paid to them, and their dissatisfaction found expression in the form of a strike in 1982-83 (exact date could not be ascertained: two or three years before the fieldwork). They were dissatisfied on two accounts: (i) wages paid to the daily agricultural labourers were too low, and (ii) the size of sheaves given to the lavas as wages was too small.

The agricultural labourers demanded that their wages should be increased from 1.75 ser foodgrains and 2 rotis daily to 3 ser foodgrains and 2 rotis daily. The lavas were given 3 sheaves of wheat for hundred sheaves harvested. They did not show any dissatisfaction with the number of sheaves. But they felt that the size of sheaves was too small because they were made by the landowners according to their will. The lavas, therefore, demanded that they should be allowed to make sheaves themselves.

The illiterate agricultural labourers of the lower castes discussed in an informal meeting the issues of wages and sheaves. The initiative for this meeting was taken by some agricultural labourers of Dhiwar caste (Hindu OBCs). They discussed the matter with the agricultural labourers of the Scheduled Castes and Other Backward Classes of Muslims and got their consent to observe a strike (hartal) till their demands were accepted. Unitedly, they refused to work in the fields of the landowners. The strike was observed at the peak of harvesting season in April. It continued for almost 4 days.

Their strike assumed an open form of class struggle. The Jat rural rich also held a meeting and decided to deal with them firmly. They imposed sanctions against the agricultural labourers. (We will discuss the phenomenon of sanctions in part IV of this Chapter.) The sanctions had an adverse impact on the conditions of the agricultural labourers. Besides the inconvenience caused to the agricultural labourers for defecation, their cattle had to starve due to scarcity of fodder.

The agricultural labourers could not sustain their strike due to the sanctions imposed against them. Yet the strike was not without consequences. It had two consequences: one, the increase in wages from 1.75 ser foodgrains and 2 rotis daily to 2.50 ser foodgrains and 2 rotis daily, and another, the replacement of the sheaf system by the grains paid as wages for the wheat harvested per bigha.

The increase in wages as a consequence of the strike is ascribed to two reasons : one, superstition, another, factionalism within the rural rich and the pressure of strike on them. The rural rich felt that starvation of cattle of the agricultural labourers caused due to sanctions, would be a curse on them ("Shap Padega"). So in order to overcome such curse they decided to increase the wages. Another reason was the factionalism among the rural rich. One Jat middle peasant, who could not afford to do without agricultural labourers increased the wages from 1.75 ser foodgrains daily and 2 rotis to 2.5 ser foodgrains and 2 rotis daily. Then it was followed by other landowners also. The strike was successful to some extent, though the wages could not be increased up to 3 ser foodgrains and 2 rotis daily as demanded by the agricultural labourers. Regarding the second demand for the right to make their own sheaves to lavas, the rural rich adopted an intelligent posture. As sheaves do not have any specific size, they may contain unlimited amount of grain, which might be disadvantageous to them. So they replaced the sheaf system with the fixed amount of grain per bigha. They decided to pay the lavas 4 dhadi (20 ser) of wheat per bigha land replacing the earlier system of paying 3 sheaves for 100 sheaves cut.

In village Jalalpur, the economy of 57.4 per cent households of the rural poor is related to selling of milk. About 92.59 per cent of their households sell milk to milkmen and only 7.41 per cent of them sell it to the dairy. On the contrary, only 23.81 per cent households of the rural rich sell milk, and all of them sell it to the dairy. There are 5 milkmen in this village.

The buffalo-keepers of this village depend on the milkmen in all ways which have been discussed in Section I of this Chapter. Due to this dependence the milkmen exploit the buffalo-keepers in many ways as discussed in the previous section.[17]

The buffalo-keepers of village Jalalpur organised a strike against the milkmen in 1973-74 for 10-12 days and in 1982-83 for 4 days on three issues :

(1) They should be paid higher price for the milk.
(2) The measuring pot - ser - should be replaced by litre.
(3) The measuring pot should be of proper shape. Its bottom should not be expanded by tampering with it.

During both the strikes the milkmen responded firmly. They adopted the following measures to counter the strike :

(1) They demanded back the money from the buffalo-keepers which was given as advance.
(2) They divided the buffalo-keepers by adopting discriminatory tactics towards those who were indebted to the milkmen, and those who were not indebted. Though they did not increase the price of milk, they started measuring milk of the unindebted buffalo-keepers with the litre.
(3) The milkmen decided to unite to face the strike but they could not form any union at the village level.[18] However, they pitched one buffalo-keeper against another. They started harassing the leaders of the strike. The leaders were asked to return the advance and the milkmen also decided not to buy their milk. This affected their economy very badly.

(4) Some milkmen attempted to intimidate physically some of the poor buffalo-keepers.

In a situation when the economy of the rural poor was dependent on milk selling to a great extent and the milkmen adopted a very tough attitude towards them, the buffalo-keepers withdrew the strike without any success. But during the strike of 1982-83 they had reached an informal agreement with the milkmen to the following effect :

(1) The ser would be replaced by the litre, though the milkmen were already using it for the unindebted buffalo-keepers, from the time of the strike of 1973-74.

(2) The bottom of the measuring pot would not be expanded.

(3) The demand for the increase in price of milk was not accepted.

The milkmen could not maintain the agreement for long. Though they now use the litre, its size is much bigger than even the ser. They have adopted two dubious means in this regard : (i) they have again expanded the bottom of the litre; and (ii) they are using the unauthorised litres which are much bigger in size than the genuine ones. These are manufactured illegally at a secret place in Meerut city.

The situation which prevailed before the strike has repeated itself in a much more exploitative nature. And whenever any buffalo-keeper demands an increase in the price of the milk and use of geniune and correct litre, the milkmen openly say that "*Hamari peshgi vapis do aur sahi dam aur thik tol lo*" ("Give our advance back and get more price and better measurement"). The buffalo-keepers now feel apathetic to organise any strike. They lack any organisation to take up their cause. Moreover, the disgusting and frustrating conditions in which the leaders of the strike were left discourages the buffalo-keepers to go on another strike. Their exploitation at the hands of the milkmen continues.

IV

The rural rich control the economic, social and political life of agrarian society by virtue of their control of the means of production. Any attempt of the rural poor to resist and defy the harassment/oppression/exploitation and domination is met by imposition of sanctions by the rural rich. In the absence of any alternative means, the rural poor are susceptible to imposition of sanctions and they have to submit to the rural rich. Even the administration and judiciary are virtually unable to help the rural poor. They do not provide any alternative; the relationships of dependence remain unchanged. The rural rich impose sanctions against the rural poor in the following ways :

(1) Stopping them from cutting grass in their fields;
(2) Stopping them from defecating in their fields;
(3) Stopping them from making bitoda (heap and dung-cakes) and dumping garbage (kuda) in the common places, *i.e.*, road-sides and graveyards;
(4) Not allowing them to unveil the sugarcane;
(5) Not giving them work in their fields;
(6) Stop providing loans and demanding the return of their loans then and there.[19]
(7) Not allowing them to pass through the dolas (boundaries of the fields);
(8) Snatching danti and khurpa (hoe and sickle) from the women of rural poor;
(9) In case of the small and poor peasants -
    (i) Stopping to sell them water from their tubewells and pump-sets, and stopping to provide other resources for agriculture; and
    (ii) Not allowing their halsots (pairs of bulls and ploughs) to pass through their fields;
(10) The rural rich adopt intimidating tactics in silencing the rural poor:
    (i) implicating them in false charges of crop theft, and
    (ii) subjecting them to physical assault.[20]

The following example will substantiate our point of view. We shall see in Chapter VI that the people of rural poor are not usually allowed to vote in the assembly and parliamentary elections by the Jat rural rich, particularly in the villages of Chobla and Tilwara Sakin. These villages fall in the Baghpat parliamentary constituency. Whenever they attempt to exercise their franchise, or resist against the prevention of their franchise, they are met with the sanctions and intimidation. The rural poor of Chamar caste in village Chobla attempted to assert their right in 1971 Lok Sabha election and they sought the help of the police and a local Scheduled Caste Congress MLA, Ramji Lal Sahayak. The Jat rural rich of the village retaliated by taking a decision in their meeting (panchayat) to impose sanctions against them. This move of the Jat rural rich in the village was called "hartal" (strike).[21] As a result, they implemented the decision to impose sanctions very firmly. These sanctions continued for 8 months. However, after the intervention of the in-charge of the local police station and senior politicians, the matter was resolved and the sanctions were lifted. On refusal to do begar, beatings of rural poor by the Jat rural rich is order of the day in this village. They are often charged with theft of crops, and cutting chilag (the sweet and mature part of the sugarcane) while unveiling the sugarcanes. The frequency of beatings and harassment of the rural poor by the Jat rural rich in this village increased when Charan Singh became the Prime Minister in 1979.

Being annoyed at the recalcitrant behaviour of the rural poor, the rural rich of village Jaisinghpur also organised a "hartal" (strike) in 1981. The rural rich deployed their family members to keep vigilance over their fields, and to prevent the rural poor from cutting grass. Whosoever went to cut grass, his/her danti and khurpa (sickle and hoe) were snatched from him/her.[22] Finally, the rural poor had to submit and agree to do begar for the rural rich as and when required by them. They also agreed to provide agricultural labour to the rural rich according to their terms and conditions. In the light of this agreement their dantis and khurpas (sickle and hoes) were returned after 4 months, and the rural poor were allowed to cut grass from their fields.

Before 1962, the village panchayat elections were held through direct voting by raising of hands. This would reveal the identity of the political choice of the voters. There were two contestants for the post of village pradhan in the panchayat election of 1952 in village Jalalpur. One was a Muslim landlord and another was a Gujar middle peasant. The Gujars were supporting the Muslim landlord against the candidate of their caste. The Gujar candidate canvassed for himself along with two Dhiwars (OBC) : one, an agricultural labourer and the other, a small peasant. These two individuals did not know the opinion of the villagers in general. They voted for the Gujar candidate by raising their hands in the panchayat election. And to their dismay all other villagers raised hands in favour of the Muslim landlord. These two persons would also have voted for the Muslim landlord had they known the opinion of the others. They had to pay a very heavy price for their support to a candidate who was supported by the rural rich of the village. They had to face the following sanctions :

(1) A Gujar middle peasant had lent out one bull to Dhiwar small

peasant. This bull was taken back by that Gujar as a punishment to him for voting a candidate whom they did not support.

(2) These two families of the Dhiwars were placed under sanctions to cut grass from their fields, enter their fields and defecate in their fields. However, they were allowed by that Gujar middle peasant whom they had supported in the election, to use his fields. Only after intervention of one Gujar Muqqdam, a panchayat was held, and sanctions were lifted.

In another example in the same village, the village pradhan, who was a middle peasant and also a moneylenders, refused to sell the water from his tube-well to two Saini (OBC) small peasants, because they dared to oppose him during the panchayat election. Their crops were ruined for want of water. They were compelled to install their own tubewell on their land (2 acres each). They had to borrow money for this purposes. So the sanction imposed by pradhan against them affected their economic condition very badly. In yet another example, the pradhan asked three Saini wage labourers to repay his loan immediately as they opposed him during the election. Three women belonging to the rural poor were implicated in the false charges of crop-theft when they opposed bids to molest them by the men of rural rich in three different incidents.

Even the attempt of the state to help the rural poor results in a fiasco, as it does not free them from the dependence on the rural rich. In the absence of any alternative which could make them free from the dependence on the rural rich, and in the face of the imposition of sanctions, the rural poor have to submit to the rural rich on their terms and conditions.

When the rural poor resist the harassment/oppression/exploitation and domination of the rural rich which emanates from the one-sided dependence, the sanctions imposed by the rural rich have unilateral impact. But if the resistance of the rural poor relates to oppression and domination of the rural rich which springs from their mutual dependence (contradictions), the sanctions and resistance affect both of them. The results would depend on the requirement and bargaining capacity of each other in a phenomenon or process involving their mutual dependence. But the relationships of one-sided dependence are more decisive than those of the contradictions between the rural rich and the rural poor in the context of the totality of all kinds of relationships

- social, economic and political.

The harassment, oppression and domination of the rural poor by the rural rich, and the exploitation of the buffalo-keepers by the milkmen can be ended only with the change in the pattern of relationships of dependence. Any attempt by the state or any other institution, short of changing the pattern of these relationships, cannot succeed in eliminating the harassment and oppression of the rural poor.

Notes

1 For discussion on literature on the patron-client relationship in India, see Jan Breman, *Patronage and Exploitation : Changing Agrarian Relations in South India, Gujarat,* New Delhi, Manohar, 1979, Chapter II.

2 *Ibid.*, p. 17.

3 For a discussion on "Everyday forms of resistance" see "Everyday Forms of Peasant Resistance in South Asia", in James C. Scott and Bendict J. Tria Kerkvliet (ed.), *The Journal of Peasant Studies,* Special Issue, vol. 3, no. 2, January 1986; James C. Scott, *Weapons of the Weak :Everyday Forms of Peasant Resistance,* London, Yale University Press, 1985.

4 The concept of contradictions has a specific meaning in the marxian terminology. It is "erroneous to equate it or confuse it with commonplace meaning of the term". See M. Basavapunnaiah, "On Contradictions, Antagonisitc and Non-Antagonistic", *Social Scientist,* Vol. 11, no. 9, September 1983. The law of contradictions or the law of unity and struggle of opposites is the basic law of the materialistic dialectic. Lenin said "in brief, dialectics can be defined as the doctrine of unity of opposites", see V.I. Lenin, "Philosophical Notebooks", in *Collected Works,* Vol. 38, Moscow, Foreign Language Publishing House, 1961, p. 223, and "dialectics in proper sense is the study of contradictions in the very essence of objects" (pp. 253-54). He further points out that "the recognition (discovery) of the contradictory, mutually exclusive, opposite tendencies in all phenomena and processes of nature (including mind and society)" underlines the law of contradictions in dialectics (pp. 359-60). The mutually exclusive opposites have "reciprocal dependence" (p. 222). If their relationships are not reciprocal, they cannot be called contradictions. Regarding this Lenin says that the lack of "mutual contact" between them (the opposites) "is the essence of anti-dialectic (non-contradictions)", p.228.

5 This contradiction has been diluted to some extent. See the postscript.

6 See Chapter III.

7 See *Ibid.*

8 See *Ibid.*

9 See also *Ibid*.

10 In village Ahera, as mentioned earlier,a milkmen is a landlord and moneylenders, who owns a brick-kiln too. This person is also the pradhan of the village. Two ex-milkmen from this village are involved in the district level politics. One of them has been a Congress (I) MLA from Khera constituency (1980-85)

11 Some of points discussed in the following paragraphs have already been discussed in Chapter III. Their repetition is inevitable in the context of discussion here.

12 In the last 10-12 years (from 1971-73) villages have seen the arrival of dairies. These dairies are either the branches of Parag Dairy or cooperative dairies. The price of milk given by the dairies per litre is more than the price given by milkmen. The milkmen pay between Rs. 85 and Rs. 90 per maund (40 sers). And the dairies pay between Rs. 130 and Rs. 140 per maund. Moreover, the masurement of milk is done by the dairies in a scientific way, while the milkmen use the traditional ways. (See also Chapter III).

13 The availability of alternative means of livelihood in such villages makes the male members of the families of the wage labourers free from depending on land. The proximity of the villages to the cities where they can go daily to work in non-agrarian sectors, and the existence of cottage industry in the village provide them alternative means of livelihood. Villages of Nagla Tashi Qasimspur and Jalalpur are located in the vicinity of Meerut city and village Behzadka is located in the vicinity of Mawana city. Besides, there are tanneries (as cottage industries) in this village, which provide employment to the Charmars.The rural poor in village Ahera are free from the dependence on the rural rich for working in their fields, as they work in the brick-Kilns.

14 We had an interesting experience while interviewing these women. The husband of one of the women could not get work in the city that day and he had to stay back at home. So we interviewed this man and three women including his wife at the same time. We asked the man if there existed any kind of harassment or oppression by the rural rich. The man replied in negative. But his wife wanted to say something. He did not allow her to express her views. But we insisted upon him to tell us if anything of that sort happened. His wife wanted to say something again. He shut her up. However, on our intervention that he should allow his wife to express her views, he allowed her. Two other women also expressed their views.

15 It is different from the views held by Rudolphs that "in the absence of ... efforts to enforce further, lower ceiling of landholding, bullock capitalists' (middle peasants') interests with respect to landholdings are

not likely to place them in antagonistic classes with other agrarian classes". See Llyod I. Rudolph and Susanne Hoeber Rudolph, *In Pursuit of Lakshmi: The Political Economy of Indian State,* Bombay, Orient Longman, 1987, p. 340. Evidence from Meerut shows that despite the lack of feasibility to lower the ceiling further, the "antagonistic" relations between the agrarian classes (the rural rich and the rural poor) exist. This does not necessarily stem from the relative small size of landholdings but from the relationships of dependence.

16 In 1980 General Election, some people of Chamar caste were beaten up by Jats in Chobla village when they refused to vote for the Lok Dal, then the Janata (SC) candidate. The Chamars moved the sessions court. But they had to withdraw the case because Jats imposed sanctions against them. In the wake of sanctions and withdrawal of the case, two families of the Chamars migrated from the village and those who stayed back in the village had to face problems.

17 A branch of the Parag Dairy exists in this village. It pays a reasonable price and measures milk in a scientific way. Despite being aware of the disadvantages of selling milk to the milkmen compared to the dairies, the buffalo-keepers sell milk only to the former.

18 In the neighbouring village Khanauda, the milkmen held a meeting and decided that they would not succumb to the pressure of the buffalo-keepers. And if any of the milkmen of that village violated this decision, he would be penalised. He would have to pay Rs. 500 as punishment; also he would be socially boycotted by others. The milkmen in Meerut district have formed an organisation. Two milkmen of Jalalpur also are members of this association. The milkmen in Meerut district went on a strike in December-January 1984-85 to demand from the private dairies in Meerut city that they should be given more price for the milk which they bring from the villages.

19 Harriss argues that the reasons/intentions behind the credit and other things which are rendered by the "dominant castes" (the rural rich) to the "low castes" (the rural poor) are that the "dominant castes" (the rural rich) have moral commitment to fulfil "obligations" towards the low castes (the rural poor). See John Harriss, *Capitalism and Peasant Farming : Structure and Ideology in Northern Tamil Nadu,* Bombay, Oxford University Press, 1982, pp. 238-44. But evidence from Meerut does not comply with this point of view. It is not the moral commitment to fulfil, the obligations which motivates the moneylenders ("dominant castes"/rural rich) to lend the "low castes" (the rural poor) money or other facilities but their social, economic and political expendiency. These "helps" are not rendered without expecting returns, unlike in a moral commitment. The indebted rural poor have to pay heavy interests to

the moneylenders for the money borrowed; they also have to oblige them in social, economic and political terms (see this Chapter Section-II, Chapter VI).

20 For the prevalence of the phenomenon of sanctions in a village of neighbouring district of Muzaffarnagar district, see M.C. Pradhan, *The Political System of the Jats in North India,* London, Oxford University Press, 1966, p.164.

21 "Hartal" (strike) has its own connotation in popular parlence of agrarian society of western Uttar Pradesh. It is used for "hartal" (strike) per se when the agricultural labourers or the buffalo-keepers or the sugarcane growers go on strike for their demands. It is also used for any action the rural rich initiate to counter the rural poor; even their decision to impose sanctions is called "hartal" (strike) in popular language.

22 Danti and khurpa (sickle and hoe) snatching is a very common phenomenon in Meerut district for preventing the rural poor from cutting grass from the fields. In local parlance snatching of danti and khurpa is called "*Danti aur Khurpa Chhinana*".'

Chapter V

Mobilisation of Agrarian Classes

The post-independence period witnessed mobilisation of peasantry on the one hand, and growth of awareness and mobilisation of the rural poor, particularly the landless proletariat belonging to the low castes, on the other. There were gradual attempts on the part of different political parties and individuals to articulate the interests of different agrarian classes and mobilise them on issues related to their respective interests. The rural rich were mobilised on the issues related to the capitalist economy, which emerged as a result of development of capitalist tendencies in agriculture, more particularly after the introduction of Green Revolution, *i.e.*, subsidised inputs, remunerative prices, better credit facilities, increase in electricity duration and reduction in electricity charges, irrigation subsidies, reduction in land tax, cheap agricultural machinery, *etc.* During the first three decades following independence, while other issues of peasantry were also taken up, it were the problems of the sugarcane growers on which the peasantry was mobilised in the most systematic way. The rural poor were mobilised on the issues related to their socio-economic conditions.

I

The main issues and problems facing the sugarcane growers in Meerut since the establishment of sugar mills in the 1930s and particularly since the 1950s have been the following : the price of sugarcane, regular and timely payment of the price, its full payment; not in instalments, timely operation of the sugar mills, mentioning the price of sugarcane on the receipts, fluctuation in the price, distribution of sugar, gur and khandsari, and corruption at the "centres" (places other than mill-gates where the sugarcane is disposed off by the sugarcane growers).[1]

Ever since the establishment of sugar mills, the Kisan Sabha had mobilised peasantry on the problems of sugarcane growers in the 1930s and 1940s.[2] While the representatives of sugarcane growers had been articulating their interests at the national and state levels,[3] the peasantry was mobilised on their problems and issues by the activists of the socialist parties - SP, PSP, SSP - and the CPI at the district and village levels.

Almost every year between December and March throughout the 1950s and 1960s the socialists and communists, and in the 1950s they along with the Hind Kisan Panchayat and Kisan Sabha, mobilised the sugarcane growers in Meerut district.[4] They organised rallies, conferences and satyagrahs of the sugarcane growers. Several local leaders of the socialist and communist parties and some independent leaders actively worked for organising the sugarcane growers' agitations.

The national leaders of the socialist and communist parties took an active part in organising the strikes of sugarcane growers in Meerut district. Acharya J.B. Kripalani, A.K. Gopalan, E.M.S. Namboodripad, Gainda Singh, Dada Dharmadhikari, Z.A. Ahmed and others visited Meerut in the 1950s quite frequently to address the peasantry . The Hindu Mahasabha also became active among the peasantry in the late 1950s. But it could not make much headway except organising a meeting of the peasants on 9 May 1959 at Kheda Hatana in Baghpat tahsil. The main speakers, local journalists - V.S. Vinod and Hardayal Devguna (editor of local Hindi daily *Vir Arjun*) - discussed the issues of consolidation of landholdings and co-operative farming. They criticised communists as "anti-nationals".[5] But the Hindu Mahasabha could not take the lead and could not continue work among the peasants.

The sugarcane growers responded with enthusiasm to the call of the socialists and communists to participate in the strikes. Sometimes a scuffle occurred between the "agents" of Congress and the agitators, the former dissuading the peasants from participating in the strikes and the latter exhorting them to participate. One of the examples of such incidents happened in December 1958. The pradhan of Idrishpur village, a Congress activist, was allegedly prevented from taking sugarcanes to the mill by the activists of the PSP and the CPI. This resulted in the arrest and foisting of charges of attacking the Congress activist on 13 persons including Shanti Tyagi (a prominent CPI leader of Meerut), B.D. Londontore (a freedom fighter, and "a revolutionary of old school" who was "with CPI for a shortwhile") and others.[6] In yet another instance on 8 December 1958, three persons - Shanti Tyagi, Nawab Singh (a socilaist organiser) and B.D. Londontore - were arrested and implicated under the charges of looting sugarcanes from the Bhola centre. The leaders were bailed out after the arrest, and they were acquitted by the Sessions Judge after 7 months' trial.[7] The arrest and trial did not demoralise the peasants; they rather boosted up their morale.[7a] Several issues of *Panchayati Raj* suggest that the leaders and activists of the socialist and communist parties continued to mobilise the sugarcane growers of Meerut district till the late 1960s, often being arrested.[8]

Following the death of R.M. Lohia in 1967, the socialist movement declined and disintegrated. The socialist leaders joined either the Congress or the BKD or became independent and politically defunct. This trend was echoed in Meerut also. It had its repercussion even on the CPI in Meerut district. Shanti Tyagi who took active part in the national movement and in the sugarcane growers' agitations in Meerut left the CPI along with 67 "progressives and socialists" to join the Congress on 6 January 1972.[9] Despite the decline and disintegration of the socialist movement, the national and state level socialist leaders continued to take interest in the problems of the sugarcane growers. Madhu Limaye visited Meerut on 7 October 1972 in connection with their problems.[10]

The socialists held a meeting on the issue of sugarcane price under the chairmanship of Gainda Singh in December 1974. Vijai Pal Singh, Surya Prasad Tyagi, Damodar Sharma, Maqsood Ali Khan and Virendra Verma attended the meeting.[11]

The activists of Bharatiya Kisan Union (BKU) formed a Sangharash Samiti under the leadership of Om Prakash Tyagi on 5 May 1973.[12] The BKU held a conference on 20 October 1973 on the issue of sugarcane price.[13]

The BKD, which was formed in 1969, filled the gap created by the disintegration of the socialist movement as an opposition. The BKD became the main champion and mobiliser of the peasantry. Even before the formation of the BKD, while being a member of the Congress Party, Charan Singh had identified himself with the backward classes and better-off sections of the peasantry. He made special efforts to consolidate his base among these sections of the eastern and central U.P. He, however, did not make the same kind of efforts in western Uttar Pradesh, although in his writings he gave priority to the interests of the western UP peasants over those of eastern UP peasants. It was only after the formation of the BKD in 1969, that his party emerged as the main mobiliser of the peasantry through agitational politics. It is interesting to note that Charan Singh as a Congress leader dissuaded the peasantry of western UP from participating in the sugarcane growers' agitations in the 1950s and 1960s, but his party became the main mobiliser of the peasantry from the 1970s till his death on 29 May 1987.[14]

By 1980, the Lok Dal had become the most important organiser of the agitations of sugarcane growers in Meerut district. The editorial of *National Herald* remarked on the Lok Dal volunteers' role in the sugarcane growers' agitation : "Behind the agitation are political rather than economic factors. Report especially from Meerut district indicates that Lok Dal volunteers are intimidating and threatening the farmers who try to take entire produce to the sugar mills".[15] While the agitations generally took the form of strikes and demonstrations, the sugarcane growers' agitation of 1978 assumed the form of a hunger strike. Twenty-six persons were on fast unto death. After 9 days their demand to increase the price of sugarcanes was accepted.[16]

The participation of sugarcane growers in agitations in large number, often resulting in the closure of sugar mills, yielded results sometimes. The fluctuation in the prices of gur and khandsari, control on inter-state circulation of gur, the economic needs of sugarcane growers, the responses of gur merchants and mill-owners, and attitudes of the government and ruling party - the Congress - often determined the duration of agitations. Notwithstanding the success or failure of the agitations, the socialists and the communists won the sympathy of peasantry and were quite popular among them during the 1950s and 1960s.

Their popularity is also borne out by the fact that they were a significant component of the formidable opposition to the Congress, though they could not become the main winning force in western Uttar

Pradesh. Their electoral performance in some parliamentary constituencies[17] of the region shows that they ranked between the first (winning five Lok Sabha seats of Kairana, Khurja, Meerut, Muzaffarnagar and Amroha in 1967) and third political force in terms of electoral performance in the general elections held between 1952 and 1967, securing between 7 per cent and 49 per cent votes. Even in 1971 parliamentary election, the Muzaffarnagar seat was retained by the CPI securing 54 per cent votes.[18] In many of the assembly constituencies of the districts of Meerut, Muzaffarnagar, Moradabad, Bijnor, Mathura, Aligarh, Bulandshahr and Saharanpur, the communists and socialists got second and third places in the general elections held between 1952 and 1967. They had won some of the seats in 1962 and 1967 elections.[19]

While the opposition parties (non-Congress parties) - the socialists, CPI, independents and BKD - mobilised the sugarcane growers till the mid-1980s, the Congress adopted a two-fold policy. On the one hand, it dissuaded the peasantry from participating in the sugarcane growers' agitations, on the other hand, it propagated its policies and "achievements" amongst the peasantry, in order to divert their attention from their problems. Banarasi Das, Co-operative Minister of Uttar Pradesh, said in a conference at Daurala "if the price of sugarcane is raised, then who will grow wheat and other foodgrains"?[20] Another Congress leader characterised the sugarcane growers' agitations as "agitations for the sake of agitations and leadership".[21] The Congress leaders often warned the peasantry against the communists and socialists, and sometimes argued on "moral lines" that "they do not respect their teachers, they would not respect their parents too", that they "are anti-socials" and they "are supporters of China".[22] The state and district level Congress leaders including Charan Singh, held public meetings, rallies and conferences frequently in the villages of Meerut district. Almost every year in the month of November, the Congress pitched its tents at the fair of Garh Ganga (the river Ganges at Garh Mukteshwar), and its volunteers worked among the pilgrims, and the leaders addressed them. Through these meetings they told the people about the importance and relevance of the zamindari abolition, mobilised public opinion in favour of consolidation of landholdings and exhorted them to support the Congress policies, and also support it during the elections.[23] But the Congress felt the necessity of taking note of the problems of the sugarcane growers in the 1970s. The All India Cane Growers' Conference was held at Meerut. Even the then Congress leaders - H.N. Bahuguna, B.P. Maurya, R.C. Vikal - addressed the conference, besides the socialists and communists, like Gainda Singh, Z.A. Ahmed and Chandra Shekhar. The Conference passed a resolution demanding the nationalisation of sugar mills, subsidised agricultural goods and payment of the sugarcane price in time.[24]

The sugarcane growers' agitation have often suffered from two problems : (i) the role of "agents" (of mill-owners) and "traitors", and (ii) casteism. More often than not, it has been the experience of the sugarcane growers' agitations that certain' "agents" of the sugar mills tended to strike a deal with the mill-owners and make attempt to disrupt the agitations.[25] In 1959, the sugarcane growers supplying sugarcane to the Shimbhawali Sugar Mill were divided on caste lines. The owner of the Shimbhawali mill was a Sikh Jat. He reminded the Jat sugarcane growers that "you are Jats", and appealed to them to discontinue the strike. Shimbhawali mill "was the first mill where strike was broken because of caste factor".[26]

Public meetings have been the most common form of mobilisation. These meetings were held at the main cities or towns where the people from nearby villages gathered. In the 1950s and 1960s, all the major political parties were well organised. The campaign by them was carried out in a well organised way. Garh Mukhteshwar at the time of fair Ganga Snan provided a wide platform for the activities of political parties, particularly the Congress. This was more spectacular in the 1950s and 1960s. But the methods of mobilisation have undergone a significant change since the 1970s. Regarding the change V.S. Dublish, a freedom-fighter and Kakori case convict said "there is a difference (in the methods of mobilisation) between then (the 1950s) and now. Then, the organisation (Congress) was strong. There were village mandals and tahsil committees...workers used to work by going on feet and cycles to the people."[27]

Most of the political parties do not have an effective organisational structure below the district level. The lowest level of political parties for all practical purposes is the district level.[28]

The usual methods of mobilising the peasants are distributing and pasting printed posters and pamphlets. The local level leaders even go from village to village appealing to the peasantry to participate in the agitations on their demands, mostly concerning the sugarcane growers.

II

Problems of the rural poor are related to their social, economic and political conditions. The rural poor, particularly the landless proletariat and the scheduled castes have become more conscious of their social, economic and political rights in the post-independence period. They revealed a consciousness of the following issues and problems: redistribution of the Gaon Samaj land, arrangement of ration, abolition of begar, provision for better wages, curb on inflation, lifting of the sanctions against them to cut grass, etc., prevention of and protection from the socio-economic harassment of the landowning classes.[29]

The rural poor, more particularly the scheduled castes, were mobilised by the non-Congress parties - socialists (SP, PSP, SSP), CPI and RPI - on the one hand, and by the Congress on the other, from the 1950s to 1960s.

The late 1950s witnessed acute food crises in the North India, which affected large sections of the rural and urban poor. The Congress policy of free trading adopted at the behest of the dominant right section within the Congress, which opposed the system of price control, generated the depletion of food stocks. Failure of the wheat crop in North India along with the rise in prices of foodgrains between 1955 and 1958, coupled with the absence of fair price distribution shops worsened the conditions of the poor. The distressed conditions of the poor found expression in the food riots in different parts of Uttar Pradesh. The poor looted grain markets in Aligarh, Meerut, Hapur and many districts of eastern Uttar Pradesh.[30]

In 1958, the Socialists and Communists organised demonstrations, and a hunger strike of the agricultural labourers and small farmers in which around 300 persons participated. Even students participated in the hunger strike. They demanded curb on inflation, availability of cheap foodgrains, and action against those responsible for mismanagement of grain stocks. They "threatened" to resort to "loot of mandies (granaries)", if the government did not take possession of the mandies which were full of foodgrains to resolve the problem of food scarcity. Most of the prominent leaders of the agitation were arrested. In 1964, a demonstration of trade unions was organised by the socialist leader, Bireshwar Tyagi, against starvation in villages and cities of Meerut district.[31] Despite their weak position, the communists organised a demonstration of landless proletariat on 3 May 1975 on the issues of allotment of home sites and redistribution of surplus land.[32]

The scheduled castes and other lower castes were mobilised by the leaders of their respective castes in order to "expose" the Congress. The RPI led by B.P. Maurya, mobilised the scheduled castes, particularly Chamars through demonstrations and rallies in western Uttar Pradesh, in the 1960s.[33] Maurya organised a demonstration and a rally of scheduled castes in Meerut district in 1964. The main demands of the demonstrators were - land to the tiller and payment of statutory minimum wages.[34] Almost at the same time Jai Prakash Kashyap organised a demonstration of the Kashyap caste (OBC).[35] In a conference on 2 July 1969, the landless labourers demanded redistribution of uncultivated land.[36] Interestingly, while the Congress propagated its policies for the benefit of the "weaker sections", the scheduled caste leaders and the students organised their demonstrations.[37]

The Lok Dal has seldom attempted to mobilise the rural poor, particularly those belonging to the scheduled castes and is generally considered to be an anti-rural poor. Yet, the Lok Dal vied with the Congress to woo the harijans in Meerut district in 1982. The Lok Dal outbid the Congress (I) when the Lok Dal scheduled caste leader Banarasi Das Chanana was allowed to install the statue of Sant Ravi Das, and the Congress (I) scheduled caste MLA Hem Chand Nimesh was disallowed by the scheduled castes. This function was attended by 2,000 harijans. Charan Singh also addressed the meeting.[38] This meeting, however, could not erase the image of Lok Dal as anti-harijan.

While the non-Congress political parties mobilised the rural poor on the socio-economic problems, the Congress adopted a three-fold policy *vis-a-vis* them: (i) it cashed on the embittered relations between the landless proletariat and the landowning classes, (ii) it propagated its policies and "achievements" among the landless proletariat, and (iii) it dissuaded them from participating in agitational politics. The scheduled castes belonging to the Congress Party held frequent meetings throughout the 1950s, 1960s and 1970s to discuss their problems.[39]

The relationships between the rural poor and the rural rich have been in conflict during the post-independence period. The conflict takes place usually when the rural poor claim a share in power, redistribution of land or challenge the harassment, oppression and domination of the rural rich. In village Kalchina under Pilakhua Police Station, a quarrel took place between the Muslim high castes and Chamars in August 1952, on the question of land.[40] In June 1956, a caste-war ensued between the scheduled castes and the dominant castes in village Sekhpur, because a scheduled caste became village pradhan, and the dominant castes could not tolerate it.[41] The harassment and oppression of the scheduled castes, and the caste-war increased in the wake of formation of the BKD and with its participation in elections.[42] In the 1970s, the number of cognizable offences increased enormously. The reason for this was the "growing self-confidence and fearlessness of the harijans as a result of the policies followed by the government".[43] In a fresh bid to win over the rural poor after the "Garibi Hatao" slogan, Congress supported the demonstration of the "dalit" in front of the residence of the District Magistrate organised by the Dalit Sangharsh Samiti on 31 August 1973.[44] Indira Gandhi, the Prime Minister of India, took recourse to implementation of the Land Ceiling Act and redistribution of land among the rural poor. This plan became more effective during the emergency period. The land distributed to the rural poor was unfit for cultivation and uneconomic. In many cases, the allottees were not allowed to take possession of the allotted land.[45]

However ineffective may be the implementation of land reform measures during the emergency, they embittered the relationships between the dominant caste rural rich and the low caste rural poor. Vulnerable socio-economic conditions of the rural poor made them susceptible to harassment and oppression of the rural rich. The rural rich dominant castes could not retaliate openly during the emergency period, but as soon as the Janata government was elected they started reclaiming the pieces of land which were given to the rural poor during the emergency. The threat to regain the land by the rural rich often resulted in caste-war in the district. The State Janata Party leaders and the Chief Minister, Ram Naresh Yadav, who visited the villages of Meerut described the news of reclaiming of land and the atrocities on harijans as "highly exaggerated", "misleading", "false propaganda", and "handiwork of vested interests". The Chief Minister further said that "not one case of atrocity was found there".[46] Thakur Balbir Singh, Agriculture Minister of Uttar Pradesh, a Rajput, who hailed from Meerut district asserted that land should be given back to the dominant castes as they were the real claimants of lands, which was taken away from them illegally.[47]

The Congress cashed on the embittered relations between the rural poor and the rural rich, particularly the supporters of Lok Dal/Janata Party. The Congress publicised the anti-harijan attitude of the Lok Dal/ Janta Party.[48] A Congress team, headed by K.C. Pant, visited the villages of Meerut district to make an on-the-spot study of the scheduled castes' forcible ejectment from the house sites and other kinds of land allotted to them under the 20-point programme. The committee found in village Rawa, under Charan Singh's constituency, cases of destruction of crops of 81 families, and in Muhammedpur Bhoomi village cases of forcible ejection from 42 plots given for house sites and of arson. Two carpenters, 2 tailors and 3 scheduled castes in village Arnawli were driven away from the village.[49]

The Congress also attempted to win over confidence of the rural poor by propagating, as in the case of peasantry, the "achievements" of implementing zamindari abolition, achieving independence, Introducing reservations for the scheduled castes, introducing welfare schemes for the rural poor, and providing security and protection to the rural poor from harassment, oppression and domination of rural rich.[50]

At the time of their visits to the drought and flood affected areas in the late 1950s and 1960s, the Congress leaders were asked for help by the rural poor. The Congress leaders often gave them assurances about solving their problems. But these promises were mostly unfulfilled. The editorial of *Panchayati Raj* commented: "The most disgraceful is that the rural people are facing acute problems (of food) at this time and the government and Congress workers are giving good advice to the people to have patience. But the hungry people want food also with patience."[51] Like the case of mobilisation of sugarcane growers, in the case of rural poor also, the Congress dissuaded them from participating in agitational politics. At a conference of the Congress activists, Ramjilal Sahayak, a scheduled caste Congress MLA exhorted the Congress workers to dissuade the rural poor from participating in any agitation against the Congress and government.[52]

III

Charan Singh's death on 29 May 1987 created a void in the leadership and political organisation, which could have articulated the interests of farmers of western Uttar Pradesh. The period preceding his protracted illness leading to his death synchronised with the emergence of the

Bharatiya Kisan Union (BKU) led by Mahendra Singh Tikait.[53] Tikait filled the void, and the cause of the farmers of western Uttar Pradesh has been taken up by the BKU since then. While the farmers' movements in Meerut, preceding the one led by Tikait, most systematically focused upon the sugarcane growers' problems, the BKU movement focused upon the general problems of the market-oriented peasantry, including those of the sugarcane growers. The movement saw maximum participation of farmers from certain districts of western Uttar Pradesh - Meerut, Muzaffarnagar, Bulandshahr, Aligarh, Ghaziabad, Moradabad, Bijnore and Saharanpur.[54] The BKU movement in western UP represents certain new trends in the farmers' movements in India in the late 1970s and 1980s.[55] It had seen a departure from the movements led by the communists and socialists, the Lok Dal and others. Unlike the earlier movements, the BKU movement in UP projected itself as "apolitical". The constitution of the BKU envisages that "the Union is an apolitical, secular and non-violent institution, a district level office-bearer of a party cannot become the office-bearer of the Union, and if an office-bearer accepts the post of a district level office-bearer of a party, he will be considered expelled from the Union."[56] Leaders with membership of or even affiliation to the political parties were not allowed to share the dias at rallies organised by the BKU at Meerut during January-February 1988 and in Delhi during October-November 1988.[57] Tikait was critical of all professional leaders; he even criticised Charan Singh when the BKU movement was in its infancy. But he had to withdraw his criticism in the face of opposition from the people.[58] Tikait, however, was appreciative of Devi Lal because of his financial donation to the BKU and his earlier announcement of the loan waiver to the peasantry of Haryana.[59] Another peculiarity of the BKU movement has been that unlike the movements of earlier decades in Meerut, the BKU meddled in all sorts of issues relating to the village society, ranging from settling village disputes to stoppage of dowry, rules about marriage customs and expenses, discipline in schools, code of conduct for women, etc.[60]

The issues which the BKU raised, and its attitude towards the problems of the rural poor and the behaviour of the supporters of the BKU towards the latter and vice-versa amply demonstrate that it is a movement of the rural rich.[61] The movement did not take up the demands of the rural poor, *i.e.*, payment of wages, stoppage of their harassment, increase in the price of milk, creation of employment (this being the most general problem of the villages).[62] However, later on, some demands relating to the rural poor, *i.e.*, fixing up of the wages of agricultural labourers at par with the salary of the army soldiers were raised during the rally of the BKU at Boat Club in October 1988. But it was done after the media-cry and the BKU's criticism of being "pro-kulak", with the purpose of erasing its image of being anti-rural poor.[63] But the seriousness of this demand is incredible and unfeasible to abide by because of the very nature of relationships between the rural poor and the rural rich (the BKU supporters).[64] It does not seem practicable that the rural rich will implement the decision of providing the agricultural labourers wages equivalent to the salary of army soldiers or they will distribute the "surplus" land to the "unprofitable land-holders" as envisaged in its constitution.

The demands for remunerative prices of the produce and subsidised inputs do not concern the rural poor. The small peasants do not grow sugarcane as the main crop and the poor peasants do not grow it at all, and they grow wheat for family consumption.[65] Moreover, they have to make distress sale, in which case increase in the price of produce is not of much help to them, since in case of such sale the prices are fixed by the dealer. Price increase would affect them adversely when they along with other rural poor buy the agricultural produce from the rural rich or market.[66] On the other hand, the BKU supporters have not been paying the dues to the state since the Shamli agitation of April 1987, following the BKU's decision of non-cooperation with government by not paying the electricity bills and revenue and not allowing the government employees and elected representatives (later on they relaxed this condition on the elected representatives) into the villages.[67] They adopt double standard in their relationships with the state and the rural poor. While they do not pay the dues to the state, they charge for the water sold and the other resources hired out to the small and poor peasants,[68] as the latter do not own enough resources.[69] In some villages, the government employees who dared to cut the electricity connection for non-payment of electricity bills were "punished" by the BKU supporters. They were gheraoed and beaten up, made to do sit-ups and tied up to the trees. The BKU had virtually set up "Kisan Raj" in the villages.[70] Even the demand for waiving off loans does not concern the rural poor. Most of the indebted rural poor do not depend for loans on government institutions. Their credit agencies are the rural rich (including milkmen). On the contrary, these are mostly the indebted rural rich who depend on modern institutions - banks and co-operatives.[71] In principle, however, the loan waiver might help those rural poor, who did not take the cash loan but took commodities like buffaloes, from the "levy". But in reality, in most cases, it will not have much meaning to them because in the process of getting buffaloes from the "levy", they get indebted to the local moneylenders/milkmen.[72]

It is quite paradoxical that the rural rich may benefit from the loan waiver by the government, but the moneylenders among them may still charge interest from the rural poor. Through our discussion with several rural rich, the supporters of the BKU, we observed that the class character of their movement is sought to be explained as a potential beneficiary to the rural poor. The argument is put forward that the improvement in the conditions of the rural rich would be tantamount to helping the rural poor, since they depend on the former for agricultural resources and wages. The improvement in the conditions of the rural rich would enable them to pay higher wages to the agricultural labourers, and reduction in electricity charges would enable them to charge less from those who buy water from them.[73] Any suggestion that the movement by and large belongs to the rural rich is scoffed as an attempt to divide the peasantry.[74]

The BKU movement is not against the rural poor *per se*. But the specific nature of relationships between the BKU supporters and the rural poor places the movement in a position whose implications turn out to be anti-rural poor or antagonistic to the rural poor.[75] The rural poor either remain indifferent to the BKU movement or support it under duress,[76] or react to it with suspicion keeping in view its consequences on their relations in the villages. They apprehend that the activisation of the rural rich through BKU agitation would lead to their encouragement to harass and oppress the rural poor.[77]

Initial threat/proposal which however was not carried out, made at the time of the rally at Meerut in January-February 1988 to cut off supply of essential commodities such as vegetables and milk caused panic among the conscious section of the rural poor whose economy depends on milk selling to a large extent.[78] The dynamics of political processes in Meerut in the post-independence period show that the rural poor and the rural rich are placed in antithetical position to each other.[79] Even the way in which the rallies were held at Meerut and Delhi for more than 20 days each time amply demonstrates the class character of the agitation. Sumptuous food, sweets, "gajar-halwa". "puri-subji', "Kesari", *etc.*, and even tobacco packed in small polythene bags which were brought from the villages can be afforded only by the rural rich in rural India.[80]

Initially it was a class-based movement, supported by the rural rich belonging to different castes, *i.e.*, Jats, Gujars, Rajputs, Tyagis, Brahmans, Saiyeds and Pathans and few low castes, Jats playing the most dominant role. Khaps and traditional leadership of these castes played important role in mobilising the farmers.[81] "Apolitical" plank was the easiest tool for bringing the peasantry of the rural rich of different castes together on their common issues. They remained as allies in the BKU movement so long as the movement retained its "apolitical character". Tikait's inclination towards any leader of a party would logically distance him from the section of farmers which supports the rival party/ leadership. Tikait could not remain "apolitical" longer.[82] He became "political" in due course. His support to the opposition in 1989 election, and before that in the Chhaprauli by-election, his support to Devi Lal (which divided even the Jats between the supporters of Ajit Singh and Devi Lal) and Chandra Shekhar, his love-hate relationship with Mulayam Singh Yadav and Congress, and hobnobbing with the politicians in the Bhopa case/agitation[83] and Rajesh Pilot, and finally his addressing the rally jointly with Devi Lal, Chandra Shekhar, Mulayam Singh Yadav demolished his "apolitical" image.[84] Tikait's behaviour with Sharad Joshi, on 2 October 1989 at the AIKCC (All India Kisan Co-ordination Committee) rally at Boat Club resulting in his expulsion from the AIKCC,[85] and later his behaviour with a senior doctor of the AIIMS,[86] his withdrawal of rallies without much achievement further eroded his credibility among the farmers. Even simmerings on the regional lines began to brew within the movement.[87] As soon as the movement started becoming "political", content of its class character got a severe blow. The dissidents within the BKU and the non-Jat leaders took advantage of Tikait becoming "political". The non-Jat leaders accused Tikait of being partisan and favouring Jats. This led to the disintegration of the BKU on the caste lines.[88] The expulsion of Lt. Col. Ram Mahesh Bhardwaj from the BKU alienated the Tyagi farmers from it. Formation of the Kisan Mazdoor Panchayat headed by Hukum Singh, a Gujar

UP Congress Minister, with famous Gujar leaders - Rajesh Pilot (also a Congress leader) and Avtar Singh Bhadana - taking interest in it, distanced the BKU from Gujars. The Congress encouraged the split in the social base of BKU by encouraging the formation of Akhil Bharatiya Kisan Mazdoor Maha Panchayat by Pilot. The Congress tried to neutralise the BKU and win over the farmers by cosmetic concessions.[89] The non-Jats started perceiving the BKU as a Jat organisation, and more particularly of the Jats belonging to the Balyan Khap headed by Tikait.[90] By 9 August 1990, the BKU movement was reduced to the rural rich belonging to Jats and supporters of the Devi Lal camp.[91]

The BKU movement in western Uttar Pradesh emerged when the farmers had almost lost faith in "politics", which to them has a narrow meaning confined to elections, professional politicians, political leaders, political activists and political parties. Failures of the political leaders and political parties to fulfil the promises made before elections or to mitigate their grievances accentuated their distrust in "politics". In our discussion with the participants in the BKU rallies and during our fieldwork in the villages in 1988, the people cutting across caste and class barriers were critical of the politicians, whom they described as "cheat, corrupt, dishonest, selfish, etc." They showed lack of confidence in the politicians. Hence they could be mobilised more effectively on an "apolitical" plank and purely on their class issues. With Tikait joining "politics", they no longer find him different from professional politicians.

The farmers supported the BKU wholeheartedly in the initial phase of the movement. During a survey in the villages - one each from Meerut and Moradabad districts - conducted in 1988, we observed that even the withdrawal of the rally at Meerut in 1988 did not dampen the enthusiasm of the farmers in supporting the agitation. But the base of BKU started shrinking predominantly to Jats as a consequence of the growth of disintegration in it and Tikait becoming "political". None of the farmers' demands was fulfilled, though they had stopped paying dues to the state as per the exhortation of the BKU for boycott. And whatever concessions were obtained by the farmers from the state were "more rhetorical than real".[92] Notwithstanding the failure of the BKU agitations, the movement brought itself in "conjunction with similar movements in other states with common aim of acquiring national attention for farmers' demands".[93] It also contributed to the growth of the level of their consciousness. The farmers in Meerut expressed their cynicism about the formation of their union just 3-4 years (during the first phase of our fieldwork in 1984-85) before the rise of the BKU. But owing to the impact of BKU agitations, they expressed the hope and need for a farmers' union in 1988 (during the second phase of our fieldwork). However, the villages do not have formally well-knit organisations even now, though the BKU office-bearers and loose sprinklings of the BKU have come to exist in some villages. Generally, the farmers have become the supporters of the BKU and participants in the movement launched by it, and not its formal members. The BKU agitations added to the realisation of the importance of the peasantry (the rural rich: "kulaks") in the 1980s,[94] which had already been made by their assertion in the movements in Maharashtra, Gujarat, Punjab, Karnataka and Tamil Nadu in the preceding decade.[95]

The attitude of Congress towards the BKU like that of other parties, was determined by its electoral considerations. A predominant section of the BKU supporters - Jats - have not been Congress supporters.[96] The Congress knew that any political activity on the part of the rural rich, particularly Jats, would push the rural poor towards it. The Congress was aware of the factions within the main opposition party, the Lok Dal: it would be easy to split the BKU's anti-Congress base, and it took advantage of this. It let the movement pass as it did.[97] It patronised division within the farmers by encouraging the non-Jat dominant caste - Gujars - to form a parallel union and it dubbed the BKU movement as that of the Jats, and finally, as we shall see in the next section, it encouraged the rural poor, Chamars, to form the BMU.

Factionalism within the Congress unit of Muzaffarnagar district got linked with the BKU agitation. The leader of one faction of Congress opposed to the UP Home Minister, Said-ul-Jama, supported the BKU in order to score points over Jama. This faction took advantage of Jama's proximity to the main accused in the Nayeema (Bhopa) case - a case related to the abduction of Nayeema, a teen-aged married Muslim woman, which triggered off an agitation led by the BKU during August-September 1989. Said-ul-Jama defended the accused on the plea that charges against him were not proved and hence he could not be held guilty. Said-ul-Jama represented the Morna assembly seat which covered the area affected by the Bhopa agitation. Jama's defence of the accused in the Nayeema case cost him popularity among the

Jat BKU supporters and upper class Muslims. Their antagonism towards Jama got channellised into the support and popularity of other Congress leader Narendra Singh, a Jat, the UP Energy Minister. Narendra Singh's involvement brought about an agreement on 10 September 1989, the government being represented by him and the BKU by its secretary, Har Pal Singh. This brought the BKU close to the Congress faction led by him. It also distanced the BKU from the non-Congress parties (opposition), while the Congress faction led by Hukum Singh had already been antagonised by the BKU since the Shamli agitation of April 1987.[98] So long as no important (holding position in the government) factional leader was siding with the BKU, the movement remained anti-Congress. One paper in its editorial remarked "the Bhopa incident goes against the Congress (I), but this does not mean the BKU is going to back the opposition in the forthcoming elections".[99] But almost after a month, with the conclusion of an agreement between the BKU and the Congress (I) minister, a pro-Congress paper in its editorial remarked: "Mr. Devi Lal has been checked while Ajit Singh had been rendered ineffective to carry forth the legacy of his father... the administration of the movement at this juncture with the active involvement of the UP government has put the Congress (I) in a strong position".[100] Several western UP Congress (I) leaders were annoyed with this agreement. They felt that whatever courtesy was shown to the BKU suppporters would not turn them into the Congress supporters. They decided to organise the scheduled castes, the backward castes, and Rajputs against the BKU in order to regain their support.[101]

IV

Even as the BKU emerged to articulate the interests of the rural rich, the Bharatiya Mazdoor Union (BMU)/the Dalit Sena/ the Shoshit Mukti Vahini and the BSP emerged to articulate the interests of the rural poor, particularly the scheduled castes (Chamars), in the latter half of 1980s.[102] They seem to be occupying the place among the scheduled castes, which the RPI did in the 1960s with the difference that the BSP like the RPI contested elections, while the BMU/the Dalit Sena/ the Shoshit Mukti Vahini, have not contested as yet.

In the wake of the formation of BKU, clashes of usual nature took place between the rural rich and the rural poor, particularly between Jats and Chamars in western Uttar Pradesh. Such clashes assumed the form of clashes between the BKU as the Jats happened to be the most dominant caste which formed its social base and the newly-formed organisation, the BMU/the Dalit Sena/the Shoshit Mukti Vahini of the rural poor belonging to the Chamars. They often culminated into imposition of sanctions by the rural rich against the rural poor. These newly-formed organisations and the BSP allied with each other in mobilising the scheduled castes during Jat-Chamar clashes. The BMU played the most leading role in mobilising the scheduled castes.[103] The BMU was formed on 16 August 1987 by a group of people belonging to the rural poor in which Jai Pal Singh Mitharia[104] played a leading role, in a meeting of the "labourers" organised at the village of Mitharia, Karheda in the Muzaffarnagar district of western UP. Around 15,000 "labourers" from three western UP districts - Muzaffarnagar, Meerut and Saharanpur - participated in the meeting. Formation of the BKU by the rural rich,and its perception by the rural poor as the Jats' organisation [105] and the clashes between the BKU supporters and the Chamars, provided enough immediate and apparent reasons for its patrons and organisers to form the BMU. Under these circumstances, the rural poor of the villages of Muzaffarnagar approached Mitharia in the first week of August or last week of July 1987, and requested him to protect them from harassment/ oppression and sanctions which were imposed against them by the rural rich following the clashes between them because of the forcible begar, under-payment of wages and beatings. The rural poor held a meeting at the Karheda village in the first week of August 1987 (the date could not be ascertained). Mahendra Singh Tikait had attended this meeting as a mediator on the request of the rural poor. But Tikait took one-sided decision in favour of the Jats at this meeting. Mitharia quoted Tikait as follows:

> *Ek dhoti wala hia, ek langoti wala.*
> *Aur langoti wala dhoti wale ko dekh kar jal raha hai.*
> One (the Jat rural rich) is wearing full clothes, another (the rural poor Chamar) is wearing underwear. The latter is jealous of the former.]

This statement of Tikait incensed the rural poor. No agreement was reached. The rural poor then decided to form the BMU. Jai Pal Singh Mitharia was elected as the national president of the union. Mitharia was already determined to form a union. Tikait's decision/statement provided him enough legitimacy/justification for its formation. Formation of the BMU was preceded by the systematic attempts by its founders in the villages of Meerut, Muzaffarnagar and Saharanpur districts to make the rural poor aware of the need of the formation of such union. The rural poor supported the BMU because they were opposed to the BKU. The emergence of the BKU scared them and they naturally supported/joined the BMU.[106]

The BMU projected itself as "apolitical". But in reality, it was not "apolitical", unlike the BKU in its initial phase. It received clandestine patronage of the Congress (I) leader and the ex-Minister, Vidya Bhusan and after his death on 12 July 1988 from Said-ul-Jamma, also a Congress minister. Mitharia also had political background.[107] The BMU provided a forum to the Congress supporters belonging to the non-Jats, *i.e.,* Gujars, Tyagis and Sainis (OBC). The non-Jat rural rich joined hands with the BMU and formed the Kisan Mazdoor Union (KMU). Achhpal Singh, younger brother of the former Congress deputy minister Narayan Singh, a Gujar from Kheda Chaugama village of Muzaffarnagar district became its president and Nahar Singh Saini (who was village pradhan, as a BMU candidate) of village Jangedi became its co-ordinator.[108] The KMU worked in tandem with the BMU. The Kisan Mazdoor Panchayat (KMP) of the Gujar Congress leaders led by Hukum Singh, a "non-political" organisation, gave a call for a meeting of the farmers. During this period, Congress leaders Avtar Singh Bhadana and Rajesh Pilot were projected in this area.[109]

The Congress (I) and the governments led by it at the Centre and in UP were jittered as the BKU and the BSP were cutting into Congress base. The BSP was weaning away the Congress base from the scheduled castes, the OBCs and the minorities.[110] In order to retain its social base the Congress adopted two-fold policy. First, it encouraged the division within the BKU on caste lines. Second, it patronised the BMU and projected as "apolitical" to dispel any impression that it had patronised the BMU.

The scheduled caste leaders irrespective of the party affiliations from Meerut, Muzaffarnagar and Saharanpur districts vied to join the BMU and take over its leadership. Hem Chand Nimesh, ex-MLA Congress (I), and Jhaggad Singh, then Janata Dal MLA, became active and visited several villages to make the scheduled castes aware of the BMU. Jhaggad Singh remained as president of the BMU unit, Meerut district, for some time. After the formation of the BMU, its meetings were organised at different places in Meerut, Muzaffarnagar and Saharanpur districts. In one such meeting in a village of Saharanpur district, the bickerings within the BMU burst into open. Jag Pal Singh, the Congress (I) MP from Hardwar constituency (SC) claimed the leadership of the BMU.[111] The union split into two factions - one led by Jag Pal Singh and another by Jai Pal Singh Mitharia. In 1988 (date and month could not be ascertained), the leaders of the BMU of Meerut district - Shiv Kumar Kataria and Sumer Singh Premi - declared their separation from the original BMU at a meeting in the village Kushar of Meerut. Finally, the BMU split into three units existing in Meerut, Muzaffarnagar and Saharanpur districts, each led by different leader independent of each other. Mitharia claimed that the union led by him is the strongest of the three. The base of the BMU shrunk and it split on the regional (district) basis.

The BMU led by Mitharia which was initially established with the patronage of Congress is now the supporter of Dalit Sena of Ram Vilas Paswan and Ajit Singh (the Janata Dal leaders). Regarding this shift from a Congress supporter to the non-Congress supporter Mithaira said that his support to a party is determined in the light of the move of the locally dominant caste group led by Tikait. When Tikait was anti-Congress, he supported the Congress and when he was supporting the Janata Dal (S), (which formed government with the support of Congress), and Devi Lal and when he became appreciative of the Congress, Mitharia switched over his support to the Janata Dal - the Ram Vilas Paswan, Ajit Singh and V.P. Singh group.[112]

Our visits to villages of Meerut, Muzaffarnagar and Moradabad districts several times since the movement of the BKU began, prove that the BMU's social base lies mainly among the Chamars, who form the most numerous group of the rural poor. But this base is confined mainly to the villages of Meerut and Muzaffarnagar districts. Although, the units of the BMU do not exist in all villages, there are its sympathisers in most of the villages of these districts. In the fieldwork which we conducted in two villages one each from Meerut and Moradabad districts in June 1988 and even before that (in the village of Moradabad district in March 1988) we observed that the rural poor of the village in Moradabad district were not aware of the existence of the BMU, unlike in the village of Meerut district. A majority of Chamars are either formal members or the supporters of the BMU in the village of Meerut.

The treasurer of the BMU unit of this village said that its units existed in almost all villages of Mawana block of Mawana tahsil. It must be noted that Mawana tahsil which provides a strong social base to the BMU in Meerut, is situated adjacent to the Jansath tahsil of Muzaffarnagar district. In this tahsil, the village Karheda, where the BMU was first formed and from where the BMU's (original) national president hails, is situated. While some of non-Chamar rural poor from the OBCs sympathise with the BMU, we found in our discussion with a large number of them in Meerut and Muzaffarnagar districts that they perceive it as a casteist organisation with its base confined to the Chamars. All supporters of the BMU have been the Congress supporters and joined or supported the BMU in reaction to the formation of the BKU. While the non-Jat dominant castes perceived the BKU as an "organisation of Jats", the rural poor (the SCs and the OBCs) perceive it is an "organisation of the rich and the Jats".

It is interesting to note that the demarcation of the social bases of the BMU, the Dalit Sena, the Shoshit Mukti Vahini, the ephermeral groups (like Ambedkar Committees) and to a large extent the BSP is blurred; their social bases overlap. Almost all of them belong to the same caste and class groups. They may be divided on political bases. But on the issue of social discrimination and other related issues they all unite. The BMU/the Dalit Sena/the Shoshit Mukti Vahini, by and large, raised the issues related to the socio-economic conditions of the rural poor - mostly the issues emanating from the relationships of dependence between the rural rich and the rural poor, *i.e.*, harassment, sanctions, etc.[113]

The clashes between the rural rich and the rural poor, between the Jats and the Chamars in western UP, received wide publicity in the wake of the formation of BKU and BMU. The Bhopa case is the most important example of such incidents. Unlike the earlier clashes between Jats and Chamars, the Bhopa clashes (second incident/development related to the Bhopa case)[114] were marked by participation of organisations, *i.e.*, the BKU on behalf of Jats and the BMU/the Dalit Sena/the Shoshit Mukti Vahini/the BSP on behalf of Chamars. The BMU had done enough groundwork among the Chamars of Muzaffarnagar district and adjoining areas of Meerut district and become a fairly well-known organisation among the Chamars of these areas. The Bhopa case (second incident/ development) started with the refusal of a labourer (Chamar) to go to work for a Jat BKU supporter, resulting in the firing, injuring 25 and killing 4 persons by the Jats on 26 September 1989. In relatiation the BMU blocked the road and the Jat students from Rakheda protested against the blockade. It developed into a clash between the BMU supporters and the Jats, which soon escalated into widespread clashes between Jats and Chamars, culminating into clashes between the organisations - the BKU and the BMU. The BKU leaders including Tikait's brother Bhopal Singh and the BKU secretary, and the BMU leader Mitharia provided leadership to Jats and Chamars respectively. The tense situation led to the deployment of the PAC in ten villages.[115] The BMU had become already incensed with the BKU during the first phase of the Bhopa case (Nayeema case: from 1 August 1989 to 10 September 1989). The BKU supporters exercised pressure upon the Chamars to join the Nayeema case agitation.[116] The killing of a labourer on 26 September 1989, added fuel to fire. The clashes took ominous turn - the BKU supporters wielding guns,[117] the BMU supporters also well prepared with arms (illegal).[118] The BMU supporters responded to the firing of the BKU with firing.[119]

The incidents which took place in the villages of Muzaffarnagar district were echoed in Meerut district. While in the villages the Jats (BKU) had an edge over the Chamars due to their dominant position and the imposition of sanctions, in the cities the rural poor (mostly Chamars) took the lead over the Jats. The activists belonging to the BMU/the Dalit Sena/the Shoshit Mukti Vahini and the BSP joined hands with each other and took active role in Meerut and in Muzaffarnagar cities (during the second incident of the Bhopa case). In Meerut, they organised a demonstration on 2 October 1989, and the participants had come from the villages of Meerut.[120] They went on rampage in Meerut city damaging public and private property.[121] The leaders belonging to the scheduled castes irrespective of party affiliations participated in the demonstration. The BKU leader, Tikait, and Jats were the main target of their abusive slogans. The demonstrators were armed with lathis, etc.[122]

It is noteworthy that the BMU meeting on 24 September 1989 at Rakheda which marked the beginning of Bhopa clashes happened just one week before the BKU rally (AIKCC or the Kisan Jawan rally) of 2 October 1989, and the BMU/the Dalit Sena/BSP took out the demonstration on the day of rally. It can be inferred that the forces opposed to the BKU could have been involved in the mobilisation/organisation of the supporters of BMU/the Dalit Sena/BSP, to take advantage of the embittered relations between the BKU and the BMU and to discredit the BKU. The Congress (I) took advantage of such relations, just as it did during the rule of the Janata Party. It patronised the BMU in the clashes.[123] The Congress was hand in glove with the BMU. Said-ul-Jama, the UP Home Minister, had lost support among the Jats and Muslims during the Nayeema case. He wanted to regain his strength by consolidating among the non-Jats and the non-upper class Muslims. He took advantage of the situation. The incident of firing on 26 September 1989 was preceded by a meeting of the harijans organised by the BMU and addressed by Mitharia on 24 September 1989. Mitharia had sought the blessings of the Congress leaders in Delhi before organising this meeting and the Congress (Said-ul-Jama) provided moral and financial support to Mitharia. "Provocative speeches" were made at this meeting.[124] The BMU with the support of Congress (I), even attempted to isolate the Jats by calling for a meeting "of 35" out of 36 castes excluding them.[125]

Mobilisation of the rural rich revolves around the issues related to the capitalist economy in agriculture mainly - the remunerative prices, subsidised inputs, writing off loans or better credit facilities, etc. Despite the development of capitalist tendencies, the mobilisation of the rural poor is seldom done on the issues emanating from the capitalist agriculture. The issues of their mobilisation are mainly related to their social discrimination and the issues which emanate mainly from the relationships of one-sided dependence.

Notes

1. These issues and problems have been sorted out from: a Hindi weekly paper, *Panchayati Raj*, 1950-1975; data from field work; interviews; proceedings of the Kisan Sabha, Meerut, 1950; Maharaj Singh Bharati, *Ganna Chini : Samasya Aur Samadhan* (Hindi), Lucknow, New Janata Press, n.d.
2. Interview : Maharaj Singh Bharati, 11 May 1985; Dev Dutt Sharma, *Jivan Ke Mod* (Hindi), Delhi, 1962, pp. 18-19.
3. See Sanjaya Baru, *The Political Economy of Sugar : State Intervention and Structural Change*, Delhi, Oxford University Press, pp. 76-80, 99-108.

4. Various issues of *Panchayati Raj,* 1950-1967.
5. *Panchayati Raj,* 29 November 1959.
6. *Panchayati Raj,* 28 December 1958. Interview: Shanti Tyagi 18 January 1992.
7. *Panchayati Raj,* 12 July 1959. Interview: Shanti Tyagi, 18 January 1992.
7a. Interview: Shanti Tyagi, 18 January 1992.
8. The socialists even mobilised the peasantry of Ghaziabad in 1963, against the acquisition of their land by the government under Master Plan, and for adequate compensation. See, *Panchayati Raj,* 8 September 1963; Paul R. Brass, *Factional Politics in an Indian State: The Congress Party in Uttar Pradesh,* Bombay, Oxford, 1966, p. 154.
9. *Panchayati Raj,* 7 January 1972.
10. *Panchayati Raj,* 8 October 1972.
11. *Panchayati Raj,* 15 December 1974.
12. *Panchayati Raj,* 6 May 1973. This BKU was in no way related to the BKU led by Mahendra Singh Tikait. It was named so because it dealt with the peasant problems. It had an ephemeral existence. Interview: Damodar Sharma, 7 December 1990.
13. *Panchayati Raj,* 21 October 1973.
14. See also Chapter VI, pp.126-29.
15. *National Herald,* 4 December 1980.
16. Interview : Bhopal Singh, 25 April 1985.
17. For example, Bijnor, Baghpat, Saharanpur, Aligarh, Bulandshahr, Hapur, Hathras, Hardwar, Kairana, Khurja, Meerut, Muzaffarnagar, Moradabad and Amroha.
18. Based on David Butler, *et al., India Decides : Elections, 1952-1991,* New Delhi, Aroon Purie for Living Media India, 1991.
19. For example in 1962, Siana, Agota, Moradabad Rural, Billari (SC), Atrauli and Muzaffarnagar were won by the SSP with votes between 31 per cent and 48 per cent and Amroha was won by the CPI with 28.7 per cent votes. In 1967 Siana (retained), Jewar (SC), Kithore, Meerut Cantonment, Charthawal (SC) were won by the SSP with votes between 33.6 per cent and 52 per cent, and Baraut and Khatauli were won by the CPI with 50.9 per cent and 19 per cent votes respectively. Based on V.B. Singh and Shankar Bose, *State Elections in India : Data Handbook on Vidhan Sabha Elections, 1952-85, Vol. 4, The North (Part 2) : Bihar and Uttar Pradesh,* New Delhi, Sage Publications, 1988.
20. *Panchayati Raj,* 29 November 1964.
21. Interview : Fateh Singh Rana, 24 April 1985.
22. *Panchayati Raj,* March 24 1953; 15 May 1960.
23. Several issues of *Panchayat Raj,* 1950-1964.
24. *Panchayati Raj,* 29 November 1970.

25. Interview : Sohanvir Singh Tomar, 8 June 1985.
26. Interview: Maharaj Singh Bharati, 28 April 1985.
27. Interview: V.S. Dublish, 25 April 1985.
28. Sanjib Kumar Baruah, *Getting A Fair Share : Politics and Poor in Rural India,* Ph.D. thesis, Chicago University, 1983, p. 260.
29. These issues have been culled out from *Panchayati Raj,* 1950-1975; the data from fieldwork. Besides the general problems of the rural poor, there were certain temporal problems which became live issues for their mobilisation. The periods between 1957 and 1964, and year 1972 were marked by recurrent natural calamities: floods due to heavy rains, pyrilla and locust which destroyed the crops and caused scarcity of foodgrains. The rural poor were affected the most. See *Panchayati Raj,* 22 September 1957; 27 August, 14, 21 September, 15 October 1958; 9 October 1960; 20 August 1961; 22 September 1963; 2 August 1974; and 30 July 1972. There also existed problems which concerned the residents of Hastinapur, Ganga Khadir - problems of the retired army officials and "political sufferers", who were allotted residential land in Ganga Khadir. These problems became very important issues for mobilisation during the 1950s and 1960s. The issues which concerned them were: (i) land given to them was not fit for cultivation, (ii) amount of revenue taken from them was higher in proportion to the quality of land, (iii) they should have been given land instead of constructed houses, (iv) they should be given the price of houses taken from them, (v) proper employment opportunities be created and a sugar mill set up and, (vi) price of land which was given to them was too high.
30. See Zoya Hasan, *Dominance and Mobilisation : Rural Politics in Western Uttar Pradesh, 1930-1980,* New Delhi, Sage Publications, 1989, p. 113.
31. *Panchayati Raj,* 25 April 1958; 7, 14, 28 September 1958; 2 August 1964. The socialists mobilised even the residents of Ganga Khadir on their problems under the banner of organisation of Ganga Khadir in the 1950s and 1960s. They organised a demonstration, in which 57 persons were arrested, and presented a memorandum to the State and Central governments in December 1961. See *Panchyati Raj,* 10, 17 December 1961.
32. *Panchayati Raj,* 1 June 1975.
33. R.I. Duncan, *Levels, the Communication of Programmes and Sectional Strategies in Indian Politics with special reference to the Bharatiya Kranti Dal and Republican Party of India in Uttar Pradesh and Aligarh District,* Ph.D.thesis, University of Sussex, 1979, pp. 266-67; see also Zoya Hasan, *op. cit.,* pp. 117-20.
34. See Sanjib Kumar Baruah, *op. cit.,* p.303.
35. Interview: Pitam Singh Rathi, 20 March 1985.

36. *Panchayati Raj,* 3 July 1967.
37. See *Panchayati Raj,* 31 August 1973.
38. *The Times of India,* 10 February 1982.
39. *Panchayati Raj,* 12 July 1952; 1, 22 July, 16 October 1955; 12 December 1965; 17 December 1972; 2 September 1973; 1 June 1975.
40. *Panchayati Raj,* 24 August 1952.
41. *Panchayati Raj,* 24 June 1956.
42. *National Herald,* 31 January 1969, 8 February 1969; *Link,* 23 February 1969, Vol. 11, no. 28, 1969. Even the Election Commission of India attributed the causes of low polling "to the intimidation of the Scheduled Caste harijans by aggressive jats (supporters of the BKD)." See R.I. Duncan, *op. cit.,* p.170.
43. *National Herald,* 3, 4 September 1976; *The Times of India,* 9 May 1976.
44. *Panchayati Raj,* 2 September 1973.
45. See Chapter II, pp. 21-22.
46. *Patriot,* 19 August 1977; *The Times of India,* 3 August 1977. See also Atul Kohli, *The state and poverty in India: The politics of Reform,* Cambridge University Press, 1989, pp. 219-20.
47. "Land Dispute or War on Meerut Harijans?", *National Herald,* 11 July 1977. See also Chapter II, p. 22.
48. Kamalapati Tripathi accused Charan Singh of being anti-scheduled castes and partial to the backward castes. Charan Singh accused Kamalapati Tripathi of supporting Brahmans. See Paul R. Brass, *Caste, Faction and Party in India Politics : Faction and Party,* Vol.I, Delhi, Chanakya Publication, 1984, p. 325. Charan Singh's Private Papers; R.I. Duncan, *op. cit.,* pp. 168-70; *Patriot,* 19 August 1977; *The Times of India,* 3 August 1977.
49. *National Herald,* 14 August 1977.
50. Several issues of *Panchayati Raj,* 1950-1975; Interviews: Fateh Singh Rana, 24 April 1985; V.S. Dublish, 25 April 1985; Kailash Prakash, 3 May 1985.
51. *Panchayati Raj,* 7 September 1958.
52. *Panchayati Raj,* 12 December 1965.
53. The original BKU was formed on 13 August 1978 in Haryana by Rai Harlal and Bal Bir Singh under the guidance of Charan Singh. It had played a significant role in mobilising the farmers to participate in the farmers' rally held at the Boat Club of Delhi in December 1978 to mark the celebration of Charan Singh's birthday. After organising the rally, the Union remained completely defunct till its resurgence in 1986-90. The BKU was revamped in 1986, and Tikait became the General Secretary of the BKU unit of Muzaffarnagar District. See Jagpal Singh, "Western

Uttar Pradesh and Farmers' Movement", *Sancha* (in Hindi), April 1988, pp. 26-27; Dipankar Gupta, "Country-Town Nexus and Agrarian Mobilisation of Bharatiya Kisan Union as an Instance", *Economic and Political Weekly*, Vol. XXIII, no. 51, 17 December 1988, pp. 2692-93; Zoya Hasan, "Self-Serving Guardians: Formation and Strategy of the Bhartiya Kisan Union", *Economic and Political Weekly*, Special Article, Vol. XXIV, no. 48, 2 December 1989, p. 2664; *Frontline*, 20 February - 4 March 1988.

54. The base of the BKU was marked by "hyper localism". Unlike Sharad Joshi's Shetkari Sangathan, the BKU did not show any inclination to transcend its regional boundaries. See Dipankar Gupta, *ibid.*, p. 2695. However, Tikait later became a member of the AIKCC (though expelled subsequently from it on 2 October 1989). And on the eve of his expulsion he made unsuccessful attempts to transcend even the "hyper localism" by making announcement to include leaders from other (than western UP) parts of the country as its office bearers; Raghuvansh Pandey from Jaunpur district of eastern UP, Kishan Patnaik from Orissa and relatively unknown leaders from West Bengal, Tamil Nadu, Punjab and Haryana. All these leaders showered praise on Tikait and declared him as the true leader of the farmers. They appealed to the farmers to rally behind him. Based on personal observation, 2 October 1989; *The Times of India*, 3 October 1989.

55. Some of these movements had their origin in the early 1970s, but culminated into their national articulation from 1980. See Gail Omvedt, "New Movement", *Seminar*, December 1988, p.39. Sharad Joshi led Shetkari Sangathan movement in Maharashtra since 1980; Nanjundaswami led Karnataka Rajya Raitha Sangha movement in Karnataka since 1980; Boopindra Singh Mann led BKU movement in Punjab since 1980 and earlier by its progenitor Khetibdari Zamindari Union since 1972; Khedyut Samaj led movement in Gujarat, Narayanaswami Naidu led Vivasayigal Sangam movement which became militant in 1972-73 and 1977-79; and Tikait led BKU movement in western UP, share some common characteristics. They emerged in the areas which have witnessed the development of capitalist tendencies; they represent the articulation of the interests of the rural rich at the national level; they mainly take up the problems of market-oriented farmers, *i.e.*, remunerative prices, subsidised inputs, etc., being the main demands. Some of them even demanded cancellation of the Acts regarding land ceiling and minimum wages to the agricultural labourers. They were mostly participated in and led by the rural rich (though in some of them even the rural poor participated). The rural-urban divide and the "apoliticism" to varying degrees especially in the beginning of these movements have been the significant symbols/tools of mobilisation. See *Seminar*, December 1988, M.V. Nadkarni,

Farmers' Movement in India, Allied Publishers, New Delhi, 1987, pp. 3-5. Kehar Singh, *Farmers' Movement and Pressure Group Politics,* Deep and Deep Publications, New Delhi, 1990. Zoya Hasan, *op. cit.;* Dipankar Gupta, *ibid.;* Jagpal Singh, *op. cit.,* pp. 28-29. But the role of traditional institutions, *i.e.,* Khap and its leadership makes the BKU movement in western Uttar Pradesh distinct from other movements. See Jagpal Singh, *ibid.,* p.35.

56. *The Consititution of the Bharatiya Kisan Union* (in Hindi). Appellant, The Bharatiya Kisan Union (Registered), Apolitical, Printer, Janata Printing Press, Shamli, Clause/point 6.1, p. 3, n.d.
57. The widow of Charan Singh, Gayatri Devi, his son, Ajit Singh and other non-Congress leaders - Virendra Varma, Swami Agnivesh, Maneka Gandhi, V.P. Singh, Kalyan Singh (BJP Chief, UP) and even Shetkari Sangathan president (Tikait considered the Shetkari Sanghatan as a "political" organisation) were not allowed to share the BKU dias. Some of them were told to resign their political positions before joining the BKU agitation when they approached the agitating farmers. *The Times of India*, 4 and 6 February 1988; *Indian Express,* 2, 3 and 9 February 1988; *The Hindu,* 31 October 1988; *Jansatta* (Hindi), 10 October 1988; see also *India Today*, 30 April 1987. Neeraja Chowdhary, "Tikait's Anti-Neta Image, His Plus Point", *Indian Express,* 6 February 1988; Dipankar Gupta, *op. cit.,* p. 2695. Tikait's "apoliticism" surpassed that of other farmers' organisations, ie., Shetkari Sangathan in Maharashtra, and Karnataka Rajya Raitha Sangha in Karnataka, Vivasayigal Sangam in Tamil Nadu. Even they had supported parties/candidates in the elections and otherwise. Zoya Hasan, *op.cit.,* p. 2665; Dipankar Gupta, *op. cit.,* p.2695.
58. Based on the discussion with a group of farmers.
59. See Dipankar Gupta, *ibid.,* pp. 2693-94; *Indian Express,* 20 May 1988. But the BKU's secretary, Har Pal Singh, announced to return Rs. 3 lakh to Devi Lal which he had donated to the BKU for installation of transformers in UP in 1988, as a mark of protest after having reached an agreement with the UP Energy Minister during the Bhopa agitation. See *National Herald* (editorial), 13 September 1989; *Indian Express,* 20 May 1988. Although the BKU could channelise the resentment and distrust of the farmers in "politics" - elections, professional politicians, political leaders, political activists and political parties into the mobilisation - "the BKU's apoliticism under Tikait's leadership was neither naive nor a matter of conviction. It was selective". "He did not lack political wisdom and sagacity." His attitude towards political parties was of "ambivalence and hostility." See D.N. Dhangare, "An Apolitist Populism",*Seminar,* December 1988, pp. 26-27. Tikait even said in an interview, "we will send our representatives to the State Assembly and Parliament as our consensus

representatives". See *News Times,* 4 February 1988.

60. See *The Times of India,* 21 February 1988, 30 July 1989; *Sunday Observer,* 21 February 1988. Fieldwork observations. *The amendment made by the BKU in 1987 to the Resolution related to Dowry passed at Sorson Conference in 1950 and 1956* (in Hindi), Courtesy : Ch. Mahendra Singh Tikait, President, the BKU, Uttar Pradesh, n.d.
61. Initially the BKU raised 11 demands which swelled up to 35 demands. See D.N. Dhanagre, *op. cit.,* p. 25; *35 Demands of the Farmers* (printed in Hindi, N.D.); see also *Indian Express,* 5 February 1988.
62. See also Dipankar Gupta, *op. cit.,* p. 2692. Zoya Hasan, *op. cit.,* p. 2692. Constitution of the BKU, however, envisages for the distribution of "Surplus" land which falls under the category of gardens (gardens are exempted from the land ceilings) to "the unprofitable landholders" and it also envisages for getting the "small industries" to the "small farmers" and putting the responsibility of selling the produced goods on the government. *The Constitution of the BKU, op. cit.,* point/clause 9, p.3. These issues, however, were not raised by the BKU in its charter of demands. Assuming that they were raised, their implementation would have depended on the will of the rural rich.
63. Even the Shetkari Sangathan in April 1988 added the demand for Rs. 20 minimum wages for agricultural labourers as "a studied move to demonstrate that the farmers' movement is not against the agricultural labourers". See D.N. Dhanagre, *op. cit.,* p. 31. See also *The Times of India,* 19 April 1988.
64. See Chapter IV.
65. See Chapter III, p. 58.
66. See *ibid.,* pp. 58-59.
67. *Indian Express,* 3 April 1987; 11, 25 February 1988; and *The Hindustan Times,* 2, 3 April 1987; *Indian Express,* 3 April 1987.
68. Interviews : with the farmers: Mehkar Singh Chaudhari, 7 December 1990, Lilapat Advocate, 7 December 1990; and Lt. Col. Ram Mahesh Bharadwaj, 8 December 1990. Tikait said "not an anna will be paid to the government by the farmers of Uttar Pradesh", *Sunday Observer,* 21 February 1988. While Tikait's supporters are consistent in not paying the dues, Tikait has been inconsistent in not respecting his announcement to pay the dues to the state. Tikait promised to appeal to the farmers to start paying dues after the agreement in Nayeema (Bhopa) case in September 1989 and again in December 1990 when he along with Devi Lal, Chandra Shekhar and Mulayam Singh Yadav addressed jointly a rally in Sisauli. See *The Times of India,* 9 September 1989, 20 December 1990. Though he had denied any intention to launch the movement after the Sisauli meeting, he threatened later to continue the agitation including

the boycott of payment of dues to the government. *The Times of India*, 9 December 1990 and *Economic and Political Observer*, 2 January 1991.

69. See Chapter III, pp.51, 55, Table 16.
70. Tikait even advised his supporters to "beat up" the government officials who would come for collection of dues from them. *The Hindustan Times*, 26 March 1988. See *The Times of India*, 28 July 1989. See also Dipankar Gupta, *op. cit.*, p. 2695. Zoya Hasan, *op. cit.*, p. 2665. Interview: Taj Pal Singh, 3 May 1987.
71. See Chapter III, pp. 51-53.
72. See Chapter VI, pp. 142-43.
73. Same argument is put forward by Sharad Joshi, see *Indian Express*, 21 February 1988.
74. Interview: Khalil Ahmad, 28 October 1988; Tikait parried the question, interview: 17 February 1988. Even Sharad Joshi does not differentiate the rural population, see Sharad Joshi, "India vs. Bharat", *The Hindustan Times*, 21 February 1988.
75. The usual clashes which occured between the rural rich and the rural poor, particularly between the Jats and Chamars assumed the form of clashes between the BKU supporters and the newly formed organisation deriving support from the rural poor (mainly chamars). See section IV of this Chapter.
76. See also Zoya Hasan, *op. cit.*, p. 2669.
77. See also Jagpal Singh, *op. cit.*, p. 29. One agricultural labourer (chamar) in village Jagua Khurd of Muradabad district quoted as to how the BKU supporters threaten the rural poor: "*Inka rehna bhi mushkil kar denge* (we (Jats) will make their (chamars') living difficult in the villages, if the BKU becomes successful)."
78. See Chapter III, pp. 53-57. See *The Hindustan Times*, 3 April 1987. Captain Bhopal Singh, the BMU's most militant leader, made tall claims that the unions of milkmen, cycle-riksha pullers, vegetable venders and workers extended support to the agitation. See *Indian Express*, 2 February 1988; *The Times of Indian*, 20 February 1988.
79. See Chapters IV and VI, Section II.
80. See also *The Times of India*, 4 February 1988.
81. In the initial phase of the movement from 1 March to 1 April 1987, the important leaders or chaudharies of khaps of different castes relating to Jats, Gujars, Rajputs and Muslims, were involved. The chaudhary of Kalsyan khap (Gujars), Mukhtiar Singh, however, became inactive in the movement, as his younger brother, Hukum Singh who happened to be the Minister in UP, was the target of criticism/attack of the BKU. See Jagpal Singh, *op. cit.*, p. 27. Interview: Tej Pal Singh, 3 May 1987.

Even the khaps of Tyagis played important role in the mobilisation of the Tyagi farmers. Interview: a group of Tyagis, 6 December 1990. For a discussion on khap see Chapter II, pp. 10-11. See also Dipankar Gupta, *op. cit.;* D.N. Dhanagre, *op. cit.,* Zoya Hasan, *op. cit.,* Kai Kriese, "Peasant Communities and Agrarian Capitalism", *Economic and Political Weekly,* Vol. XXV, no. 29, 29 September 1990, pp. A140-A141.

82. Interview: Mehkar Singh Chaudhary, 7 December 1990; Shanti Tyagi, a senior leader from Meerut, expressed apprehension - "the minute Tikait turns political, there will be scramble for tickets and his movement will split into pieces". Quoted in "Farmers on March", *Indian Express,* 21 Februrary 1989. Though there is no "scramble for tickets" yet, the movement no doubt, has "split into pieces".
83. The Bhopa case/agitation refers to two important political incidents/ developments which took place in the Bhopa village and its surrounding area in Muzaffarnagar district, i.e., one, the agitation led by the BKU (1 August-10 September 1989) on the issue of abduction of Nayeema (see this Chapter, pp. 102-3); another, the clashes between the Jats and Chamars (between the BKU and the BMU/the Dalit Sena/the Shoshit Mukti Vahini/the BSP) during 26 September 1989 and 2 October 1989, following the decline and withdrawal of the agitation of the BKU regarding the Nayeema case. (See this chapter, pp. 107-9). It is usually unnoticed that the meaning of the Bhopa case among the scheduled castes and their leaders refers to the incidents of clashes between the Jats and Chamars in the wake of the Nayeema case.
84. See *The Times of India,* 2 February 1988; *The Telegraph,* 2 November 1988; Interview: Mehkar Singh Chaudhari, 7 December 1990.
85. *The Times of India,* 3 October 1989; *The Telegraph,* 3 October 1989.
86. See *The Times of India,* 14 December 1989.
87. We observed during our survey in the village of Moradabad in June 1988 that some farmers accused Tikait of giving importance to the regional demands of Muzaffanagar (i.e., fixing up of electricity bills in proportion to the water level in area; the farmers said that this demand suited the interests of farmers of Meerut and Muzaffarnagar districts as there the water level was higher). They, instead, preferred fixing up of electricity bills according to the quality of land (less for the inferior quality land and more for the better quality land. The land in Meerut and Muzaffarnagar districts is supposed to be of better quality than the land in Moradbad district) and the reading of electric meter. Ashok Sirohi, the leader of the dissident group of the BKU from Bulandshahr criticised the support of Tikait to Chandra Shekhar, Devi Lal and Mulayam Singh Yadav group and said that the concession announced by Yadav at the rally-meeting of 11 December 1990 held at Sisauli, would benefit Muzafarnagar district,

implying that it would result in regional discrimination. See *The Times of India,* 14 December 1990.

88. Despite its division on caste lines, the movement remains secular. Ever since the movement began, efforts were made to involve Muslim leadership in agitation with a view to make it secular. Interviews: Tej Pal Singh, 3 May 1987; Hafiz Khalil Aḥmad, 9 March 1988; see also Dipankar Gupta, *op. cit.,* pp. 2693-94; Jagpal Singh, *op. cit.,* p. 27; *The Times of India,* 8 August 1989. Slogans symbolising the religious faiths of Hindus and Muslims, i.e., "*Har Har Mahadev*" and "*Allah Ho Akbar*" were shouted at the rallies of the BKU in order to demonstrate the communal harmony.

89. See *The Times of India,* 8 September 1989; Zoya Hasan, *op.cit.,* p. 2668.

90. Interview: Mehkar Singh Chaudhari, 7 December 1990; discussion with some Tyagis, 6 December 1990; and with a group of Gujar farmers, 8 December 1990. Interview: Lt. Col. Ram Mahesh Bharadwaj, 8 December 1990. (Lt. Col. Bharadwaj claimed that he is supported by Ajit Singh and Tyagis along with other castes). Alleging Tikait of "dictatorial" attitude even the BKU dissidents held a parallel meeting at Saidpur village in Bulandshahr district on 16 November 1988. *The Times of India,* 14 December 1990.

91. Tikait who began his agitation with "apoliticism" marked by "hostility" and "ambivalence" to the political parties, shifting love-hate attitude towards V.P. Singh and Devi Lal and hatred to Congress (sometime to one faction of it and sometime to the entire Congress) ultimately became an ally of Devi Lal, Chandra Shekhar, Mulayam Singh Yadav (and appreciative of the Congress). As opposed to this alliance, there existed a counter alliance of different factions of the BKU and other political leaders (the Ajit Singh and V.P. Singh group). See *The Times of India,* 12 December 1990; and *Indian Express,* 12 December 1990.

92. See Zoya Hasan, *op. cit.,* p. 2667.

93. *Ibid.*

94. Despite receiving humiliating treatment, the political leaders (mainly non-Congress) who wanted to share the BKU platform, showed their concern for the BKU agitations. V.P.Singh declared the 1980s as the farmers' decade. Devi Lal lamented his inability to join the movement because of the "constitutional constraints" and donated Rs. 3 lakhs for installation of transformers in UP. Ajit Singh threatened agitation for the "just demands" of the farmers, issued statement in support of the agitation and criticised the government for ignoring the agitation. Lok Dal (A) workers and Janata Dal leader, George Farnandes, were arrested when they sat on dharna at the UP Chief Minister's residence during the Meerut siege; the BJP leader, L.K. Advani and the Delhi University Students Union's president

belonging to the ABVP expressed support to the agitating farmers. Seven opposition parties, the BJP, the Janata Party, the Jan Morcha, the Muslim League, the Lok Dal (A), the Lok Dal (B) and the Congress (S) had given a call for bandh in support of the BKU agitation; the Janata Dal assured farmers that if elected in 1989 election, it would give concessions to the farmers and give priority to agriculture; and belatedly the Congress also, declared to give priority to agriculture in Eighth Five-year Plan and initiate legislation to put agriculture at par with industry. The Congress government in UP took note of the issues of the farmers in its budget of 1988, which did not impress Tikait. Culled from *Indian Express,* 2, 6, 9 and 15 February 1988; *The Times of India,* 4 February 1988, 31 October 1989; *The Hindustan Times,* 5 February 1988; 21 March 1988; *The Hindu,* 8 March 1988; Rakesh Joshi, "Political Pampers Cash in on Tikait's Mean Appeal", *National Herald,* 16 February 1988; Zoya Hasan, *ibid.,* p.2668; and Dipankar Gupta, *op. cit.,* p.2693.

95. See M.V. Nadkarni, *op. cit., Seminar,* December 1988.
96. For social bases of political parties, see Section II, Chapter VI.
97. See also D.N. Dhanagre, *op. cit.,* p. 28; *The Times of India,* 6 March 1988. The UP Chief Minister Vir Bahadur Singh said that such agitation did not "pose challenge" to his government. *Indian Express,* 6 February 1988. Complaining against the Congress' attitude towards the BKU for not taking action against the Tikait's supporters during the Nayeema case (Bhopa case), M.P. Daga, the working president of the Congress unit of Muzaffarnagar district said that it would embolden the BKU supporters who have been anti-Congress and it would antagonise the landless persons and poor peasants, which would prove disastrous for the Congress in the election of November 1989. *The Hindustan Times,* 10 August 1989.
98. Based on: *The Hindustan Times,* 4, 6, 10 and 11 August 1989; *The Statesman,* 22 August, 9 September 1989; *National Herald,* 9 and 10 September 1989. BKU was so overwhelmed by its agreement with the minister, who represented one faction of the Congress that its secretary even announced to return the money which it had received from Devi Lal as donation. See *National Herald* (editorial), 13 September 1989. Even the leaders of 30 farmers' organisations from 12 states including Sharad Joshi and Swami Agnivesh, who visited the site of the Bhopa agitation, were not entertained by the BKU. *The Times of India,* 18 August 1989.
99. *The Hindustan Times,* 6 August 1989.
100. *National Herald,* 5 September 1989.
101. *National Herald,* 14 September 1989.
102. The BSP appeared in western UP during the 1985 assembly election.

In this election it fielded candidates as independents. It professed to capture the state power by the majority section (Bahujan Samaj) of the society including the non-high caste Hindus and minorities to the complete exclusion of high castes - Brahmans, Kayasthas, Khatriyas, Rajputs and Banias. It did not envisage any economic and social policies for the "Bahujan Samaj". It, instead, appealed to the casteist passions with the purpose of mobilising them for capturing power. The party organised meetings and rallies of its supporters which were addressed by its leaders. The bases of BMU/the Dalit Sena/the Shoshit Mukti Vahini, are rather narrower than the base of the BSP. They are confined mostly to the chamars who constitute a very large part of the population and are politically most vocal among the lower castes of western UP. These organisations aim at mobilising the rural poor, especially the scheduled castes on their social and economic problems. The Dalit Sena has the patronage of Ram Vilas Paswan. He is the National President of the Sena. The Sangharsh Mukti Vahini was founded by politiclally conscious and ambitious scheduled caste leaders - Samer Chand Premi and Virendra. Intervew: Lilapat Advocate, President of the Dalit Sena, Meerut 12 December 1990. But the emergence of such organisations of the rural poor in Meerut, Muzaffarnagar and Saharanpur districts does not conform to the observation, which Kohli made in the context of western Uttar Pradesh that "the landless labourers" are getting "unionised under various left of the centre leadership". See Atul Kohli, *op. cit.*, p.219.

103. See also Zoya Hasan, *op. cit.*, p. 2669.

104. Jai Pal Singh Mitharia, son of a poor peasant of chamar caste, is now in his 30s and hails from the village Karheda of Jansath Tahsil of Muzaffarnagar district. He had seen "the harassment of the SC students in the school days", which he "could not tolerate". He got initiated into the politics during his college days in 1971 (in the SD Degree College in Muzaffarnagar) by taking up the cases of "harassment of harijan students". In 1973 he had joined the Regional Food Corporation (RFC) in Muzaffarnagar as a Junior Accounts Clerk (JAC). During his service he was "discriminated" and "one Jat Kamdar (lower level official) tried to insult" him and Mitharia "beat up (this) high caste boy" and left service in 1973 because he "was given an ultimatum". Having left the service, he started contractorship and became active in the DS4 (The Dalit Shoshit Samaj Sangharsh Samiti), the progenitor of the BSP. In 1984 he became the first president of the District unit of the BSP of Muzaffarnagar and contested unsuccessfully as a BSP candidate for the assembly seat from Jansath constituency in 1985. But he soon developed differences with one of the very important leaders of BSP who "briefed Kanshi Ram against me (Mitharia)". He became inactive in the BSP, though he attended

its functions. As soon as the bitterness between the Jats and the chamars intensified with the emergence of the BKU in 1986-87, he "(then) tried to make an organisation ... (did) set up an organisation, beginning with my (Mitharia's) village" and he founded the BMU. Based on interview: Jai Pal Singh Mitharia, 9 December 1990.

105. See this Chapter, p. 107.

106. Interview: Jai Pal Singh Mitharia, 9 December 1990.

107. Interviews: Jai Pal Singh Mitharia, 9 December 1990; Tej Pal Singh, 31 October 1989; Mahavir Singh Azad, 8 December 1990. *The Times of India*, 29 September, 1990.

108. Interview: Jai Pal Singh Mitharia, 9 December, 1990. This union got the patronage of Hukum Singh and Rajesh Pilot - both Gujars and Congress (I) leaders. Interview: Tej Pal Singh, 31 October 1989. *Deccan Herald*, 8 October 1989; see also this Chapter, pp. 100-1.

109. *The Times of India*, 14 March 1990.

110. The Scheduled Castes and the OBCs formed a strong base of Congress in western UP. The BSP as an alternative to the Congress would deviate them from the latter and would spilt its base. See Chapter VI, Section II.

111. Interview: Jai Pal Singh Mitharia, 9 December 1990. Jagpal Singh, *op. cit.*, p. 27.

112. Interview: Jai Pal Singh Mitharia, 9 December 1990.

113. See also this Chapter, p.111, fn.29, Even at the meeting organised at Karheda village, on 16 August, 1987, such issues apparently led to the formation of the BMU. Interview: Lilapat Advocate, 7 December 1990. The BMU even demanded the sanctioning of gun licences to the "working class" for their security and taking over all licences in the villages where group clashes between the rural rich and the rural poor take place. *Muzaffarnagar Bulletin* (Hindi daily, Muzaffarnagar), 31 August 1987. The BMU got the response from its supporters mainly on the sensitive issues involving the relationships between the rural rich (Jats) and the rural poor (Chamars). It, however, also took up other issues, i.e., establishment of "college" for children of "labourers" since they are harassed and denied admission in the village schools by Jats, implementation of the Mandal commission Report, fulfilment of reservation for the SCs and STs, cancellation of debt up to Rs. 10,000 of the "working class", and the problems of brick-kiln workers. *Demand Charter: The Bharatiya Mazdoor Union* (Reg. No.42), Muzaffarnagar, presented to the District Magistrate, Muzaffarnagar and the Chief Minister, Uttar Pradesh, 16 August 1990.

114. Bhopa case/agitation refers to two incidents/developments : one, the Nayeema case, and second, the clashes between Jats and chamars. See footnote 83, p.117.

115. Based on interviews: Lilapat Advocate, 7 December 1990; Jai Pal Singh Mitharia, 9 December 1990. *The Times of India,* 30 July, 27 and 29 September 1989; *Deccan Herald,* 8 October 1989.
116. Interview: Jai Pal Singh Mitharia, 9 December 1990.
117. *The Hindustan Times,* 28 September 1989; *Deccan Herald,* 8 October 1989.
118. Interview: A BMU member who participated in the clashes (name and date withheld).
119. *Ibid.*
120. Interview: Tej Pal Singh, 31 October 1989; Lilapat Advocate, 7 December 1990; Interview: A participant in the demonstrations of 2 October 1989.
121. *The Times of India,* 3 October 1989. Because of the problems created by them, the district administration in Meerut even banned the entry of harijans into the Meerut city on 6 October 1989. *The Times of India,* 7 October 1989.
122. Interview: Tej Pal Singh, 31 October 1989.
123. Interview: Tej Pal Singh, 31 October 1989; Mahavir Singh Azad, 8 December 1990. Congress (I) dominated the scene. Even Kashi Ram, the BSP leader, who has been opposed to Congress was not allowed to share the BMU dais. He had to erect a separate dais to address the audience. *Jansatta* (Hindi), 30 September 9 October 1989.
124. *The Times of India,* 29 September 1989; *The Hindustan Times,* 29 September 1989; *Deccan Herald,* 8 October 1989; *National Herald,* 14 September 1989; Interview: Mahavir Singh Azad, 8 December 1990.
125. *Indian Express,* 5 October 1989.

Chapter VI

Social Bases of Political Parties

The social bases of political parties form a significant part of rural politics. The social base of a political party is considered to be those classes and castes which support that party not only at the time of elections but also at other times when elections do not take place.[1] The social bases of political parties have generally been studied as their "vote banks" and as part of the election studies. Though the studies have considered the multi-variables as factors which influence/determine the "vote banks", caste has been their main concern. While the policies of political parties, their failures/successes have been dealt with to varying extent,relationships among social groups have been viewed in a restrictive sense as the factors which influence/determine the "vote banks". They have been viewed in terms of patron-client relations, factions within the castes (especially dominant castes), failures/successes of the caste/faction leaders to mobilise support of the respective castes/caste groups.[2] The relationships among the social groups have not been viewed in totality; in the case of patron-client relationships influencing the political behaviour of the clients, one-sided approach - an approach which gives primacy only to the role of "patrons"- has been followed. It has been observed in many studies that the refusal of "clients" to vote as asked by the "patrons" results in the use of coercion on the former by the latter. But it has been overlooked as to how the "clients" react to the coercion in terms of choice/perception of the political parties or candidates. Moreover, the perception of the voters and "how it ('the ignorant population') rationalises its choice" for a party has been ignored.[3] Alam, however, has attempted to study the perception of masses and the rationalisation of the perception.[4] But his main focus was on people's perception of emergency. There is an absence of studies on different parts of India, which deal with the implications of totality of relationships on the choice/rejection/perception of the political parties - dealing not only with the inter and intra-caste factions but also with the perception of the rural poor in reaction to the oppression/coercion of the rural rich. Therefore, any attempt at generalisation regarding the factors which influence the social bases of political parties needs to be made with caution. It calls for an attempt also to understand in different parts of India the voters'/masses' perception of political parties in the light of the nature of totality of relationships or in reaction to the oppression of/coercion on the rural poor. However, on the basis of Nayar's observation from Punjab,[5] Kohli's observation from Meerut[6] and other studies (although not covering totality of relationships), it may be said that the policies of the political parties and nature of relationships among the social groups influence/determine the social bases of the political parties.

The political support for the leading political parties is influenced by two sets of factors: the policies and programmes pursued by parties and the social relations among the classes which prevail at the local level. These social relationships determine not only day-to-day relationships among agrarian classes but their political relations also. Political relations like the social and economic relations are one of the reflections of the relationships at the local level. Social bases of the political parties exist even at times when elections do not take place. Elections only show the shifts or continuities in the support structure of political parties.

I

Unlike the non-Congress parties, the Congress commands support in entire UP to varying degrees. It has been "a coalition of classes under the hegemony of national bourgeoisie". The party attempted to reconcile the interests of bourgeoisie and landlords with the interests of workers and peasants. The party mobilised support on the basis of promises such as the establishment of socialist society, socialist co-operatives, introduction of land reforms, ceiling on land, consolidation of landholdings, distribution of surplus land among landless and protection to tenants against exploitation of landlords. It ensured the continuance of the "landed interests" at the cost of "poor peasants".[7] The landlords by virtue of being part of the decision-making body, and the bourgeoisie by means of financing the Congress have influenced its programmes in such a way that they either did not harm or affect their interests adversely. The Congress government nationalised banks and abolished the privy purses in the late 1960s. It took recourse to populism to win back the poor in the 1970s. It raised the slogan of "Garibi Hatao" during 1971 parliamentary election, and introduced the 20-point programme during the emergency and the IRDP in the 1980s.

The district leadership of the UP Congress has been drawn from "dominant castes" of Brahmans and Thakurs, and in countryside the leadership has been drawn from "the locally dominant rural communities'.[8] Unlike the council of ministers of Samyukta Vidhayak Dal (SVD) government, headed by Charan Singh, in which backward castes were given maximum representation, Congress gave representation to the "high castes", *i.e.*, Brahmans, Kayasthas, Rajput and Vaishyas in the executive committee of Provincial Congress Committee, district level posts of the party, and in the legislatvie assembly.[9]

The electoral base of Congress has been broader than its leadership in UP. The support base of Congress consists of a "coalition of castes" or "alliance of extremes". The Congress derives its support from the socially and economically deprived classes, belonging to the scheduled castes, lower backward castes, Muslims and from the people of higher castes and sections, of "middle status cultivating castes".[10] It derives its support from two groups of classes which occupy opposite and extreme socio-economic position; from those who have landholdings below 2.5 acres in entire Uttar Pradesh and from those who have landholdings above 30 acres in central and eastern Uttar Pradesh and from those who have landholdings between 8 and 20 acres in western Uttar Pradesh. The greatest support for the Congress has been in the areas "where disadvantaged groups are concentrated and in the areas where large proprietors are concentrated".[11]

Independent candidates have played a very significant role in the politics of Uttar Pradesh. The success of independent candidates shows a kind of discontentment against the organised parties, particularly

Congress. They have derived their support from peasantry with the landholdings between 5 and 30 acres in elections held during the 1950s and 1960s. However, in the 1969 election, the support to independent candidates declined. Much of their support was transferred to BKD after its emergence. The support base of independents was very strong in western Uttar Pradesh, where the middle present proprietors are concentrated.[12]

In Uttar Pradesh, the RPI, socialists, communists and independents who had their social bases in the countryside were replaced by BKD which became the main opposition party in 1969 assembly election. It captured 98 seats out of 425 in the legislative assembly with 21.29 per cent of votes. It emerged as the largest opposition party in 43 out of 54 districts.[13] The Congress won 211 seats with 33.68 per cent of votes. In fact, the defeat of Congress was an outcome of the dissatisfaction with the party, which could not fulfil the political aspirations of important groups, such as the middle and backward castes. They had benefited from the economic policies of the Congress government and were now interested in seeking political power. Charan Singh's defection from the Congress Party on 1 April 1967, and the formation of BKD in 1969 provided them an opportunity and a vehicle to pursue their interests.

Charan Singh adopted a two-pronged policy to build the social base of BKD in the countryside: first, he articulated the interests of peasant proprietors; second, he had projected himself as the leader of backward castes. Even when he was in the Congress, he pursued this strategy to widen his individual support base. His role in the abolition of zamindari won him the support of the peasants of backward castes, like Yadavs, Kurmis, Lodhas, etc., in eastern and central Uttar Pradesh. They were the tenants of zamindars and taluqdars of Rajput, Brahman and Bhumihar castes before the abolition of zamindari. His opposition to co-operative farming except in terms of cooperation of service, mechanisation, tractors, new varieties of minerals and seeds, and his emphasis on the image of an ideal farmer "having his own pair of oxen" suggest that he supported the "middle peasant" thesis or the self-cultivating proprietors without making any mention of it.[14] However, as discussed in Chapter III, it is very difficult to locate the ideal peasant proprietors or middle peasants of Charan Singh. It should be noted that even as a leader of the Congress, he articulated the interests of the relatively better off peasants. He opposed the resolution on land ceiling passed at the Nagpur session of Congress in 1959 and the proposal to increase 50 per cent irrigation charges by the G.B. Pant ministry in 1953 on the bhumidhars. But he proposed to put this increase on the Sirdhars, who, in fact, were those peasant-proprietors who could not acquire bhumidhari because of their inability to pay 10 times of the rent.[15] In 1962, the C.B. Gupta Government proposed an increase of 50 per cent on land revenue. Again, he strongly opposed this and suggested that this surcharge be imposed on Sirdhars instead of bhumidhars. However, he agreed to the imposition of 25 per cent surcharge, exempting the small peasants from this, in the wake of Chinese attack on India on 20 October 1962.[16] All these actions indicate that Charan Singh supported the "peasant-proprietors" against the "poor peasants".

As the majority of peasantry in western Uttar Pradesh, particularly in Meerut district, dominated by ex-bhaiachara system, did not benefit from zamindari abolition, Charan Singh attempted to please them along with the rural inhabitants in general. He sought to identify three kinds of interests in Uttar Pradesh: interests of the western UP peasants over the eastern UP peasants, rural interests over urban, and interests of bhumidhars over Sirdhars.[17] The BKD further projected itself as the defender of "rural democracy". On the eve of elections, BKD also resorted to populism. Though Charan Singh had opposed the proposal of land ceiling and redistribution of land at the Nagur session of Congress in 1959, just before 1969 election he accepted the need for ceiling on landholdings and redistribution of land and it was included in the election manifesto of BKD. He proposed 27.5 acres as the ceiling and distribution of the surplus land to landless and those peasants who held landholdings below 2.5 acres.[18] He had not been consistent on certain issues. For example, he opposed the increase in land revenue when C.B. Gupta was Chief Minister of UP during his first tenure. He agreed to abolish the land revenue on peasants with the landholdings of 5 bigha (a little less than one acre) or below the area for a gradual procurement policy. Although Charan Singh stood for the middle caste peasantry, yet his opposition to the abolition of privy purses showed him favouring the ex-zamindars and taluqdars. He condemned the Congress decision to abolish the privy purses as a "political stunt" and a threat to "private ownership of property". Three BKD Members of Parliament opposed the Bill to abolish the privy purses in the Rajya Sabha.[19]

Charan Singh sought to identify himself with the backward castes peasantry of eastern Uttar Pradesh ever since the 1950s, following the abolition of zamindari. Although the backward castes of eastern Uttar Pradesh had supported the socialists in the 1950s and 1960s and opposed the Congress, they supported Charan Singh (then a Congressman) personally during that period, because he identified himself with their interests. Throughout the 1950s and 1960s he visited the villages of eastern Uttar Pradesh frequently addressing the "middle castes" and propagating the policies of Congress and particularly its role in the abolition of zamindari.[20] Because of his popularity among the backward castes peasantry, he was invited even by the non-Congress Yadav leaders to address them on a number of occasions. On one such occasion, he was invited by Ganesh Ram Yadav, who contested against a Congress candidate in the 1952 general election and Thakur Bans Narain Singh, a Congress MLA, to a meeting convened at Bhadoi in Banaras district, with a view to celebrate the abolition of zamindari. On the recommendation of the Chief Minister Govind Ballabh Pant, he attended the meeting held at Bhadoi on 1 July 1953.[21] Besides, Charan Singh favoured the distribution of tickets to the backward castes, especially the Yadavs, in the 1957 election.[22] He gave due representation to the backward castes, such as "Ahirs" (Yadavs), Kurmis and Gujars, besides Jats in his cabinet in 1967 and 1970 when he was the Chief Minister of Uttar Pradesh. The backward castes received 29.63 per cent representation in the first coalition ministry headed by him.[23] His proteges - Ram Naresh Yadav in Uttar Pradesh and Karpoori Thakur in Bihar - introduced reservation for the backward castes during the rule of Janata Party. Though it resulted in large scale violence in both states, Charan Singh and his chief lieutenants became the undisputed leaders of the backward castes through this measure. A study of the implications of the reservations for backward castes in Bihar reveals that the reservations were likely to benefit only the "Upper Backwards", *i.e.*, Yadavs and Kurmis.[24]

Charan Singh's attempt to favour the backward castes and his identification with peasantry brought him into conflict with the Congress leadership since the 1950s. Some of the Congressmen levelled charges of casteism against him, alleging that he was promoting the interests of backward castes. He, in turn, accused the Congress leadership of harbouring the "high castes". No doubt, his popularity among the backward castes intensified owing to the faction-fighting within the Congress. Attempts were made by the high caste Congress leaders to dissuade him from attending the meetings of the backward castes, and they demanded action against him when he did not heed them. He was blamed for the defeat of Congress in the by-election of 1953.[25] Charan Singh's differences with his colleagues in Congress led to his resignation from C.B. Gupta Ministry on 1 April 1967, and subsequently he formed the SVD government on 3 April 1967. He took this decision when Congress was isolated from the masses which was reflected in its defeat in 1967 election in 8 states. Also, by then, the socialist movement had almost died down with its leaders joining other political parties. The absence of a party of peasantry, created by the decline of socialist movement in the eastern and western Uttar Pradesh provided Charan Singh an opportunity to fill this gap. He formed Bharatiya Kranti Dal in October 1969, and incorporated his views in its programme. His party came to be seen as the party of peasants and backward castes, and it enlisted the support of the "middle caste peasants": Jats, Yadavs, Kurmis and Lodhas. Its strong position among the backward castes of eastern Uttar Pradesh was further strengthened by the merger of SSP into it in 1974, when the party came to be known as Bharatiya Lok Dal.[26] As we have discussed in the last chapter, the Congress exploited the anti-poor image of the Lok Dal and cashed on the embittered relations between the supporters of Lok Dal/Janata Party and the rural poor of Meerut in mobilising the latter.[27]

In Uttar Pradesh, there has been a gradual decline in the performance of Congress in the successive elections since the 1950s. Its decline was most spectacular in Upper Doab.[28] While it was declining by varying degrees in the entire state, it faced opposition from different political parties in different parts of Uttar Pradesh. The Jan Sangh provided opposition to Congress in Awadh, Socialists in eastern UP and Lower Doab, and independents in western UP (Upper Doab and Rohilkhand).[29] The decline of Congress also reflected in Meerut district, both in terms of the seats won and percentage of votes polled in the successive assembly elections since 1957 (See Tables 17 and 18). Though this decline in the percentage of votes polled by Congress was marked by the relative increase in the percentage of votes polled by the opposition parties, in terms of the number of seats won, Congress performed much better. The independents, socialists and Jan Sangh provided the main opposition to Congress between 1952 and 1962. In 1957 Jan Sangh became the second opposition party replacing the socialists. It was only in 1967 that any opposition political party could win any seat, though independents (they do not form any party) could win one seat in 1957 and four seats in 1962. In 1967, the general trend of the Congress defeat in 8 states was echoed in Meerut too, when out of the 14 seats Congress could win only 4.

Table 17

Percentage Distribution of Votes Polled by Political Parties in Meerut District for the UP Legislative Assembly, 1952-1985*

Political Party	1952	1957	1962	1967	1969	1974	1977	1980	1985
1. Congress/ Congress (I)	26.91	55.71	40.74	39.72	28.60	44.40	37.25	45.37	42.25
2. NCO/Cong. (J)						5.19		4.15	5.38
3. Congress (S)									0.28
4. Socialists and KMPP	24.51	2.76	13.72	15.67	5.59				
5. Communists	1.36	3.69	6.39	7.73	1.75	1.81	0.15	0.36	0.51
6. BKD/BLD/Lok Dal/Janata (SC)					35.86	28.79		32.32	34.30
7. Jan Sangh/BJP	9.95	9.17	8.89	14.16	10.52	8.45		6.00	4.61
8. Janata							53.38		2.88
9. Janata (S)								1.78	
10. Janata (JP)								3.19	
11. Independents	35.67	28.60	23.55	4.67	3.77	6.23		6.81	9.41
12. Republican Party of India			2.92	17.80	10.97	0.69			
13 Others	1.59	0.12	3.78	0.65	2.92	4.44	8.77	0.03	0.38
Total	100.00	100.00	100.00	100.0	100.00	100.00	100.00	100.00	100.00

Source : Reports of the Eighteenth Communism of India, 1952, 1957, 1962, 1967, 1969, 1971, 1974, 1977, 1980, 1984 and 1985.

* The boundaries of constituencies are not coterminous with the administrative boundaries of districts. Some of the constituencies overlap the boundaries of neighbouring districts. Hence these data are about the dominant and relative performance of parties in each district.

Table 18

Seats won by Political Parties to U.P. Legislative Assembly from Meerut District : 1952-1985

Political Party	1952	1957	1962	1967	1969	1974	1977	1980	1985
Congress	15	14	11	4	2	9	2	9	6
SSP	-	-	-	2	2	-	-	-	-
-									
Janata	-	-	-	-	-	6	9	2*	-
BKD/BLD/ Lok Dal	-	-	-	-	8	-	-	-	5
CPI	-	-	-	1	-	-	-	-	-
Republican Party of India	-	-	-	3	-	-	-	-	-
Independents	-	1	4	3	-	-	-	-	-
Jan Sangh/BJP	-	-	-	1	2	1	-	-	-
Total	15	15	15	14	14	16	11	11	11

* Janata(SC)

Note : In 1952 and 1957 assembly elections there were 3 seats with double membership. In 1952 all three double member seats were won by Congress, while in 1957 one of the 3 double member constituencies was won by an independent candidate and others were won by Congress.

Source : *Report of the Election Commission of India*, 1952, 1957, 1962, 1967, 1969, 1974, 1977, 1980 and 1985.

The year 1969 became a watershed in the electoral history of Meerut. The opposition which was provided to Congress by socialists, independents and RPI before 1969, was now shared by BKD[30] and Jan Sangh, the progenitor of BJP, in terms of votes polled by the opposition. It is noteworthy that among the opposition parties the rise of BKD was marked by the simultaneous decline in the performance of Jan Sangh. And Jan Sangh remained in the second position to BKD only after 1974. The BLD remained the most important opposition party between 1974 and 1985. The Congress, however, regained its pre-eminent position in terms of the percentage of votes polled during this period.

There was a gradual decline in the performance of Congress even in the parliamentary elections between 1952 and 1967. The decline in the performance of Congress was accompanied by an improvement in the performance of socialists and independents. Since 1971, the BKD provided the main opposition to Congress (See Table 19). Till 1962, all the three seats were bagged by Congress. But in 1967, as a reflection of general trend elsewhere, Congress lost all the three seats one (Meerut) to SSP and two (Hapur and Baghpat) to independents. Again the Congress regained these seats in 1971. In 1977, when there were only two seats, Janata Party won them. In 1980 and 1984 Lok Dal and Congress bagged Baghpat and Meerut seats respectively.

Table 19

Percentage Distribution of Votes Polled by Political Parties in Parliamentary Elections in Meerut District 1952-1984

Political Party	1952	1957	1962	1967	1971	1977	1980	1984
1. Congress/ Congress (I)	61.18	63.41	42.23	26.18	54.85	34.87	36.62	44.36
2. NCO					10.87		0.20	
3. Socialists and KMPP	16.77	7.75	18.52	18.58	0.16	-	-	-
4. Communists	-	6.0	2.11	5.52	-	0.53	-	-
5. BKD/BLD/Lok Dal/Janata (S)	-	-	-	-	27.25	-	48.35	43.27
6. Jan Sangh/BJP	5.92	22.84	7.34	3.07	-	-	-	6.10
7. Janata	-	-	-	-	-	64.17	11.42	1.53
8. Independents	10.22	-	21.53	29.53	4.09	0.13	3.07	4.63
9. R.P.I.	-	-	-	12.81	1.56	-	-	-
10. Others	6.02	-	8.71	4.31	1.22	0.30	0.35	-
Total	100.00	100.00	100.00	100.00	100.00	100.00	100.00	100.00

Source : *Reports of the Election Commission of India,* 1952, 1957, 1962, 1967, 1971, 1977, 1980 and 1984.

II

In the sample, 96.48 and 92.92 per cent households could provide information regarding their support to the political parties in the Lok Sabha and legislative assembly elections respectively.[31]

In Lok Sabha elections most of the electorate supported the Congress. Around 78 per cent supporters of the Congress belonged to the rural poor (and miscellaneous category). Only 15.72 per cent of the electorate supported Lok Dal. The outstanding feature of Lok Dal is the enormous support received by the party from the rural rich. The middle peasants are the leading supporters of the party (See Table 20). All supporters

Table 20

Percentage of Distribution of Households of Different Classes in Relation to Party Support in Parliamentary Elections

Class	No. of Households	Congress	Lok Dal	BJP	Never allowed to vote/allowed only once/never seen even the ballot paper.
The Rural Rich					
1. Landlords	23	3.97	15.94	-	
2. Rich Peasants	9	0.33	11.59	-	-
3. Middle Peasants	93	17.55	49.80	24.78	3.77
Total (a)	125	21.85	76.81	24.78	3.77
The Rural Poor and Miscellaneous					
4. Small Peasants	96	22.85	17.39	53.33	6.93
5. Poor Peasants	9	2.32	-	-	3.77
6. Agricultural Labourers	68	12.91	2.90	-	50.94
7. Wage Labourers in non-agrarian sectors	83	24.50	-	20	11.30
8. Traditional Occupation Holders	22	4.64	-	-	15.09
9. Miscellaneous	36	10.93	2.90	1.89	8.20
Total (b)	314	78.15	23.19	75.22	96.23
Total (a+b)	439	100.00	100.00	100.00	100.00
Percentage of households out of total households	96.48	68.79	15.72	3.42	12.07

of the BJP belonged to Saini caste. The Congress is a party supported both by the landowners and the landless. Among the supporters of Congress 42.38 per cent own land and the rest of them do not own land at all. The Lok Dal is a party exclusively supported by the landowners: 94.2 per cent of them own land, and only 5.8 per cent do not own land at all.

In terms of caste, the supporters of Congress and Lok Dal in the parliamentary elections can be broadly divided into non-Jats and Jats. Around 95 per cent supporters of Congress are non-Jats: the non-Jat dominant castes, *i.e.*, Brahmans, Banias, Tyagis and Gujars, the Muslim high castes, and the low castes, *i.e.*, the scheduled castes and the other backward classes of both Hindus and Muslims. The low castes of Hindus and Muslims form the majority of Congress supporters. Only 4.64 per cent supporters of Congress are Jats. They support Congress because of the factionalism within their caste. On the other hand, around 90 per cent supporters of Lok Dal are Jats and Meenas. As we have discussed in Chapter III, the Meenas, who inhabit only 4 villages of Meerut district and are mainly inhabitants of Rajasthan identify themselves with the Jats in Meerut. A small section of the supporters of Lok Dal belongs to non-Jats, *i.e.*, Brahmans, Scheduled Castes, and OBCs of Hindus and Muslims. In 1984 Lok Sabha election, 3.42 per cent households, who are otherwise supporters of Congress, supported BJP. All of them belong to Saini caste. They switched support from Congress to BJP, because BJP candidate belonged to their caste (See Table 21).

The pattern in the assembly elections is substantially similar to that of Lok Sabha elections. In the assembly elections most of the electorate usually supported the Congress. Around 75.17 per cent supporters of Congress belonged to the rural poor (and miscellaneous category). Only 16.76 per cent of the electorate supported the Lok Dal. Most of the supporters of the Lok Dal belonged to the rural rich. Middle peasants formed 50 per cent of Lok Dal supporters. Around 6 per cent electorate supported Congress (J) in 1985 assembly elections (See Table 22).

Table 21

Percentage of Distribution of Households of Different Castes in Relation to Party Support in Parliamentary Elections

Caste	No. of Households	Congress	Lok Dal	BJP	Never allowed to vote/allowed only once/never seen even the ballot paper.
Non-Jats					
1. Brahmans	13	2.65	1.45	-	7.55
2. Banias	3	0.66	-	-	1.89
3. Tyagis	2	0.66	-	-	-
4. Gujars	57	18.87	-	-	-
5 Muslim High Castes	4	1.32	-	-	-
6. OBCs (Hindus)	116	25.17	1.45	100.00	41.51
7. OBCs (Muslims)	49	11.26	5.80	-	20.75
8. SCs	119	34.77	1.45	-	28.30
Total (a)	363	95.36	10.15	100.00	100.00
Jats					
9. Jats	72	4.64	84.06	-	-
10. Meenas	4	-	5.80	-	-
Total (b)	76	4.64	89.86	-	-
Total (a+b)	439	100.00	100.00	100.00	100.00
Percentage of households out of total households	96.48	68.79	15.72	3.42	12.07

All supporters of Congress (J) belonged to the Chamar caste. In fact, they have been traditionally the supporters of Congress, and in 1984 Lok Sabha election they supported Congress. They deviated from their usual support for Congress to Congress (J), as they felt that it was led by Jagjivan Ram who belonged to their caste, and also because

Table 22

Percentage of Distribution of Households of Different Classes in Relation to Party Support in Assembly Elections

Caste	No. of Households	Congress	Lok Dal	Congress (J)	Never allowed to vote/allowed only once never seen even the ballot paper
The Rural Rich					
1. Landlords	24	4.25	16.22	-	-
2. Rich Peasants	10	1.06	9.46	-	-
3. Middle Peasants	93	19.50	50.00	3.57	-
Total (a)	127	24.81	75.68	3.57	-
The Rural Poor and Miscellaneous					
4. Small Peasants	93	24.82	14.86	3.57	19.30
5. Poor Peasants	10	2.48	1.35	3.57	1.75
6. Agricultural Labourers	70	11.70	4.05	17.86	50.88
7. Wage Labourers in non-agrarian sectors	85	23.05	1.35	50.0	8.77
8. Traditional Occupation Holders	22	4.25	-	-	17.54
9. Miscellaneous	34	8.87	2.70	21.43	1.75
Total (b)	314	75.17	24.31	96.43	100.00
Total (a+b)	441	100.00	100.00	100.00	100.00
Percentage of households out of total households	99.10	63.95	16.76	6.35	12.93

of the factionalism in the Congress scheduled caste leaders of the district. As in case of Lok Sabha elections, in the assembly elections also, Congress is the party of both the landowners and the landless. Around 52 per cent supporters of the Congress own land and the rest do not own land at all. Similarly, in the assembly elections the Lok Dal supporters consist exclusively of landowners, predominantly middle peasants, *i.e.*, 91.9 per cent of them own land, and only 8.1 per cent of them do not own land.

In the assembly elections too, the supporters of Congress and Lok Dal are divided into non-Jats and Jats. Around 95 per cent supporters of the Congress are non-Jats. However, 4.61 per cent Jats preferred Congress in 1985 assembly election. They did so because of the factionalism within their caste and their reservations about Charan Singh. Around 90 per cent supporters of Lok Dal belong to Jats and Meenas. Only a small minority of the supporters of Lok Dal belong to the non-Jats (See Table 23).

Table 23

Percentage of Distribution of Households of Different Castes in Relation to Party Support in Assembly Elections

Caste	No. of Households	Congress	Lok Dal	Congress (J)	Never allowed to vote/allowed only once/never seen even the ballot paper.
Non-Jats					
1. Brahmans	13	2.84	1.35		7.02
2. Banias	4	1.06	-	-	1.75
3. Tyagis	2	0.71	-	-	-
4. Gujars	57	20.21	-	-	-
5. Muslim High Castes	4	1.42	-	-	-
6. OBCs (Hindus)	111	30.14	2.70	-	42.11
7. OBCs (Muslims)	49	11.70	4.05	-	22.81
8. SCs	122	27.30	2.70	100.00	26.32
Total (a)	362	95.38	10.8	100.00	100.00
Jats					
9. Jats	75	4.61	83.78	-	-
10. Meenas	4	-	5.41	-	-
Total (b)	79	4.61	89.17	-	-
Total (a+b)	441	100.00	100.00	100.00	100.00
11. Percentage of households out of total households	99.10	63.95	16.76	6.35	12.93

Tables 20, 21, 22 and 23 show that 12.07 and 12.93 per cent respondents have never been allowed or allowed only once to vote or have not even seen what a ballot paper looks like in the Lok Sabha and assembly elections respectively. They are prevented from exercising their franchise by the Jat supporters of Lok Dal. Interviews and field-work reveal that these electorate who are deprived of their right to vote are the potential supporters of Congress. Most of them belong to the rural poor and the low castes such as scheduled castes and other backward classes of Hindus and Muslims. The following examples of statements are noteworthy in this regard:

> We even do not know how the vote is cast.
>
> Till today we have not voted.

This respondent asked us:

> What is the vote (meaning thereby ballot paper) like? Where is it cast?

He further said:

> (Jats) give us dummy slips, cast our votes. Till today we do not know what is the vote (ballot paper) like. The police come and eat pudding (in the houses of Jats) and return. They do not help us.
>
> [Agricultural labourer, sweeper, Tilwara Sakin]
>
> We are Congressites. But (the Jats) do not let us vote. (We) voted in one or two elections.
>
> [Agricultural labourer, Muslim oilman, Tilwara Sakin]
>
> Neither anybody allows (us) to enter the fields nor does anybody let (us) vote. Till now nobody has let (us) vote. (Jats) say that (our) votes have been cast.
>
> [Agricultural labourer, Chamar, Chobla]
>
> From 1952 till now (we) have not voted.
>
> [A 60-year old agricultural labourer, Chamar, Chobla]
>
> For M.P. or M.L.A. (Jats) do not let (us) vote. Our votes are cast already.
>
> [Agricultural labourer, Chamar, Chobla]
>
> (Jats) themselves cast our votes. If we ask for the police (help), they (Jats) beat us up.
>
> [Share-cropper, Chamar, Chobla]
>
> (We) face problems in voting. My uncle (chacha) went to Neik (polling station) for casting vote. My uncle was beaten up (by Jats)

as to why he went to cast vote.

[Agricultural labourer, Chhippi (Printer), Chobla]

Three years ago I fought a court case. (We) had come after voting; beatings took place (*Mar-peet Hui*). Harijans and my uncle, etc., were beaten up. Earlier I could vote, telling lies. But this time I could not vote. I was not allowed to enter (the polling booth).

[Agricultural labourer, Hindu weaver, Chobla]

I have been beaten up two-three times because once I had criticised Charan Singh.

[Agricultural labourer, Dhiwar, Chobla]

There is no liberty of any kind in voting for MLA, MP. We are not allowed to vote.

[Wage labourer in the non-agrarian sector (brick-kiln), Kumhar, Chobla]

Whenever we are in a position to vote, we vote for the Congress.

[Traditional occupation holder, Muslim Washerman, Chobla]

Even the minority high castes, *i.e.*, Banias and Brahmans irrespective of their class positions are often not allowed to vote in the Jat-dominated villages. One Brahman, a small peasant of Chobla said:

Our votes are already cast.

Another Brahman, a middle peasant of the same village said:

Coercion is used (*Jabar Dasti Hoti Hai*) in the election of MLA, MP. They (Jats) cast our votes themselves. We fight to cast our votes (*Jhagda kar-kar ke vote Dalte Hain*).

One Bania shopkeeper of Tilwara Sakin said:

Who will let us vote?
It is a village of Jats.

Prevention from voting of non-Jats, particularly the rural poor or booth capturing by Jats, is more common in the villages of Tilwara Sakin and Chobla of our sample. These villages fall in the parliamentary constituency of Baghpat, which was represented by Charan Singh between 1977 and 1987. The victory of Charan Singh in the parliamentary elections owed a great deal to the fact that Congress supporters were not allowed to vote. Break-up of the votes polled by Charan Singh and Congress (I) in the assembly seats which constitute the Baghpat parliamentary seat shows that Charan Singh polled more votes in the Jat-dominated assembly constituencies of Chhaprauli and Barnawa than in the non-Jat dominated assembly constituencies of Siwal Khas (SC),

Khekra and Baghpat (See Table 24). It is interesting to note that whenever the Jats and non-Jat dominant castes vote for the same political party, the rural poor of low castes and the minority high castes do not face problems in casting their votes. In 1985 assembly election, many Jats and non-Jats of Tilwara Sakin village of Chhaprauli assembly constituency and of Jansinghpur village of Kithor assembly constituency voted for the same party - Congress (I). The following examples show that the non-Jats did not face problems at the hands of the Jats during this election. The respondents expressed this point in the following statements:

> This time (1985 assembly election) there was no problem in casting votes because there was a Congress wave (*jaur*) in the village. But in the earlier years (elections), (the Jats) never let us vote. [Agricultural labourer, Muslim oilman, Tilwara Sakin]

Table 24

Assembly Constituency-wise Distribution of Percentage of Votes Polled by Charan Singh in Baghpat Parliamentary Seat : 1980-1984

Assembly Constituency	1980	1984
1. Siwal Khas (SC)	Not Known	40.45 (48.86)
2. Khekra	49.63 (46.66)	38.20 (46.80)
3. Baghpat	54.97 (42.18)	45.16 (38.58)
4. Barnawa	73.12 (23.59)	58.81 (33.81)
5. Chhaprauli	90.46 (7.49)	80.63 (14.37)

Note : Figures without bracket show the percentage of votes polled by Charan Singh and the figures in bracket show the percentage of votes polled by Congress (I).

Source : Data collected from the election section, collectorate, office of the District Magistrate, Meerut.

> There was no problem in voting this time (1985 assembly election). There was problem in the last election when Chaudhary Charan Singh contestd, they (Jats) voted themselves (on our behalf). The government even conducted enquiry many times before the elections, but nothing happened. If somebody comes to conduct enquiry, he

is fed *(Khila-pila diya jate hai).*

[Agricultural labourer, Harijan weaver, Tilwara Sakin]

Ever since the voting started, (we) voted for the first time in this election (1985 assembly election). Earlier (our) votes used to be cast. (Jats) did not let (us) even go to the polling station.

[Agricultural labourer,Dhiwar, Tilwara Sakin]

(We) have been Congress supporters.

(Jats) do not let us vote. We do not go to cast vote. (We) cast vote for the first time this time - to Sompal (Congress candidate). (We) were not allowed to vote at the time of Charan Singh (when Charan Singh was the candidate).

[Traditional occupation holder, Barber, Tilwara Sakin]

During the last two elections irregularity (*Gadbadi*) did not take place. Earlier (Jats) used to cast our votes, (They) used to say "your votes have been cast".

[Small peasant, Chamar, Jaisinghpur]

Only this time (1985 assembly election) we have had liberty to vote; because of Bhim Singh (Congress (I) candidate).

Earlier, we were never allowed to vote.

[Poor Peasant, Chamar, Jaisinghpur].

We have been free to vote for the first time in this election (1985 assembly election). (We) were not free to vote before.

[Small peasant, Gadaria, Jaisinghpur]

(Jats) did not let us vote till some years ago.

[Middle peasant, Gadaria, Jaisinghpur]

Voted only this time (1985 assembly election).

[Small peasant, Gadaria, Jaisinghpur]

There used to be lots of irregularities (*Gadbadi*) in casting votes earlier (in the pre-1985 assembly elections). (Jats) did not allow (us) voting. This time (1985 assembly election) Jats were supporters of the Congress as well as Lok Dal. We did not want to vote earlier (because of the trouble at the hands of Jats).

[Middle Peasant, Brahman, Tilwara Sakin]

No booth capturing (by Jats) took place this year (1985 assembly election). It used to happen before. It has been prevalent in the Chhaprauli area from the beginning. They (who do booth capturing) are supporters of Charan Singh, but their number is decreasing.

[Riksha-puller, Brahman, Tilwara Sakin]

This time (1985 assembly election) there was groupism (*partibaji*) among them (Jats). We did not vote earlier (to this election). They (Jats) used to say "your votes have been cast".
[Shopkeeper, Bania, Tilwara Sakin]

Basically two important factors can explain the support structure of the Congress and Lok Dal. These are policies of the political parties or governments led by the respective parties, and the nature of domination and dependence which characterise the social relationships among castes and classes that form the social basis of various parties.[32]

As far as the Congress is concerned, the government policies after independence have helped the party to establish support among the rural poor. This was evident from the interviews of respondents of the rural poor who indicated that they preferred Congress because of its pro-poor policies. It should, however, be noted that all of them were not satisfied with the policies of Congress, and that in many a case the policies of the Congress government have brought more harm than benefit to them. Our field work reveals the presence, in almost all villages, of the malpractices in the process of distribution of the (Congress) government "help" to the rural poor. The "help" of the government does not reach the genuinely needy directly. It reaches them through many layers of intermediaries - village pardhans, VLWs., Patwaries, Veterinary doctors and other petty bureaucrats. The distribution of buffaloes inter-alia under the 20-point programme presents the most common case of such exploitation. Buffaloes are given to the rural poor through the VLWs and the medical fitness certificates of the buffaloes are the necessary requirement. The VLWs and veterinary doctors take some percentage each of the market price of the buffaloes as bribe for their respective "services". In many cases the village pradhans also take their "dues". Since the buffalo-borrowers do not have cash to bribe the public servants, they borrow it either from the milkmen (who exploit them tremendously)[33] or the moneylenders. The moneylenders take some valuables of the borrowers on mortgage. The buffalo-borrowers are supposed to repay the cost of buffaloes to the government in instalments of cash. Unable to pay the instalments on time, they have to face the opprobrium of the police; they have to face physical torture, illegal lock-up and pay bribe. A borrower even loses the item, which he mortgages to the moneylender. In the ultimate result, the buffalo costs him more than its original price and he loses more than what he gains. In some cases the "help", in fact, is usurped by any trustworthy or relative of the village pardhan, while the loan/"help" is officially registered in the name of the genuine rural poor. Even the Food For Work Programme (FWP) had a limited scope in the districts of UP including Meerut, and the public money allocated for Gaon Sabhas and Panchayats has been usurped in corrupt and non-developmental practices.[34] But the rural poor still feel that the Congress is better than other parties, and that Congress government generally introduces "good policies" favourable to them. They believe that it is the local influentials and the bureaucracy which prevent the implementation of these policies. No doubt, measures introduced by the Congress government have benefited the poor to some extent, though they did not change their conditions substantially. Popular measures created a public image of the Congress as the better alternative available to them.

More specifically the respondents from the rural poor in the sample identified the following reasons for their support to the Congress:

(1) The Congress Party achieved independence for the country, and that they feel more secure in free India than in the British India. The respondents appreciated Congress for achieving Independence in the following way:

Indira Gandhi got independence, Gandhi got independence.
[Sweeper, Jalalpur]

(We) vote for the Congress because all are living happily ever since the Congress Government (Raj) came. What used to happen during the time of zamindari does not happen now.
[Small Peasant, Chamar, Jalalpur]

Congress keeps us comfortable (*Congress se Suvidha Hai*). Nobody can scold us.
[Shopkeeper, Chamar, Jalalpur]

(We) vote for Congress, all other parties were born out of Congress, Congress got the country independence.
[Small Peasant, Gujar, Jalalpur]

(We) vote for Congress, Congress got independence.
[Poor Peasant, Dhiwar, Jalalpur]

Congress got us independence, removed untouchability.
[Agricultural Labourer, Khatik, Jafarnagar Begamabad]

Till now (we) have been voting for Congress. Congress got independence.

[Small Peasant, Carpenter, Ahera]

Since the achievement of independence, nobody can coerce us to work. The zamindars used to make us change houses three times in a year (*teen-teen bar*). (We) had to change houses every six month.

[Poor Peasant, Chamar, Jaisinghpur]

(We) have been voting for Congress since before. (We) have got all the benefits from Congress; (we) can sell our garbage (*kuda*), we can sell our house, can sell our site (place).

[Agricultural labourer, Weaver, Jaisinghpur]

The abolition of zamindari has made a difference; (we) can stop begar (forced/unpaid labour) for anybody. If (Jats) say that (they) will eliminate (us) from the village (*Gaon se kho deinge*), we say the world is very big.

[Small Peasant, Gadaria, Jaisinghpur]

The zamindari was abolished because of Congress. (My family) got 15 bigha land (after the abolition of zamindari).

[Poor Peasant, Kumhar, Nagla Tashi Quasimpur]

The condition has improved after the abolition of zamindari, (my) sons got educated, (my family members) do not render labour to anybody, (we) do not do begar for anybody.

[Wage Labourer in non-agrarian sector (construction worker), Chamar, Nagla Tashi Quasimpur]

The Congress liberated the poor people from the zamindari.

[A person, who had become a peasant-properietor after the zamindari abolition and who has acquired the position of a landlord in due course, Carpenter, Nagla Tashi Qasimpur]

All have been living happily from the day when Congress government (raj) was first established. What used to happen at the time of the zamindari does not happen now.

[Small Peasant, Chamar, Jalalpur]

All restrictions were removed after the abolition of zamindari. The goat and the lion are drinking water from the same shore.

[Small Peasant, Chamar, Jaisinghpur]

Because of the abolition of zamindari (we) do not render begar to the zamindar. At that time (before the abolition of zamindari), (we) had to go to Baghpat (the nearby town where the landlord resided) to render begar to the Nawab.

[Traditional Occupation Holder, Potter, Ahera]

(2) The respondents noted that zamindari abolition freed them from social and economic repression of the zamindars. But zamindari abolition did not free them from political and social domination of the dominant caste peasant-proprietors. Yet, they support the Congress on the grounds that it helped them to become owners of their houses, provided them freedom to cut trees, etc.

(3) The Congress has helped them through introduction of policies such as reservation and scholarships for the Scheduled Castes (this fact is resented by the non-Scheduled Caste rural poor but it does not prevent them from supporting Congress). The Congress government has given them plots, subsidised means of self-employment, buffaloes, carts and credits at subsidised rates of interest. They discussed the benefits derived from Congress rule in the following ways:

Congress helped us, gave scholarships to our children, gave them education.

[Wage labourer, who works in the open labour market, Chamar, Jalalpur]

Reason (for supporting Congress)? It helped us. I could not have educated my sons. But they could be educated because of the fee concession and scholarship.

[Horse-cart runner, Chamar, Jalalpur]

(We) have been voting for Congress since before. We have got reservation because of Congress.

[Middle Peasant, Khatik, Jafarnagar Begamabad]

Congress gave us support; (we) got concession (from Congress government). Congress has made everybody equal (*Congress ne eik kar diya*). Now (everybody) can drink tea in the same cup.

[Agricultural Labourer, Chamar, Jafarnagar Begamabad]

(We) have been voting Congress since long. Congress helps the harijans.

[Wage Labourer in the non-agrarian sector, sweeper, Nagla Tashi Qasimpur]

Congress gives (us) loan.

[Wage Labourer in non-agrarian sector, Chamar, Nagla Tashi Qasimpur]

Indira Gandhi did a lot for us. But (the vested interests) did not let the help reach us.

[Vegetable vender, Gadaria, Nagla Tashi Qasimpur]

Jawaharlal, Indira, her son did good things. Indira even sacrificed her life. (Congress) gave loan for the buffaloes. But allotment of our buffalo was cancelled. There is lot of corruption (*Dhandledbaji*). (We) have been voting only Indira from the beginning.

[Cycle mechanic, Faquir, Nagla Tashi Qasimpur]

Congress got us levy (loan) and plot. We vote for Congress because we benefit from it.

[Wage Labourer who constructs roads, Chamar, Jalalpur]

Congress helped us; gave us levy (loan), gave us plot.

[Wage Labourer in non-agrarian sector, Chamar, Jalalpur]

We will sing praise (*Gun Gayeinge*) of those (Congress), who (which) have (has) elevated us.

[Small Peasant, Chamar, Jalalpur]

(We) vote for Congress because Congress helps us.

[Agricultural labourer, Saini, Jafaranagar Begamabad]

(I) got the house made by the loan provided by the (Congress) government. The government gave (me) 2000 bricks, one door, one window, 5 stone plates. Rupees fifty was given (by me) as bribe for each item. (I) do not know who ate the bribe. (We) have been voting for the Congress till now.

[Wage labourer in non-agrarian sector (brick-kiln), Chamar, Ahera]

We benefit from the government. Nobody beats us up.

[Wage labourer in non-agrarian sector (brick-kiln) Chamar, Ahera]

(I) got a cart as loan (given by Congress government). The cart is standing unused. The cart and the he-buffalo were bought for Rs. 4500.

[Wage labourer in non-agrarian sector (brick-kiln), Jogi, Ahera]

The block (lower level administrative unit) officials got (our) house made. (They) gave (us) 2000 bricks, 18 roof-poles, 5 stone plates, 4 bags of cement and 2 windows. We supplied rest of the items on our expenses. (We) have been voting for Congress.

[Wage labourer in non-agrarian sector (brick-kiln), Kumhar, Ahera]

Many of the non-scheduled caste rural poor, however, complain that the government has favoured the scheduled castes more than them:

The government has worked only for the harijans.

[A woman belonging to the wage labourer in non-agrarian sector (construction work), Gadaria, Nagla Tashi Qasimpur]

No help has come from the government yet. Chamars-chudhas (Chamars-scavengers) have got full help. (We) vote for Congress.

[Agricultural labourer, Muslim tailor, Ahera]

(We) do not have space. Chamars have been given space. We have not got.

[Agricultural Labourer, Dhiwar, Jaisinghpur]

Harijans have been given concessions (*chhut*). We have got nothing. No party has done anything for the Jogi caste.

[Mobile vender of cosmetics, Jogi, Nagla Tashi Qasimpur]

(4) The Congress has given them self-respect, removed untouchability and hierarchy. Regarding this point, the respondents made the following statements:

Congress is better than other parties; (it) removed the hierarchy (*unch-nich*)

[Middle Peasant, Saini, Nagla Tashi Qasimpur]

Congress is useful to us. Nobody can scold us (*koi hamein dhamki nahi dikha-sakta*). Congress taught us how to speak. Now we can sit beside anybody, can talk to anybody. (Congress) even gave us loan.

[Shopkeeper, Chamar, Jalalpur]

This is under the Congress rule that we can sit in the head-side (sirana)[35] part of their (high castes') cots. This is only because of Congress. During the zamindari period we were not even allowed to stand near (the high castes).

[Wage Labourer in non-agrarian sector (construction worker), Chamar, Jalalpur]

Congress removed the untouchability.

[Agricultural labourer, scavenger,Jafarnagar Begamabad]

This respondent further emphasised the Congress's role in removing untouchability, and pointing out to us (assuming that we belong to the higher social order), he said:

You can sit near us. This is Congress' obligation *(Aap hamare paas Beith Sakte Hain. Ye Congress ki Meharbani Hai).*

[Agricultural Labourer, Chamar, Jafarnagar Begamabad]

(5) The Congress government abolished land revenue taken from the small and poor peasants.

(6) It is interesting to note that some kind of "misconception" prevails among the rural poor regarding the achievements of Çongress. Whatever subsidy or help they get from the government or any other institution, they think it is because of the Congress. For example, we came across the response among many cases that the scheduled castes vote for Congress because Ambedkar introduced the reservation and he removed untouchability, and they believe that Ambedkar was able to do so because he was in the Congress, which is not true. Regarding this one sweeper of Jalalpur said: "*Ambedkar Ne Chhua Chhut dur Karvai* (Ambedkar got the untouchabality removed)."

Again a tannery owner, Chamar of Behzadka assuming that Ambedkar was in Congress, said: "*Ambedkar Ne Naukrion me Jagah Surakshit karvai*. (Ambedkar got the reservation in the jobs.) Some of the respondents attributed their support for the Congress to Jagjivan Ram who is presumed to have introduced the reservation, while the fact is that Jagjivan Ram was not involved in the formulation of reservation policy for the scheduled castes. For example, one government employee, Chamar, of Nagla Tashi Quasimpur said: Jagjivan Ram got the reservation implemented, the policy (of reservation) was formulated by Ambedkar.

(7) Few of the respondents, particularly belonging to the rural poor of other backward classes said that since there was no better alternative to the Congress, they opted for the ruling party. They expressed their desire to support a better alternative, if available.

(8) We have seen in the first part of this chapter that the Lok Dal articulated the interests of the backward castes/classes and peasantry, and that it is supported by the backward castes/classes including the OBCs and peasantry in eastern Uttar Pradesh and Bihar. But in the case of Meerut district, the OBCs do not support Lok Dal, despite the fact that the Janata government headed by Ram Naresh Yadav introduced reservation for them in 1979. In fact, they support Congress more because of their embittered relations with the Jats than because of the policies of Congress or Lok Dal.

The relationships of dependence between the rural poor and the rural rich are reflected in electoral politics at two levels: (i) Lok Sabha and legislative assembly elections, and (ii) the Panchayat level elections. It should be noted that though the relationships of dependence exist between the rural poor and the rural rich in general, it is the relationships of dependence between the rural poor and the Jat rural rich, which are most sharply reflected in the Lok Sabha and assembly elections. However, the relationships of dependence between the rural poor and the non-Jat rural rich like the ones between the rural poor and the Jat rural rich, affect the village Panchayat elections. The political parties do not have their units below district level in Meerut district. For all practical purposes the lower level of party organisation is the district level unit.[36] Hence the Panchayat elections are never contested on party basis. The candidates, however, may belong to one or another political faction or may be sympathisers of one or another political party. The candidates belonging to the Jat and non-Jat rural rich behave in the similar way with the rural poor at the time of the Panchayat elections. Even before the elections, the candidates, as they happen to be the moneylenders and landowning rural rich mostly, ask those rural poor who are dependent on them to vote for them. And they threaten the rural poor with dire consequences in case of their failure to oblige them. Some candidates contesting for the post of village pradhan, however, plead with "folded hands" to the rural poor for votes. The aftermath of the village Panchayat elections is a nightmare for the rural poor. The defeated candidates create all kinds of problems for the rural poor including imposition of sanctions and intimidation. We have got several examples of harassment of the rural poor by the rural rich of both Jats and non-Jats, at the time of Panchayat elections from seven villages of our sample. Such cases of harassment are less prevalent in the villages where the rural poor have got some means of livelihood and form quite a substantial part of the village population.

After the formation of BKD in 1969, the Jat peasantry identified itself with Lok Dal and rallied behind that party. Being the numerically dominant caste among the "upper castes" and controlling the maximum land in Meerut, the Jat peasantry made it a point to ensure the victory of Charan Singh's party. By virtue of their domineering socio-economic position, Jats mounted pressure on the low caste rural poor and the minority high castes of Brahmans and Banias, irrespective of their class position to vote for Lok Dal. Otherwise they are not allowed to vote and sanctions are imposed and coercion is exercised on them. In the villages, where they are generally not allowed to vote, these groups would prefer to vote for Congress, if they were given an opportunity to vote. Some kind of suspicion and insecurity exist in the minds of the rural poor about the supporters of Lok Dal. They feel that they would face problems in their day to day life if the candidates of Lok Dal won. Even if they do not face problems after the victory of Lok Dal candidates, their suspicion about the supporters of Lok Dal persists. Moreover, Charan Singh's ascendancy to power encouraged his supporters to behave rudely with the rural poor. This fact further strengthened the suspicion and apprehension of the latter. When Charan Singh became the Chief Minister of Uttar Pradesh in 1967-1969 and again when he became the Prime Minister in 1979, the Jats behaved ruthlessly with the rural poor in the Jat-dominated villages. During the time of Janata government, they reclaimed the land from the rural poor, which was allotted to them during the emergency. This resulted in large scale violence. The Janata Party leaders sided with the Jat rural rich. The Congress took advantage of the situation.[37] The attitude of Jats towards low caste rural poor and non-Jat minority high castes has made the Jats and non-Jats into two distinct political units in terms of their support to political parties. The rural poor, who predominantly consist of the hierarchies of low castes, act as a social group, subordinating their caste differences in order to defend their interests against the Jat rural rich.

The rural poor in Jat-dominated region expressed their suspicion about the attitude of Jats towards them, and stated that voting for Congress would give them a sense of security. They expressed their suspicion and apprehension towards the supporters of Lok Dal and reasons for their support to Congress in the following ways:

> *Koi hamein nahi dhamkavega Congress ke Jitne pe. Yohi Vajeh he ham Congress ko Vote devein.* (Nobody, meaning thereby Jats, can threaten us after Congress comes into power. That is why we vote for Congress).
>
> [Wage labourer in non-agrarian sector (road construction worker), Jogi, Jaisinghpur]
>
> *Unki tyori badel jayagi.* Their (Jats') eye-brows will change (when Lok Dal candidate wins).
>
> [Wage labourer who goes daily for construction work in Meerut city, Chamar, Nagla Tashi Qasimpur]
>
> *Halaki Congress ne Jyada Kuchh nahien kiya Hamare Liyo, Fer bhi ham Congress ko vote Devein* [Although Congress has not done much for us, yet we vote for the Congress (implicitly because

Jats vote for Lok Dal and low caste harijans for Congress)].
[Traditional Occupation Holder, Barber, Behzadka]
Congress ne Kuchh Nahi Kiya Fir bhi Congress ko Vote Devein. Meene Lok Dal Ko Vote Devein. (Congress has done nothing for us, yet (we) vote for the Congress. Meenas (whom we have likened with Jats in our analysis) vote for Lok Dal.
[Agricultural labourer, Khatik (Harijan), Jafarnagar Begamabad]
Jab Jat Stavein, Congress ke Dhore Javein (Whenever Jats harass us, we take help of Congress).
[Poor Peasant, Chamar, Jaisinghpur]
Yadi Jat ho gye to gaon chhorna parega, Isi karan Congress ko vote dete hein [if Jats (Lok Dal) win, we will have to leave the village. That is why we vote for Congress].
[Agricultural Labourer, Dhiwar, Chobla]
Yadi Congress Jit Gayi to hamari Bhau Betion ke Tang Nahi kiya javega. [If Congress wins, our women will not be harassed (by Jats)].
[Agricultural Labourer, Chamar, Chobla]
Jo Congress jit gai to ham logon ko gaon me tang nahi kiya javega. [If Congress wins, we will not be harassed in the villages (by Jats)].
[Traditional Occupation Holder, Carpenter (Khati), Chobla]
Congress Ko Vote Dete Hain Kyonki Charan Singh Ke Jitne pe Jat Samasya Karte Hain [We vote for Congress because Jats create problems after the victory of Charan Singh (Lok Dal)].
[Poor Peasant, Kumhar, Nagla Tashi Qasimpur]

Narrating his personal experience how a Jat encouraged after the victory of Lok Dal, beat him up, an agricultural labourer of weaver caste of Chobla village said:

Jab Charan Singh Hua to ek Admi Kehne Laga "Nyar Uthvao, Gobar Hatvao". Meine Kaha "Ye Kam tu Khud Karle". Usne Mere Panch-Char Chante Mare. Uske Bhai ne kaha "Aur Mar Sale Ko" [After Charan Singh (Lok Dal) had won, one man (Jat) asked me to "cut fodder, lift the dung". I said, "You do this work yourself". He gave me four-five slaps. His brother said, "beat this bastard more"].

Echoing the sentiments of the rural poor of Jat-dominated villages, a small peasant of Saini caste of Jalalpur village, which is dominated by Gujars (and where Jats form a small section of the households), said:

Charan Singh ke Banane par Jaton ke Gao Me Jat Badi Dhons se kam lete hain. [After winning of Charan Singh (Lok Dal), Jats use coercion (on the rural poor) to get their work done].

These statements show the deep suspicion of the rural poor against the Jat suppored Lok Dal, which is rooted in the relationships between them and the Jat peasantry. The Congress may not save them from harassment and oppression of the Jats, yet they support Congress in order to avoid degradation suffered at the hands of Lok Dal supporters.

Besides, in their day to day behaviour, Jats make loose statements many a time in unparliamentary language, as to what they would do to the "riaya" (the rural poor) in case Lok Dal candidate wins. This attitude of Jats scares the rural poor and strengthens their suspicion about the Lok Dal. The anti-rural poor statements, particularly the anti-Chamar statements of Jats, gain currency at the time of elections. Many a time such statements are made at public places. Although these statements are made by individuals belonging to Jats, they are perceived by the rural poor as the statements of Jats in general. Such statements boomerang and create anti-Lok Dal feelings among them. Given below are examples of statements and expression of Jats.

In the course of our discussion, a Jat landlord of Jaisinghpur village scorned the Congress for helping the rural poor. He said:

Congress ne raya ko chada ke inka dimak kharab kar diya (Congress has elevated the riaya and has spoilt their mentality).

On the eve of 1980 assembly election, a group of Jats and Chamars were sitting in the compound of a school of village Khanauda and chatting about the election. In the course of the conversation, one Jat middle peasant got agitated and said:

Janata Party (SC) jit gayi to Chamaron ko thik kar deinge (If Janata Party (SC) wins, we will mend the Chamars).

The persons belonging to Chamar caste quoted this statement among the people of their caste. The Chamars, as well as other low castes of the village came to know about the statement. This strengthened their anti-Lok Dal attitude.

Likewise, in our discussion with a group of the rural poor of Chamar caste in Nagla Tashi Qasimpur, one of the participants, a student, quoted a Jat middle peasant as:

Lok Dal jit gaya to Chamarion ka khet me ghas khodna band kar denge. [If Lok Dal wins, we will stop the chamaris (women chamars) from cutting grass in our fields].

Besides, they make statements particularly about the women of the rural poor in extremely derogatory language.

The Jats and non-Jat rural rich enjoy a dominating position over the rural poor, but the non-Jat sections of the rural rich align themselves with the rural poor to support the Congress. The question arises why should the non-Jat rural rich and the rural poor become allies. This is largely because the non-Jat rural rich have an axe to grind against the Jat rural rich. The contradiction between the non-Jat and Jat rural rich accounts for the political division between them. The non-Jat rural rich and the rural poor find a common political force in the Congress to counter the Jat supported Lok Dal.

Brahmans, irrespective of their class position, support the Congress, because they feel that Congress has been led by the Nehru family. The common reply from the Brahman respondents for their support to Congress was that they "are Brahmans".[38] Moreover, the Congress has always patronised the Brahman caste in Meerut district by giving district level political and non-political posts to them.[39] Besides in the Jat-dominated villages, as we have noted in this chapter, Brahmans are a minority caste and hence not allowed to cast vote. This kind of political suppression has compelled them in the entire district to rally behind the "Nehru family led Congress" against the "Jat supported Lok Dal". Likewise, the Banias support Congress in the villages for similar reasons.

Tyagis and Gujars are the two main dominant castes which provide a semblance of challenge to the Jats in the countryside in Meerut District.[40] Congress Tyagi leaders of the district keep in touch with Tyagis in the villages. It is their sheer rivalry with the Jats over the domination of the district politics which makes them support the Congress. However, it should be noted that whenever Lok Dal gives ticket to a person from Tyagi caste, they support Lok Dal. For example, Tyagis of Jafarnagar Begamabad village, which falls under the Muzaffarnagar parliamentary constituency supported the Lok Dal candidate, Dharam Vir, who happens to be a Tyagi. Ram Chandra Vikal, a prominent Congress leader of Gujar Caste and an ardent rival of Charan Singh, is one of the motivating factors which makes the Gujars support the Congress. However, whenever Lok Dal allots ticket to a Gujar candidate in any constituency, their votes get divided between the Congress and Lok Dal even in the neighbouring constituency. In Jalalpur village which falls under the Muzaffarnagar parliamentary constituency, the Gujars supported Lok Dal (Janata Party (SC)) candidate, Ghayoor Ali Khan in 1980 parliamentary election because it allotted ticket to Harishpal, a Gujar, in the neighbouring Lok Sabha constituency of Meerut. But they opposed Lok Dal in 1984 parliamentary election, when Harishpal was denied the ticket to contest Meerut constituency, and they opted for Dharam Vir Singh of Congress. In fact, having been denied the ticket by Lok Dal in 1980 general election, Harishpal had campaigned for Congress.[41]

Moreover, Gujars feel that Congress policies have benefited them. Both Gujar inhabited villages, *i.e.*, Jalalpur and Ahera, of our sample, are the ex-zamindari villages. Gujars were mostly the tenants of the zamindars in these villages before the zamindari abolition. They were the tenants of the Nawab of Baghpat in Jalalpur and the landlord of Harchandpur in Ahera. They feel that it was the Congress policies because of which zamindari had been abolished and they became the owners of their land. Like the rural poor they also feel that the Congress won them independence, and its policies are helping the farmers. The Muslim respondents could not give specific reasons for their support to Congress. One of them who is a landlord and a Congress activist, however, said that his family supports Congress because they have connections in the Congress and that it is a secular political party.

Jats of Meerut district alongwith the Tyagis supported the opposition even prior to the formation of Lok Dal, probably because they were adversely affected in the ex-bhaiachara villages by the zamindari abolition. However, the Jats of Chhaprauli region supported Charan Singh personally even when he was in Congress. He had been representing this region ever since he began his political career. The Lok Dal provided a common political party to the Jats of Meerut district to rally their support. Jats did not get any specific benefit from the policies of Congress when Charan Singh was in it. They did not benefit from the zamindari abolition in the ex-bhaiachara villages. Since they are not included in the category of the OBCs, they did not benefit from the reservations introduced by the Janata government headed by Charan Singh's protege Ram Naresh Yadav unlike the Yadavs, Kurmis and Lodhas. Yet, they have supported Charan Singh both as a Congressman and Lok Dal leader. Charan Singh articulated and defended the better-off sections of the peasantry of all castes especially the middle castes. He, however, patronised the Jats in Meerut by giving posts in the district unit of Lok Dal. The Jats pointed out the following reasons for their support to Lok Dal:

(1) Most of them feel that they support Lok Dal because of its policies and achievements. They feel that it is a party of kisans, that Charan Singh abolished zamindari, that he was a "son of kisan", that he removed patwaris and that "he got the roads built" linking the villages with main road (we got this reply in the village Chobla of Baghpat parliamentary constituency which was represented by Charan Singh). Some elements of "misconception" exist among the supporters of Charan Singh, just as they exist among the rural poor with regard to their support for Congress. Whatever help or benefit they got, many of them feel that it was given by him, or because of his efforts. They feel that even land revenue on the small landholdings was abolished by him, and price of their produce was increased due to his efforts.

(2) Though they generally support Lok Dal, very few of them were ready to accept that they support Charan singh because of caste. However, the relationships of Jats with the non-Jat rural rich in the district, so far as domination of the district politics is concerned, lead us to infer that Lok Dal provided a political forum to the former to counter the latter who support the Congress generally. Therefore, the caste and class have brought them together to support Lok Dal. The caste has divided the rural rich between Jat supporters of Lok Dal and non-Jat supporters of Congress.

(3) Just to oppose the Congress Party also they support the Lok Dal. They feel that Congress is the party of Sarmaidars (capitalists) and Brahmans, and it supports the Chamars.

(4) When we pointed out to them that Charan Singh has done nothing substantially for them, they said Charan Singh was a "lone man", "his voice was not heard" and he was discriminated. They asked back "what can he do alone?", "*kya ham use Ikla Chhod dein* (should we leave him alone?)".

Thus, Jats support Lok Dal mainly because it is a party which is concerned with the problems of the peasantry and which was led by a leader from their caste. Charan Singh championed the cause of peasantry, and Lok Dal provides them a forum to counter the non-

Jats politically.

The social bases of political parties exist at times even when elections do not take place. Elections only show the shifts or continuation in the social bases of political parties. Under special circumstances the "traditional supporters" of Congress and Lok Dal shift their support. This happens because of factionalism, caste, and availability of a better political alternative in the form of a party or leader. In 1984 parliamentary and 1985 assembly elections, 4.61 per cent of the Jat households, and in 1985 assembly election 6.35 per cent of the total households, all belonging to Chamar caste deviated from their respective traditional support because of the intra-caste factionalism. Factionalism within Chamars divided them into the supporters of Congress (I) and Congress (J). In 1984 Lok Sabha election Sainis deviated in their support from the Congress to BJP, since BJP candidate belonged to their caste.[42] Gujars and Tyagis also deviate in their support from the Congress to Lok Dal, if the Congress does not allot ticket to the candidate from their respective caste but the Lok Dal does.[43] The scheduled caste Congress supporters deviated to RPI in 1967 and 1969 assembly elections, and its traditional supporters supported the Janata Party in 1977 general election. But as soon as the supporters of the party get dissatisfied with the new alternative or as soon as the new alternative ceases to exist, they swing back to support the party, which they have been usually supporting.

Even in the 1989 assembly and Lok Sabha elections, several supporters of the Congress deviated to support the newly emergent party, the BSP. In BSP, they found a better alternative than the Congress, as it claimed to be the champion of the low castes. They may remain with the BSP so long as it retains its identity and the low castes/SCs feel satisfied with it. But they may swing back to the Congress, if BSP loses its identity or ceases to exist, as they did in the cases of the RPI and the Janata Party.

Notes

1 We will be using Congress (I) and Congress synonymously on the one hand, and the BKD, Lok Dal, Janata Party (SC), and DMKP also synonymously on the other hand, in our discussion.

2 For the issues influencing/determining the social bases/"vote banks" of the political parties dealt with in the studies, see Paul R. Brass, *Caste,*

Faction and Party in Indian Politics, Vol. II: Election Studies, New Delhi, Chanakya Publications, 1985; Iqbal Narain and S.P. Varma (ed.), *Fourth General Election in India,* Vols. 1-2, Bombay, Orient Longman, 1970; Iqbal Narain, *et al., Election Studies in India: : An Evaluation,* New Delhi, Allied Publishers, 1978; Susheela Kaushik, *Elections in India : Its Social Bases,* Calcutta, K.P. Bagchi and Co., 1982; see also for the issues studied in case of elections in Andhra Pradesh, Marguirite S. Robinson, *Local Politics: The Law of the Fishes: Development Through Political Change in Medak District Andhra Pradesh (South India),* Delhi, Oxford University Press, 1988, Chapters V and VI.

3. Susheela Kaushik, *ibid.,* p.5.
4. See Javed Alam, *Domination and Dissent : Peasants and Politics,* Calcutta, Mandira, 1985.
5. Nayar observes that conflictual nature of relationships between the Jat Sikhs and the Scheculed Castes in Ludhiana district of Punjab determines the choice of political parties to a significant extent. See Baldev Raj Nayar, "Religion and Caste in Punjab : Sidhwan Bet Constituency", in Myron Weiner and Rajni Kothari (ed.), *Indian Voting Behaviour: Studies of 1962 General Elections,* Calcutta, Firm K.L. Mukhopadhyaya, 1965.
6. Kohli also observes that the nature of Jat-Jain conflict in Meerut determines their choice of support to the BLD and Jan Sangh respectively. See Atul Kohli, *State and Poverty in India : The Politics of Reforms,* Cambridge, Cambridge University Press, 1987, p. 209.
7. See C.P. Bhambhri, "Ideology and Political Parties In India", *Economic and Political Weekly,* Vol. III, no. 16, 20 April 1968, pp. 643-46.
8. Paul R. Brass, *Caste, Faction and Party in Indian Politics : Faction and Party,* Vol. I, Delhi, Chanakaya Publications, 1984, p.242.
9. See Saraswati Shrivastava, "Uttar Pradesh : Politics of Neglected Development", in Iqbal Narain (ed.) *State Politics in India,* Meerut, Meenakshi Prakashan, 1976, pp. 334, 352-54.
10. See *ibid.,* pp. 242, 247, 330; Paul R. Brass, *op. cit.,* Vol. II, pp. 15, 170. Atul Kohli finds such a categorisation of Congress as "misleading". He argues that the Congress is not the party of "alliance of extremes" because it has been supported by the landowners of all classes (as there does not exist correlation between the electoral performance of Congress and size of the landholdings), its politics of Green Revolution benefitted "backward caste" cultivating "middle peasantry" and its support base has regional variations. He concedes that many in the rank of "middle peasantry" were alienated from the Congress due to its " broad-based" approach. See Atul Kohli, *op.it.,* p.206.
11. See Paul R. Brass, *ibid.,* pp. 105-25. See also Pradhan H. Prasad, "Rising Middle Peasantry in North India", *Economic and Political Weekly,* Vol.

XV, nos. 5-7, February 1980, p. 217. Prasad shows that in North India the party activists of Congress are drawn from "middle and poor peasantry", "industrial working class" and "petty bourgeoisie"; and its leadership is drawn from "top peasantry", especially landlords, and the "industrial bourgeoisie".

12. Paul R. Brass, *ibid.*, pp. 127-30.
13. Craig Baxter, "The Rise and Fall of the Bharatiya Kranti Dal", in Myron Weiner and John Osgood Field (ed.), *Electoral Politics in the Indian States : Party Systems and Cleavages,* New Delhi, Manohar Book Service, 1975, p. 136.
14. See Paul R. Brass, *op. cit.*, Vol. I, pp. 212-16; Charan Singh, *Land Reforms in U.P. and the Kulaks,* New Delhi, Vikas Publishing House, 1986. Charan Singh, in fact, fitted into the tradition of "populist and neo-populist" ideas and was an "organic" intellectual of "the rich and middle peasantry". For a discussion see T.J. Byers, "Charan Singh, 1902-87 : An Assessment". *The Journal of Peasant Studies,* Vol. 15, no. 2, January 1988, pp. 139-89.
15. Even the occupancy tenants and tenants-at-will (sirdhars) in the neighbouring district, Aligarh, were unable to pay 10 times of revenue. See Zoya Hasan, *Dominance and Mobilisation : Politics in Western Uttar Pradesh, 1930-1980,* New Delhi, Sage Publications, 1989, p. 59.
16. See Paul R. Brass, *op. cit.,* Vol. II, pp. 69-70.
17. Paul R. Brass, *op. cit.,* Vol I, p. 306.
18. *Ibid.*, p. 316.
19. *Ibid.*, pp. 320-21. Charan Singh's opposition to the abolition of privy purses led to trading of charges between him and the Congress. The Congress accused him of accepting money from the mills. He refuted this charge in a letter dated 2 September 1970 written to Indira Gandhi. The BKD and other coalition partners also had differences on this issue. See *ibid.*, p. 332, footnote 32.
20. Charan Singh's Private Papers.
21. Charan Singh, *Land Reforms in UP, op. cit.*, pp. 64-65.
22. Paul R. Brass, *op. cit.*, vol. I, p. 309.
23. See M.H. Johnson, *Relations Between Land Settlements and Party Politics in Uttar Pradesh, 1950-1969 - With Special Reference to the Formation of the Bharatiya Kranti Dal,* University of Sussex , Ph.D. thesis, 1975, pp. 242-65. See also Saraswati Shrivastava, "Uttar Pradesh", *op. cit.*, pp. 333-34.
24. Harry W. Balir, "Rising Kulaks and Backward Classes in Bihar: Social Change in the Late 70s", *Economic and Political Weekly*, Vol. XV, no. 2, 12 January 1980, pp. 66, 69.
25. The District Congress Committee of Banaras passed a resolution con-

demning Charan Singh for attending the Bhadoi meeting in 1953, and asking the UPCC to take action against him. However, no action could be taken against him as he attended the meeting with the consent of the Chief Minister, G.B. Pant. He was not not given co-operation by the district Congress leadership in a meeting held in Banaras on 17 May 1953. See Charan Singh, *Land Reforms*, *op.cit.*, pp. 64-65. Thakur Hukum Singh wrote a letter to the Chief Minister, G.B. Pant, holding land reform policies of Congress and thus Charan Singh indirectly responsible for its defeat in the by-election. Sampurnanand also wrote a letter to the Congress cabinet meeting held on 15 June 1953, pointing out the reasons of Congress' defeat in by-election of 1953. He wrote that the defeat was due to the land reforms policies of Congress government, which "antagonised practically *every class which has so far possessed education, wealth, social status and consequently influence... the classes to which I refer, in general, belong to the Brahmin, Rajput, Bhumihar, Kayastha and Vaishya communities...higher castes...*" (emphasis added) He further said that the policies of Congress "had the definite tendency of affecting adversely the interests of the higher castes...from whom the Congress has derived the greatest measure of support in the past." Holding Charan Singh responsible indirectly, he said that "...our public acts have benefited... the backward classes", who "have been activised by Sosit Samaj Sangh." He wrote: "Whatever advantages we may confer upon them they are not likely, as a body, to come into our fold....The kind of leadership which can reach them easily, is that represented by groups like the PSP or the communists". He advised, "we must, therefore, make up our minds to channellise the contending forces into revolutionary channels, *the game of baiting higher classes must be suspended*", (emphasis added), pp. 60-64. The Congress leaders were issued circular not to attend the meeting of the backward castes in 1956. See Zoya Hasan, "Power and Mobilization: Patterns of Resilience and Change in Uttar Pradesh", in Francine R. Frankel and M.S.A. Rao (ed.), *Dominance and State Power in Modern India: Decline of Social Order*, Vol. I, Delhi, Oxford University Press, 1989, p. 177. Charan Singh wrote a letter that the persons of the backward castes whom he was alleged to be supporting, hardly represented in the senior posts in the entire administration in Uttar Pradesh. *National Herald*, 20 September 1970.

He accused Nehru and Indira Gandhi of favouring Brahmans and discriminating against Jats. See Atul Kohil, *op.cit.*, p. 199.

26. Paul R. Brass, *op.cit.*, Vol. II, p. 144.
27. Though the rural poor supported the Janata party in 1977 election, they were dissatisfied after the formation of the Janata Party government. They considered it as a stereotype of the Lok Dal. The support of landowning

classes to the Janata Party in 1977 election was a continuation of the support of its constituent parties among the leading peasant proprietors in Uttar Pradesh. See *ibid.*, p. 149. After the split in the Janata Party in 1979, Lok Dal assumed its independent shape. The regions and social base of its support remained the same as existed before its merger with the Janata Party.

28. See *ibid.*, pp. 86-87.
29. See *ibid.*, pp. 127-31, 134-37. The socialists and communists were quite popular even in some areas of western Uttar Pradesh. See Chapter V, pp. 90-91.
30. In Uttar Pradesh BKD drew upon the base of independent candidates in 1969. See Craig Baxter, *op.cit.*, p. 115. But in Meerut, interestingly, it cut into the bases of the socialists and RPI as well, besides the base of independent candidates.
31. We did not intend to study any particular election. Our main emphasis in interviewing the respondents has been to ascertain the political parties which they usually support in the Lok Sabha and assembly elections over the years, and reasons for their support. However, we could get information from all the eight villages about the 1984 Lok Sabha election, as we began our household survey in January 1985. Though in three of eight villages we conducted the household survey before the 1985 assembly election, we could get information in all the villages about the support and preference of the respondents regarding the political parties.
32. The implications of the relationships of dependence on the choice of votes have usually been explained in such a way as if the dependent (the rural poor) accept the domination/dictate of those on whom they depend (the rural rich) willingly and that they do not resist the domination and also as if they (the dependent) vote as desired by the rural rich willingly. See Lloyd F. Rudolph and Susanne Hoeber Rudolph, *In Pursuit of Lakshmi: The Political Economy of the Indian State*, Bombay, Orient Longman, 1987, p. 52; *The Modernity of Tradition: Political Development in India*, Bombay, Orient Longman, 1967, pp. 24-25; Atul Kohli, *op.cit.*, p. 205. The influence of the rural rich might make them seek the consent of the rural poor (dependent) in the tradition of the "patron-client" relations in certain cases/parts of India, but this cannot be presented as a case of generalisation.

    Our observations show that the rural poor are not willing to accept the domination of the rural rich, on whom they depend. Rather, they accept their domination unwillingly and they strive to resist this domination. (See Chapter IV).

    Even when the rural poor ally with the non-Jat rural rich to support the Congress in the parliamentary and assembly elections, it is not because of any kind of "patron-client" relationship between them. It is more because of the nature of relationships - which both the rural poor and non-Jat rural rich have with the Jats.

33. See Chapter III, pp.56-57 and Chapter IV, pp. 69, 73-74.
34. See Atul Kohli, *op.cit.*, p. 219.
35. The parts of the cot (charpoy) denote the social position of the individual sitting on the cot in western UP villages as in some other parts of North India. A person who occupies superior position in the caste hierarchy in relation to the inter-caste relations, and a person who is older in relation to the intra-caste relations sits in upper portion of the cot (sirana). The lower portion of the cot (panayat) is meant for sitting of a person belonging relatively to lower social order and younger persons. The chamars and some other lower castes are not allowed to sit on the cot of the relatively higher castes in most villages of the district. Violation of this code is considered as disrespect to the person of higher castes and older persons. This code, however, is getting eroded in certain areas. But in most parts of western UP it is strictly adhered to.
36. See Sanjib Kumar Baruah, *Getting A Fair Share: Politics and Poor in Rural India*, Ph.D. Thesis, Chicago University, 1983, p. 260.
37. See Chapter II p.22, Chapter V., pp.95-96.
38. With regard to the Brahmans' support to the Congress, one elderly Congress leader said: "Like the bonded labourers Brahman votes are Congress votes." Interview: Uma Dutt Sharma, 2 May 1985.
39. Even the Jats along with Gujars and Ahirs of Aligrah district resent the control of the local institutions, *i.e.*, land development banks and credit societies by the 'upper castes' - Brahmans and Rajpus because of their domination over Congress. See Zoya Hasan, *op.cit.*, p. 123.
40. The leaders of Congress (I) and Lok Dal/BKD belonging to Tyagi and Jat castes have been patronising the "anti-social" elements with criminal records belonging to their respective caste. These "anti-social" elements have been "used" by the leaders of one caste supporting a particular political party against the leaders of another caste supporting the rival party and *vice versa.*
41 Harishpal contested unsuccessfully on the Janata Party (SC) ticket from Meerut parliamentary seat in 1980. He defected to Congress (I) in 1984 on being denied ticket by Charan Singh for this seat. He swung back to the Janata Dal (with the former Lok Dal as one of its components) and fought the 1989 election successfully from Meerut parliamentary seat, defeating the former Union Minister Mohsina Kidwai.
42. See this Chapter, pp.133-137.
43. See *ibid.*, pp.153-54.

Chapter VII

Conclusion

Two features form the dominant and decisive aspects of the agrarian economy of Meerut. They are - the development of capitalist tendencies and the relationships of dependence. The capitalist tendencies developed mainly since the late 19th century and got accelerated with the introduction of Green Revolution. The emergence of the issues related to capitalist economy, *i.e.*, the remunerative prices, subsidised inputs, fertilizers, machines, seeds, *etc.*, cut in the electricity charges, better agricultural conditions and the related demands place Meerut in the category of other regions like other districts of western Uttar Pradesh, Punjab, Haryana, Maharashtra, Karnataka and Tamil Nadu, where such tendencies and issues have emerged. Most of these regions have been the arenas of the political activities of the commercial farmers. Their assertion in the 1970s and 1980s, in the form of agitations of BKUs in Punjab and western Uttar Pradesh, Shetkari Sanghthan in Maharashtra, Khedeyut Samaj in Gujarat, Karnataka Rajya Raitha Sangha in Karnataka, Vivasayigal Sangham in Tamil Nadu and the way they have articulated their interests, testify the fact that they are the most resourceful and influential sections of the rural society in these regions. They have benefited most from the state policies, and particularly from the Green Revolution. The commercial farmers in Meerut are the rural rich consisting of the landlords, rich peasants and middle peasants.

They are part of the capitalist economy, and the forces of market and capitalism affect them to varying degrees. Despite the differentiation and contradictions among them and their unequal capacity to interact with the market forces, the rural rich share certain common characteristics in terms of their control on the resources and hiring in of the labour power, excepting the middle peasants (though during the harvest season, even they hire in the labour power). The moneylenders and milkmen also belong to the rural rich.[1] The commonalities among the rural rich bring them together so as to dominate the rural poor - the small and poor peasants, and landless proletariat. The relationships between the rural rich and rural poor are those of dependence. Some of these relationships developed along with the new trends in the agrarian economy, and some of them have been existing for centuries. The relationships of dependence are of two types – the mutual or two-sided dependence or contradictions and the one-sided dependence. In the case of the mutual dependence (contradictions), both groups of classes depend on each other in the particular processes or phenomena involving their relationships of dependence. The existence of their relationships of dependence depends on their mutual interests. In such cases of mutual dependence, the rural poor can bargain with the rural rich. But in the case of one-sided dependence on the rural rich for cutting grass from the fields, defecating in the fields, passing through the dolas (boundaries of the fields), throwing rubbish, *etc.*, the rural poor cannot bargain. The existence of the relationships of one-sided dependence depends on the discretion of the rural rich. In Meerut, the relationships of one-sided dependence play more decisive role in determining the political, social and economic relations between the rural rich and the rural poor than the relationships of two-sided dependence (contradictions).[2]

The relationships of dependence determine the social, political and economic relationships between the rural rich and the rural poor. The rural poor are not allowed to cast votes, their women are molested and raped, they are forced to do begar, they are abused, they are asked to behave "properly", etc. Any attempt to defy the rural rich or resist their harassment results in the imposition of sanctions against them. In the absence of any alternative which can free them from the dependence they have to submit to the rural rich.[3]

In the context of the relationships of dependence between the rural rich and the rural poor, the cleavages, factions and contradictions within each group get subordinated and they behave as if they are two opposite social groups.[4]

The harassment of the rural poor is minimised to a large extent in those villages where they have some alternative means of livelihood either because of their nearness to the main city or due to the availability of some cottage industry at the village level. This is also true of those villages where the rural poor form quite a large section of the village population and where they have zamindari background (three out of eight such villages of our sample surveyed in 1984-85 have the zamindari background). But the harassment/oppression/exploitation of the rural poor is more intense in the villages, which have bhaiachara background. However, there are certain exceptions among this sort of villages. Behzadka, one of the five ex-bhaiachara villages, presents an exception in our sample, because there the scheduled castes (the rural poor) form the majority and a large number of them have tannery as an alternative means of livelihood.[5]

The availability of the alternative means of livelihood, however, does not eliminate the harassment and oppression of the rural poor completely. Such alternatives do not abate all kinds of dependence.[6]

The larger numerical proportion of the middle peasants (20.44 per cent) and their control on quite larger proportion of resources along with the smaller number of agricultural labourers (15.60 per cent) present a paradoxical case in an agrarian economy marked by the presence of capitalist tendencies. But these middle peasants are not the ideal middle peasants of the Chayanovian school. They are subject to the conditions of capitalist economy. They share many common characteristics with the landlords and rich peasants. Hence, the economy of Meerut cannot be called "middle peasant economy" or the mode of production as the "middle peasant mode of production".[7] The numerical dominance of the middle peasants along with the presence of very small proportion of agricultural labourers indicate that though the agricultural wages form a very important issue in Meerut, they are not the main or priority issue of the rural poor.[8] The main problem of the rural poor and also of many of those belonging to the middle peasants is to seek employment. Apart from the unemployment, the main issues of the rural poor emerge from their relationships of dependence reflected through their social, political and economic harassment and oppression. The level of the unemployment is obvious from the fact that though the percentage of the rural poor is as high as 63.07, only 15.60 per cent form the agricultural labourers who derive subsistence mainly or solely from agricultural labour, 18.90 per cent are engaged as wage labourers in non-agrarian sectors and 5.27 per cent are engaged in the traditional occupations. The miscellaneous (8.79 per cent) are socially, economically and politically closer to the rural poor. The rural poor do not get employment for all twelve months in a year.[9]

The smaller number of agricultural labourers marked by the numerical dominance of the middle peasants forecloses the possibility of a formation of well-knit enduring union of the agricultural labourers.[10] However, there might emerge sprinklings of such unions with ephemeral existence. Over-decisiveness of the one-sided dependence and the fear of consequent sanctions further mar the formation of such unions. No doubt, low caste rural poor particularly belonging to the Chamars, quite often get organised under the Ambedkar Committees in the villages of Meerut district.[11] Also they are often organised or mobilised by some political organisations/groups/parties like the BMU and several short-lived organisations like Dalit Sena/the Shoshit Mukti Vahini and by the parties like RPI, BSP, and Congress. They usually raise issues related to discrimination, harassment and oppression of the low castes, mainly Chamars, particularly at the hands of the local dominant castes - Jats (mostly), Gujars, Tyagis, Rajputs and Muslim high castes. Most of their problems emanate from the nature of relationships of one-sided dependence, not from the mutual dependence or contradictions. The response of the rural poor to such mobilisation shows a level of social and political consciousness among a section of the rural poor.[12]

Alavi discusses "the roles played by different sections of peasantry" in "revolution".[13] He observes that the "poor peasants", share-croppers and farm labourers depend on the "landlords and rich peasants". In his "purely tentative" arguments he holds that the "poor peasants" have "servile habits, backward mentality... servile mentality" because of the "dependence" and their relations with their "masters" (the "landlords or the rich peasants") which are based on the "paternalistic" norms, are "initially" "the least militant class of the peasantry". "The middle peasants" are described to be enjoying "economic independence" (from the landlords and rich peasants) who unlike the "poor peasants" are self-sufficient in terms of the resources and labour power. They are "initially most militant" and are described as "a powerful ally of the proletarian movement in the countryside especially in generating the initial impetus of the peasants revolution" and "the militancy of middle peasants" builds up "anti-landlord and anti-rich peasant sentiment" in a "revolutionary situation". In such a situation, the morale of the "poor peasants" is said to be raised and the "poor peasants" are "more ready to respond to calls" (of the "middle peasants") to action.[14] Such views of Alavi are based on his observations in the context of "revolution" in Russia, China and India (the Telengana and Tebhaga movements are categorised as "revolution"); the "middle peasants" play a leading and an "independent" role in such contexts. They are credited to play such roles even in the context of "social and political upheavals".[15] But in western Uttar Pradesh, particularly in Meerut, where the situation is not ripe for "revolution" and where "social and political upheavals" are not likely to occur (in near future), where the agrarian history was marked by the predominance of the peasant proprietors of the bhaiachara having its bearing on the agrarian system of the post-independence period, where the middle peasants form quite a dominant section of the village society but do not fit into the Chayanovian model of the middle peasantry, where they are mostly relatively independent (and those who depend for resources, do not depend only on the landlords and rich peasants: unlike the middle peasants discussed by Alavi, they also depend on those middle peasants who control the needed resources), where the middle peasants alongwith the landlords and rich peasants have benefited most from the policies of the state, where there does not exist a well developed class of agricultural labourers, and where they also harass/exploit/oppress the rural poor in social, economic (not necessarily in terms of wages always) and political terms - the middle peasants cannot be an "ally of the proletarian movement in the countryside". Nor can they be "anti-landlord and anti-rich peasant". On the contrary, they are hostile towards the rural poor and the allies of the landlords and rich peasants.[16]

In Meerut, as in several other districts of western Uttar Pradesh, the poor peasants like other classes of the rural poor depend not only on the landlords and rich peasants but (unlike the "poor peasants", share-croppers and farm labourers as described by Alavi) also on the middle peasants. The majority of the middle peasants (except those who are not self-sufficient in all resources) are independent like the landlords and rich peasants. They do not form an absolutely distinct class. They have social, political and economic relationships with other classes.[17] The middle peasants of western Uttar Pradesh, unlike those discussed by Alavi, do not act independently and in dissociation from other classes of the rural rich. Commonness of their issues and characteristics related to the capitalist and village economy make their alliance possible.[18]

The "dependence" of "the poor peasants" on "the landlords and rich peasants" is said to cause the "vertical" mobilisation of the "poor peasants" by the latter.[19] In the case of the non-electoral politics (dependence, resistance and sanctions, and mobilisation for agitations of the rural rich and the rural poor) the "vertical" mobilisation - alliance between the rural poor and the rural rich - normally does not take place. The rural rich and the rural poor get mobilised separately on the issues, which concern them exclusively, and which are not necessarily class-issues always. However, the poor peasants might get "vertically" mobilised in non-electoral political processes. Their strength and participation remain much smaller than those of the rural rich in such processes. The middle peasants make an alliance with other classes of the rural rich in the political activities related to the non-electoral politics and on issues related to the agrarian economy.[20] Even in their social and economic attitude towards the rural poor they behave in a similar way,[21] as other sections of the rural rich.

Electoral politics, however, is marked by a departure from the non-electoral politics. The rural rich and the rural poor get divided on caste lines in the electoral politics. The non-Jat rural poor and rural rich join hands in their choice for Congress and the Jat rural rich and rural poor join together in their choice for the Lok Dal. Here also, not only the other classes but the middle peasants are also divided on the caste lines, *i.e.*, between Jats and non-Jats - the former joining the other agrarian classes of non-Jats and the latter joining the other agrarian classes of Jats. Thus, the "vertical" mobilisation of Jats and that of non-Jats takes place cutting across the class barriers.[22] Alavi and Harriss opine that "paternalistic" relations (and "moral commitment" ; Harriss) induce the "clients (rural poor)" to support the "patron" (rural rich).[23] This may be true of their observations (Alavi's observations from Punjab of Pakistan and Harriss' from North Arcot of Tamil Nadu) but our case does not comply with this view. The causality of the support of the rural poor to the rural rich (including the non-Jat middle peasants) lies not in their "paternalistic" relations, but in the nature of their relationships of dependence (which are not "paternalistic") and policies of the parties or the governments led by them.[24]

The possibility of the alliance of the rural rich - the landlords, rich peasants and middle peasants - as a whole or of any of the constituent class of the rural rich with the rural poor - the small peasants, poor peasants and the landless proletariat - as a whole or with any section of the rural poor, and particularly with the landless proletariat, for any political activity might vary in the context of issues and level of politics of mobilisation in western Uttar Pradesh and particularly in Meerut district. If the issues raised in an agitation concern only the rural rich, the rural poor and the miscellaneous would not join. Similarly, if the issues raised in an agitation concern only the rural poor, the rural rich would not join. But if the issues concern both of them wholly or any constituent or constituents of each of them equally (like elections), the larger section, of the rural poor side with those rural rich who can pose a challenge to the more dominant rural rich, (the non-Jat rural poor and rural rich allying with other to support Congress and the Jats (most of them are rural rich) supporting the Lok Dal.[25] But the political (electoral) division of the rural rich into Jats and non-Jats and the alliance of the latter with the non-Jat rural poor in terms of electoral politics does not divide/abate the intensity of harassment of the rural poor by the rural rich (Jats and non-Jats both).[26]

While the rural rich and the rural poor can be organised/mobilised on their respective demands separately, they are not likely to be united on these demands/issues. The nature of relationships among them forecloses such a possibility. There is, however, a potentiality of the alliance between the rural rich and the rural poor: that means the possibility of alliance of the entire rural sector/classes on the questions related to the agrarian society/rural sector as a whole. Such issues involve corruption (though a segment of the rural rich is part of the corrupt practices), better medical, transportation, education and other facilities, creation of employment opportunities, *etc.*, in the villages, and issues of democracy (which require high level of consciousness and politicisation of the classes). Such issues may be of concern to the agrarian classes to different extent, but they really matter to them all. However, the possibility of such potentiality of alliance is fraught with the problems of realpolitik. Despite the commonness of the issues to the entire village society - nature of the local level relations, factionalism, the political parties deriving support from different social bases, etc., - may hamper the possibility of an alliance of all agrarian classes even on the issues which concern the entire rural sector. Such an alliance can take more broad-based/progressive form when the issues of agrarian society are linked with those of entire political economy. The problems of the agrarian classes have to be identified with those of the corresponding classes in the cities.

Majority (82.22 per cent) of the rural rich belong to the dominant castes of Hindus - Brahmans, Tyagis, Banias, Meenas, Jats and Gujars, and Muslim high castes. These castes form 36.50 per cent of the village population and control 83.38 per cent land and monopolise other resources. And majority (83.3 per cent) of the rural poor belong to the low castes of Hindus and Muslims. The scheduled castes form maximum of all castes.[27]

Is it the caste factor which makes the dominant castes of rural rich so dominant that they harass, oppress and dominate the rural poor belonging to the low castes/lower strata? It is not the caste which makes the rural rich so strong. Instead, it is the relationships of dependence (mainly one-sided), which account for their domination/dominant position. But the harassment/oppression/exploitation of the low castes - the scheduled castes and the OBCs of Hindus and Muslims (most of whom belong to the rural poor), get minimised in the villages which have zamindari background, where the rural poor have availability of alternative means of livelihood, and have relatively larger strength of the low castes. Had the caste been the main or only factor in determining the dominance of the dominant/high caste rural rich, their dominance/ domination would not have got relatively minimised in the villages where such conditions prevail.

Castes or caste groups derive their respective strength or vulnerability in the village society from their respective position regarding the control and distribution of resources and from the nature of their relationships of dependence. Their respective material conditions determine their positions in such matters as involving the relationships of domination and subordination, harassment/oppression of the low caste men and women, prevention of casting votes, etc. The dominant castes of Hindus and Muslims become so dominant because they form the majority of the rural rich and control the maximum of resources and are placed in the domineering position with respect to the relationships of dependence. On the contrary, the low castes - both Hindus and Muslims - are placed in the subordinate position because they either do not control or some of them control inadequate resources and are placed in the vulnerable position in the relationships of dependence.[28] Jats are politically most assertive caste of the district. This is so because after the scheduled castes (37.63 per cent) they are the second largest caste (16.49 per cent) of the village population and they form 44.54 per cent of the rural rich and control more than 50 per cent of the land.[29]

Caste, however, maintains its identity at the psychological level. And it assumes an autonomous position in the context of conflicts and political matters. Positions of caste/social groups and their relations are perceived (by the villagers and leaders) in the caste language (idioms).[30] Even the conflicts, irrespective of their nature, involving two individuals or groups of individuals of different castes or incident of harassment, etc., find echo in the respective caste or caste groups cutting across class and regional (district) lines.[31] Their casteist perception is sharpened by the growing politicisation of caste by the political parties and pressure groups/social groups. The Congress/RPI/BSP explain any conflict between the low castes and Jats as the harassment/oppression of the former castes by the latter. Similarly, Lok Dal, though not mentioning any special concession to the Jats in its policies, favours Jats in its party structure and consciously consolidates its position amongst them.

Caste even deviates the electorate from their traditional choice of a political party. The low castes do not hesitate to vote a candidate of dominant caste fielded by the Congress. But if they find a candidate of their caste fielded by any other (important) political party, they deviate from their traditional choice and vote their caste candidate. Sainis (OBCs), traditionally Congress supporters, voting for a Saini candidate fielded by BJP in 1984 parliamentary election, Chamars voting for Janata Party in 1977 election because of Jagjivan Ram's appeal, and their opting for the RPI in the 1960s, and for the BSP in the 1984 and 1989 elections form some examples of such deviations.[32] Jats, irrespective of the class, had rallied behind the Charan Singh's party, one of the reasons being that Charan Singh belonged to their caste. Brahmans cutting across the class barriers have generally perceived the Congress as party of Brahmans and "Nehru family (Brahmans)".[33] Caste, in fact, cuts across the religious boundaries too in certain circumstances. The Muslim electorate usually side in their choice with their caste counterparts in the Hindu community. While the Muslims traditionally opted for the Congress, their attitude mainly was determined by the question as to which party fielded a Muslim candidate. If Congress which they usually supported did not field a Muslim candidate, and Lok Dal did, quite large section of them deviated to Lok Dal. But if both parties fielded candidates from the same religious community, the Muslims voted/chose/supported the party/candidate on the lines of their caste counterparts among the Hindus. The Muslim OBCs join hands with the Hindu OBCs. We have observed that in Chhaprauli assembly constituency, the Muslim Jats join hands with the Hindu Jats in their support to the Lok Dal.

The dominant/high caste rural rich - both Hindus and Muslims - behave almost in a similar way with low caste rural poor (both Hindus and Muslims). But the competition between different dominant castes for the domination of district politics divides the rural rich on caste lines.[34] Even the rural rich of same caste get divided on gotra and family lines.[35] The division within the rural rich on the caste and family/gotra lines leads to "vertical" (hierarchical) mobilisation at the level of Panchayat elections. But once the elections are over, even the candidates whom the low caste rural poor voted behave in the usual way of the rural rich with them.[36] In Jat-dominated villages, the non-Jats belonging to the minority high castes like Brahmans and Banias face the same fate as do the low caste rural poor (rural rich from the low castes almost being absent in such villages) during the elections. Even the minority high castes irrespective of their class-position are not allowed to vote. Jaisinghpur, Chobla, Tilwara Sakin present such cases; Chobla and Tilwara Sakin are the den of booth-capturing by the Jats.[37] If the non-Jat high castes are allowed to vote in such villages, they would prefer to vote the same candidate/party along with the low caste. Caste even eroded the unity of the sugarcane growers.[38]

Caste, however, works as a unifying factor under certain circumstances. But this unifying function of the caste is restricted in its class appeal. During the agitation led by BKU, the caste functioned as a unifying factor in the initial phases of mobilisation. The khaps of different castes - Jats, Gujars, Rajputs and Muslims brought the rural rich who shared common class problems together on the class lines. But this unifying function of the caste remained confined to the rural rich; it could not bring the rural poor of different castes with them. The unifying function of caste was a short-lived one. It existed as long as the BKU movement remained apparently "apolitical", untouched by the tangible involvement of the professional political parties and leaders. But as soon as the political parties/leaders/the ruling party (Congress), the opposition (BKU's support to the Janata Dal in 1989 Chhaprauli by-election and 1989 general election, and Devi Lal and Chandra Shekhar) got linked with the BKU, it got divided on caste lines.[39]

To sum up, the root cause of the social, political and economic harassment/oppression/exploitation and domination/discord in the villages is the over-decisiveness of the relationships of one-sided dependence. But what is the way out? Can the problem be solved? Does the solution lie in the mobilisation of the rural poor into a class war/struggle against the rural rich? Or does it require the forceful intervention of the state which can provide some alternative, not only to the rural poor but also to the needy of the rural rich? The mobilisation of the rural poor into the class struggle is possible on those issues which involve the relationships of contradictions. The strikes of the lavas (agricultural labourers doing harvesting) on the issues of sheaves (wages in kind) in village Tilwara Sakin and of the buffalo-keepers on the issues of price and measurement of milk in village Jalalpur present examples of mobilisation involving the relationships of contradictions.[40] But that would not resolve the problem because of the over-decisiveness of the one-sided dependence. The resolution would lie only in the elimination of the relationships of dependence, particularly those of the one-sided dependence. This dependence can be eliminated by providing alternatives which would make them so independent that they do not have to cut fodder from the fields of the rural rich, defecate in their fields, make dung-cakes and throw garbage in the common land, and pass through the dolas (boundaries of fields). The harassment, oppression and the domination of the rural poor by the rural rich, which are commonplace in Meerut and in other districts of western UP, can be overcome only with the change in the pattern of relationships of dependence (particularly one-sided dependence). If the relations are of mutual dependence (contradictions), the rural poor can at least bargain. Any attempt by the state or other institutions (including court and police), short of changing the pattern of these relationships, cannot succeed in eliminating the harassment and oppression of the rural poor. When there does not exist a fully developed class of agricultural labourers, when there are large number of people without secure means of livelihood and when the land reforms are not the issue, what is the way out? How to change the pattern of such relationships and provide alternative to the rural poor? Is co-operative farming necessary for such an exercise? Or is industrialisation the solution to such problems? For any measure to be introduced, economic disparities of the whole country have to be taken into consideration. As to what has to be the alternative-co-operative farming, industrialisation, cottage industries or anything else, - requires serious deliberation and is beyond the scope of this book.

Notes

1. See Chapter III.
2. See Chapters IV.
3. See *Ibid* and Chapter VI, Section II.
4. See Chapter IV.
5. See *ibid.*, pp.70-71.
6. See *Ibid.*, pp.67-68, 72-73.
7. See Chapter III.
8. In an interview to Baruah, a senior knowledgeable leader from Meerut, who had been in the CPI, said: "Wage is not much of a question" of the rural poor in Meerut. Their main problems are "social justice". See Sanjib Kumar Baruah, *Getting a Fair Share : Politics and Poor in Rural India,* Ph.D. thesis, Chicago University, 1983, p. 322.
9. See Chapter III, and Table 10.
10. Even Baruah's interview with the leaders points out the absence of the union of the agricultural labourers and impossibility of their formation and success in Meerut district. Sanjib Kumar Baruah, *op. cit.*, pp. 315, 318.
11. See also *ibid.*, pp. 302, 308.
12. See Chapter V, Sections II and IV.
13. See Hamza Alavi, "Peasants and Revolution", in Kathleen Gough and Hari P. Sharma (ed.), *Imperialism and Revolution in South Asia,* New York, Monthly Review Press, 1973.
14. *Ibid.*, pp. 333-34; see pp. 293-95, for the description of terminology to categorise different sections of peasantry by Alavi.

15. See Eric R. Wolf, "On Peasant Rebellions", in Teodor Shanin (ed.), *Peasants and Peasant Societies,* Harmondsworth, Penguin, 1984.
16. See Chapters III and IV.
17. See also John Harriss, *Capitalism and Peasant Farming : Agrarian Structure and Ideology in Northern Tamil Nadu,* Bombay, Oxford University Press, 1982, pp. 266, 279-81, Harriss observes that the"middle peasants" are not as distinct in Tamil Nadu as in Pakistan (Alavi's field). Using Utsa Patniak's phrase he says, "they are organically connected to other classes". But as mentioned earlier, those middle peasants who are not self-sufficient in terms of the resources in Meerut depend not only on the landlords and rich peasants but also on the self-sufficient middle peasants (Harriss observes that the "middle peasants" in Northern Tamil Nadu depend on "the big farmers and merchants or financial capitalists"; he makes no mention whether they depend on the resourceful "middle peasants" or not.)
18. See Chapter V, Sections I and III; see also Chapter IV.
19. See Hamza Alavi, *op. cit.*, p. 332.
20. See Chapters IV and V.
21. See Chapter IV, Sections III and IV.
22. See Chapter VI, pp.132-37.
23. See Hamza Alavi, *op. cit.*, p. 33. John Harriss, *op. cit.*, pp. 238-44
24. See Chapter IV, pp.138-53.
25. See Chapter VI, Section II.
26. See *ibid.*, p149.
27. See Chapter III, Tables 11 and 12.
28. See Chapter IV.
29. See Chapter III, Tables 11 and 12.
30. On this point see also Sanjib Kumar Baruah, *op. cit.*, p.308.
31. See Chapter V, p.108.
32. See also Chapter VI, pp.134-37, 153-54.
33. See *ibid.* pp.153, 155.
34. See *ibid.* p.153.
35. During our fieldwork in 1984-85, we observed that the dominant castes mainly Jats and Gujars in seven and Chamars in one out of eight villages are divided into factions on the gotra (sub-caste) and family (minimal lineage) lines.
36. See Chapter VI. p.149
37. See *ibid. pp.*138-40.
38. See Chapter V. p.92.
39. See *ibid.* pp.100-101.
40. See Chapter IV, Section III.

Postscript

Post-Ayodhya Developments: Some Emerging Trends

I

Since October 1990, the rural areas of western UP have witnessed two unprecedented but related developments. First is the rise in the level of the consciousness of a Hindu identity among the Hindu agrarian classes. Second is the birth of communalism among a section of them. The consciousness of Hindu identity shows the existence of belongingness to the Hindu religion. Such a consciousness is not necessarily antagonistic to other religions. The consciousness of communalism on the other hand means not only existence of feelings of belonging to a particular religious community but also that of intolerance, contempt and hatred towards other religions and their followers. It may be noted that while both these tendencies have been existing in the urban areas and in the villages situated in their peripheries (for example Malyana village of Meerut district), it is perhaps for the first time that they have come to exist among the agrarian classes.[1]

These tendencies became more prominent, especially following the developments related to Ayodhya such as performance of the "kar seva" and firing at the "kar sevaks" during 30 October and 2 November 1990 (henceforth Ayodhya developments). The BJP and its allies, in fact, have been trying to politicise the consciousness of Hindu identity and generate communal feelings, especially from February 1986 onwards following the opening of the temple at Ayodhya through various ways to mobilise the Hindu opinion, *e.g.*, carrying Ram Shilas (bricks with Ram engraved on them), L.K. Advani's Rath Yatra, provocative speeches of Uma Bharati and Sadhavi Ritambhara, distributing cassettes of their speeches and video-cassettes showing police firing at "kar sevaks". These developments provoked communal riots in many parts of the country. Wide publicity given to the Ayodhya and pre-Ayodhya developments by the mass media, BJP and its allies played decisive role in strengthening the feelings of Hindu identity and communalism on the eve of 1991 general election in which the Bharatiya Janata Party emerged as the leading party followed by the Janata Dal with the Congress (I) faring poorly in UP.

We conducted the fieldwork in September 1991 in Jalalpur and Khanauda villages, and in Barwala village of Meerut and Muzaffarnagar districts respectively.[2] The former fall under Muzaffarnagar parliamentary and Sardhana assembly constituencies and the latter falls under Kairana parliamentary and Morna assembly constituencies. In these constituencies like most parts of Uttar Pradesh, BJP and the JD have emerged as the two main political parties. For the first time BJP has fared impressively in the villages. This evidently shows that the voters have deviated from their traditional political choice, *i.e.*, Congress (I) to BJP (Hindus) and JD (Muslims, some OBCs and SCs). In fact, field observation also shows that some of the supporters of JD in the last election have shifted to BJP. The BJP has cut into the social bases of both Congress (I) and JD. Whether the supporters of BJP/JD will shift to their traditional political choice is yet to be seen. It will depend on how the future processes will unfold themselves.

II

Unlike Congress and JD, the social base of BJP lies among the Hindus of all agrarian classes. This may be attributed to the following factors:

(i) The BJP's promise to construct the temple; rise in the level of consciousness of Hindu identity;

(ii) Dissatisfaction with Congress (I), and JD (Mandal Commission), and search for an alternative/giving BJP a chance, to "test" BJP;

(iii) Growth of Hindu Communalism;

(iv) BJP's strategy to win some castes/social groups; and

(v) changing nature of contradictions between the peasantry and the traders.

BJP's promise to construct the temple appears to be the most important factor which mobilised the support for it. Not only did the Hindu communalists respond to this issue, but also other sections of Hindus supported BJP.

Dissatisfaction with Congress (I) and JD among their traditional supporters was another reason for their support to BJP. The following statement is noteworthy in this regard:

> The Congress (I) never focused its attention on the villages. It has encouraged casteism and helped only specific castes - Mohammadans and scheduled castes. It has mainly encouraged corruption. I think BJP will show its interest in the problems of villages. The BJP will be helpful in weeding out corruption.
>
> [Small peasant, "loadman" in a factory at Meerut, Saini, Jalalpur].

The respondents expressed in the following way their will to "test" the BJP:

> We have tested all parties - Congress (I), JD, etc., in the past. (We) wanted to test BJP this time.
>
> [Brother of Thamba Barwala, head of unit of the Balyan Khap of Jats of Barwala, middle peasant].

Again, a poor peasant, potter of Jalalpur said:

> (We) want to test it (BJP) this time. We have tested others. Let us have the alternative also. We were Congress supporters till now.

Two issues - introduction of the Mandal Commission Report, and Mulayam Singh Yadav, the then Chief Minister's stand on the temple issue, particularly the firing on the "kar sevaks" - caused much resentment among the Hindus against the JD. While the Mandal Commission Report annoyed the high castes and evoked a mixed reaction among the OBCs, the stand on the temple issue, particularly the Ayodhya developments incensed almost every section of the Hindus. The JD's stand on the temple issue was perceived by the Hindus as an act of appeasement of the Muslims. As a result, the Hindus who had supported the JD in the 1989 election, voted for the BJP in 1991 election. The temple issue even overshadowed the Mandal Commission Report. Lower OBCs were mostly unaware of it and those who knew about it felt that it would help only the better off people. They preferred the temple issue (BJP) to the Mandal issue (JD). The landed/upper OBCs, on the other hand, were though influenced by the Mandal Commission and were appreciative of the JD/V.P. Singh, yet the temple issue overshadowed their political preference. The Gujars (the landed OBCs) of Jalalpur village, for example, supported the Hindu JD candidate Thakur Vijay Pal Singh for the Sardhana assembly seat because of the Mandal issue. But they supported BJP candidate Naresh Kumar Balyan for the Muzaffarnagar parliamentary seat because the JD candidate Mufti Mohammed Sayeed was a Muslim. These respondents would have voted for the JD candidate even for the parliamentary seat, had he been a Hindu. The BKU president Tikait's speech at the anti-Mandal rally at the Boat Club, on 2 October 1990[3] also indicates that the peasantry - the rural rich, mostly Jats - which supported BKU, were opposed to the Mandal Commission Report. Most of the respondents expressed dissatisfaction with the JD/V.P. Singh/Mulayam Singh Yadav, in the following ways:

Mandal Commission was also the reason for voting against the Janata Dal.
[Brother of Thamba Barwala].

We are not affected (impressed) by Mandal Commission Report. We want temple, not job.
[Middle peasant Registered Medical Practitioner, Saini, Jalalpur].

(Janata Dal/V.P. Singh/Mulayam Singh Yadav) got the Hindus butchered (during the firing at the kar sevaks). I saw the video film in our village.
[Village Pradhan, Middle Peasant, Saini, Jalalpur].

(We) wanted to defeat V.P. Singh because he got the Hindus killed by firing (at kar sevaks at Ayodhya) and by deploying army (there). Most of the people got annoyed with Janata Dal (because of firing).
[Middle peasant, Jat, Jalalpur].

We should have voted for Janata Dal because of the Mandal Commission, but (we) did not vote for Mufti (JD candidate) because he was a Muslim.
[Middle peasant, Gujar, Jalalpur].

A section of the Hindus (23 out of 64 Hindu respondents) supports the BJP mainly because this party claims to espouse the cause of the Hindus, and it is anti-Muslim. This section is very assertive, vocal and offensive in expression. This section believes that the Muslims had oppressed the Hindus in the past and they continue to do so wherever they are in majority; that the Muslims by nature are violent and inhuman (anti-Hindus); that they kill animals (cattle) and inflict atrocities on "human beings" (Hindus); that mosques are the centres of injecting anti-Hindu feelings among the Muslims and of inciting them against programmes like family planning; that a Muslim cannot be a trusted friend and that the minorities (Hindus) in Pakistan are highly discriminated while the minorities (Muslims) in India are appeased.

It must be noted that the views of Hindu communalists are based mainly on myths and rumours. When asked about the source of their views, a majority of the respondents replied "Suna Hai (heard about it)". Some of them, however, conceded that they saw video films on the firing on "kar sevaks", heard tape-recorded speeches of the BJP leaders and listened to some BJP leaders telling them about such things, while some others claimed to have either read or heard about the fatwa (religious decree) of Saiyed Imam Bukhari, the Imam of Jama Masjid, Delhi. This fatwa is said to have instigated the Muslims against the Hindus. It should be noted, however, that the Imam made no such decree. But he did, in fact, make an appeal to the Muslims to vote for the JD in the 1991 election.[4] The so-called fatwa which the respondents referred to was a concoction. Some of the respondents said that this fatwa was given to them by the BJP leaders. To prove that the Muslims are anti-Hindu and ruthless, the Hindu communalists cite the exploitation/oppression of the Hindu tenants in the past by the Muslim landlords and karindas. They project such exploitation/oppression which emanated from the nature of agrarian relations as that of the Hindus by the Muslims. The following statement by a Gujar middle peasant from Jalalpur represents such an opinion:

> Wherever the Muslims were in a position to exploit the Hindus, they did it. They plundered the Hindus wherever they were landlords. The karinda of zamindar used to take rent, forcibly take nazranas (allowances), used to place the leg of the cot on our hands and sit on it, and used to take away the milk of our buffaloes.

Similar was the reply of a Jat employee of an educational institution, hailing from Muzaffarnagar district. He said:

> In our village, the Muslim zamindars were ruthless. They sucked the blood of Hindus (tenants). How can we forget that? The Muslims are atrocious and ruthless.

Talking about the untrustworthiness of the Muslims, a medical practitioner, Deepchand Saini, ex-Pradhan of village Meethepur, and a local BJP leader, who plays an active role in organising the panchayat of Sainis in support of the BJP, said with reference to endogamy prevalent among the Muslims:

> The Muslims who cannot be faithful to their own sisters, how can they be faithful to our (Hindus') sisters.

Being contemptuous he further said:

> Muslims are inferior to Hindus in every sense: they are dirty, their food habits are also peculiar. For example, they eat cattle, which are treated by the Hindus with mercy (daya).

Another respondent, a Saini middle peasant from Jalalpur said that the mosques in the area carry the propaganda that - the family planning does not apply to the Muslims and it applies to Hindus only; that the Muslims who support family planning, will go to hell; that if a Muslim kills one hundred kafirs (Hindus), this act will be equal to doing one thousand Haj; that the Hindus who favour us (Muslims) should be circumcised and made the followers of Islam; and that beat a Hindu who opposes Muslims till he stops worshipping idols and accepts Islam.

The comparison between the minorities of Pakistan (Hindus) and those of India (Muslims) is also made. Some of the respondents also said that the Muslims have no right to stay in India as they have got Pakistan. They also said that since Hindus in Pakistan are second class citizens and are discriminated against, the Muslims in India should also be treated in the same way.

Apart from mobilising Hindus on the temple issue through the use of rumours and myths and by a strong publicity network, the BJP has adopted a well-thought-out policy to create its social base. Over the last 5-6 years the BJP has systematically been attempting to penetrate into various sections of society, *i.e.*, caste groups, peasantry, women, etc. Its attempt to woo the Sainis and Jats of Meerut and Muzaffarnagar districts is one such example.[5]

The Sainis of Jalalpur village did not have any idea of the BJP till the general election of 1984. For the first time it fielded Ram Pal Singh Saini for the Muzaffarnager parliamentary seat in this election. Sainis are an agriculturist caste, mostly belonging to the middle, small and poor peasants. They belong to the lower and other backward caste/class. In western Uttar Pradesh they form quite a substantial part of the population. In Sardhana assembly constituency of Meerut district which forms a part of Muzaffarnagar parliamentary constituency, they inhabit around 19 villages and form a large section of the electorate. They can determine the victory or defeat of a party, especially when majority of them are said to vote on similar lines. The BJP realised that the Sainis could become its potential supporters. As a result, the BJP leader Kalyan Singh, in a public meeting of the Sainis organised at Saini dharmashala (inn) at Meerut, on the eve of 1984 election, impressed upon the Sainis and promised them that the ticket for the Muzaffarnagar parliamentary seat would be given to a Saini. And Ram Pal Singh Saini was fielded as a BJP candidate.[6] Since then the Sainis of this region have been supporting the BJP. They identify themselves with the BJP because it fielded candidates from their caste if not in all constituencies, at least in some of the constituencies of western UP. The reasons for the growth of the social base of the BJP among the Sainis is explained by Kude Singh Saini, a leading member of the caste panchayats as follows:

> In 1984 BJP fielded Shri Ram Pal Singh Saini for the Muzaffarnagar parliamentary seat and the Sainis participated in that election overwhelmingly. The reason was that the BJP fielded a Saini as a candidate for the Lok Sabha seat in Meerut commissionary for the first time.[7] The BJP started this (fielding the Saini candidate for the parliamentary seat in the Meerut commissionery). So the intellectuals of Saini society[8] held special discussion on politics and the decision which emerged was we will support the party which takes us (Sainis) towards progress.

It is worth emphasising that most of the communal Hindus belong to the Sainis [out of 23 such respondents 14 (out of 17 of them) are Sainis]. They supported the BJP in 1984 election due to caste factor but it transformed into the support due to the communal feeling in 1991 election. During 1984-85 fieldwork none of the Sainis of Jalalpur village who supported the BJP in 1984 election for the Muzaffarnagar parliamentary seat had attributed their support to the factor of Hinduism or Hindu communalism. They had then supported the BJP solely because of the caste factor.[9] This shift during 1984-1989/91 points towards the integration of the Sainis into BJP's politics.

Like Sainis, Jats also supported BJP in 1991 election. They preferred the BJP Jat candidate to the Jat candidates of other parties. But they voted for the non-BJP Jat candidate, if the BJP candidate was a non-Jat.

The BJP's attempt to woo the Jat peasantry (predominantly) was first observed at the first rally of BKU at Meerut during January-February 1988. The BJP had then put up make-shift clinics for the farmers who had come to the rally. But the BKU rally at Meerut was marked by communal harmony.[10] The BJP came closer to the farmers/BKU in July 1990 and acted as their well-wishers when the Mulayam Singh Yadav government prevented BKU supporters and its leaders from holding a rally at Lucknow. The government lodged BKU leaders and supporters in different jails of Uttar Pradesh. The BKU was already annoyed with Congress. Now JD and its leadership also became its enemy. And with Ajit Singh not resigning from the ministry on the issue "the BKU was looking for an alternative to counter Ajit Singh, and Tikait found it in the BJP."[11] The BJP leader, Kalyan Singh, met the farmers in the jails of UP, the BJP activists provided the farmers with medical facilities and other basic amenities. This move was much appreciated by the farmers lodged in jails.[12]

Tikait maintained a diplomatic silence over the BKU's support or opposition to the BJP before the election. In this context he said: "*Hum To Chup Hain* (I am silent)." Nevertheless, he gave "enough indications (to his supporters) that he is (was) inclined to support the BJP."[13] He, in fact, denied having supported the BJP after the election was over.[14] But the convenor of the BJP election office in Muzffarnagar, Mahendra Acharya, confirmed "we (the BJP) even fielded candidates of his choice for two assembly seats".[15] There is no doubt that the BJP followed a well thought out strategy to penetrate the important social groups/classes of the villages of western Uttar Pradesh. Our interviews with the Jat respondents show that the BJP's strategy of fielding Jats has paid dividends. Though fielding candidates from a caste which dominates a particular constituency or forms the substantial section of population there is not a new phenomenon, the BJP did so when Hindus became more conscious of their Hindu identity and a section of them got communalised. In this regard the following statement of a Jat rich peasant from Barwala is noteworthy:

> This time even BJP gave tickets to the Jats. Had the BJP candidates been Banias, they would not have won. For the first time the BJP gave tickets to the farmers. Because of this reason the farmers voted for the BJP.

The support of BKU to BJP in 1991 election alienated the Muslim farmers from it.[16] The social base of BKU, which initially consisted of the market-oriented peasantry of different castes, had already been reduced to the Jats.[17] Alienation of Muslims further shrank it to mainly Hindu Jats; even the Muslim Jats (Mule Jats) got alienated. About this process a Mule Jat (Muslim Jat) middle peasant said:

> Muslims are not with the BKU. It is a party of *goondas*. Although the Muslims started getting alienated from BKU from the beginning, after the BKU started supporting BJP it became an additional factor for their alienation from the BKU.

The nature of contradictions between the peasantry and the traders has always affected the nature of political relationships between them. The traders have usually been perceived by the villagers and the peasantry in particular as the exploiting class. This perception when translated into the caste terms, has been seen as a contradiction between the peasant communities mainly Jats, Gujars, Tyagis, etc., on the one hand, and the Banias on the other. This contradiction (rural-urban divide) has been used during the mobilisation of the peasantry[18] at the time of conflict between the peasant-communities and Banias.[19] The progenitor of the BJP, the Jan Sangh, and until the 1991 election even the BJP were considered as the parties of traders, mainly the Banias, as well as of the capitalists. As a consequence, agrarian classes of Meerut and Muzaffarnagar never supported Jan Sangh and BJP. But during the 1991 election, the Hindu agrarian classes cutting across class lines supported the BJP. How could it be possible? While the temple issue played a subjective role, the changing nature of contradictions between the peasantry and traders played an objective role. The changing nature of contradictions between them had made an alliance possible. Till the introduction of the policy of direct procurement from the producers in the late 1960s[20] the economic contradictions between the peasantry and traders were sharp. The peasantry had to sell out main produce, *i.e.*, wheat, gur and other essential produce even when the existence of sugar mills had provided market for the sugarcane. In the process the peasants were exploited by the traders.

By providing one more alternative market alongwith the existing granaries (mandis), the introduction of the policy of direct procurement from the producers diluted the nature of economic contradictions between the peasantry and traders to the extent that the traders are no more considered as exploiters in the same sense as they were till the late 1960s. Moreover, emergence of some of the rich peasants and landlords as traders has further made it possible for a political alliance between the traders and farmers.[21]

The resentment which used to be against the traders earlier was now directed against the state. The development of capitalist tendencies and issues related to the capitalist economy, *i.e.*, remunerative price, subsidised inputs, etc., have become particularly the main issues since the 1970s. The following statement of a Gujar middle peasant from Jalalpur shows the extent of the dilution in the nature of contradictions between the peasantry and the traders:

> The BJP is no more a Bania party. Except Muslims all castes are in it.

A similar opinion was expressed by a middle peasant Saini of the same village:

> So long as it (BJP) was Jan Sangh, there was hierarchy. But with the BJP, there is no hierarchy. All Hindus are same.

The growing resentment among the Hindu peasantry against the non-BJP parties, the rising communalism and the well thought-out strategy of the BJP to win over the agrarian classes have made the latter overlook the cultural differences with the traders (urbanites) during the 1991 election. But the dilution of economic contradictions has not affected the cultural contradictions between the traders (urbanites) and the peasantry. In case of conflict between them and in case of the mobilisation of peasantry against the state, the cultural differences are made use of.[22] Even the diluted nature of economic contradictions are further projected as the main contradictions.

The BKU supporters who had supported BJP in 1991 election were dissatisfied with it, particularly after the Pilona and Dhaulri incidents[23] and the refusal of the Kalyan Singh's government to grant Tikait permission to hold a rally at Lucknow in September 1991. The BKU supporters who had no qualm in supporting the BJP during the election, have started rethinking it as a party of traders. The following statement of a Jat rich peasant of Barwala is noteworthy:

> BJP is a party of *Lalas* (Banias; traders) and capitalists. But this time the feelings of Hinduism clouded this fact.

III

There is a possibility that those who supported the BJP because of the consciousness of Hindu identity might not remain its sympathisers in future. Despite voting for the BJP and appreciating the BJP government's action against criminals, they are not very firm in their support in future, and they have started developing certain reservations about the BJP. They had supported it just out of religious feelings. They were incensed by the firing on the "kar sevaks" at Ayodhya. Some of them even are not very firm on construction of the temple; they feel that the temple should be constructed but at the same time the mosque should not be demolished. They also feel that if no solution is in the offing, the temple-mosque should be declared a national monument.

IV

Significantly the Ayodhya issue and the consequent growing trends of Hinduisation and communalisation have created feelings of helplessness among the Muslims. Though they are rarely willing to discuss the Ayodhya issue, yet it has provided them a new perspective on the political parties. They are no longer the supporters of the Congress Party. They hold it responsible for "sowing the seeds" of the Babari Masjid-Ram Janambhumi dispute. They perceive the BJP as anti-Muslims and the party of the Banias (traders) and capitalists. Having rejected both the Congress and the BJP, the largest section of Muslims have shifted their support to the JD. In the pre-1991 elections, the Muslims usually preferred a Muslim candidate to a Hindu candidate irrespective of his/her political party, while broadly remaining Congress supporters. But in the 1991 election in the Sardhana assembly seat they preferred a JD Hindu candidate to a Muslim Congress (I) candidate. For them V.P. Singh, Mulayam Singh Yadav and the JD mattered more than the Muslim of a non-JD party. V.P. Singh's decision to quit his prime ministership in order to "protect the mosque" following the withdrawal of support to the JD government by the BJP impressed the Muslims further and they have become the supporters of the JD. It is significant that despite the emergence of anti-Muslim feelings among a section of Hindus, the Muslims by and large were not found to be anti-Hindus. Their reaction, in fact, was a kind of giving justification to their disagreement on the temple-mosque issue. In this regard, the following statement of a landless wage labourer, Muslim oilman, of Khanauda is noteworthy:

> The fire was lit by the Congress (by opening the temple with the court order in 1986). Had the Congress (I) not got the temple opened, this situation would not have come. Advani is dividing people. It is for votes. V.P. Singh sacrificed his chair for protecting mosque. We will vote for V.P. Singh.

A similar opinion was expressed by a middle peasant, Mule Jat (Muslim Jat) of Barwala, who said:

> We are opposed to the BJP. If somebody wants to demolish the temple in the village, how will the Hindus feel? Even if nobody performs worship in the temple, the Hindus will be annoyed. If somebody attacks our homes, we will have to oppose it. The BJP is splitting the hearts. We oppose it. We are supporters of the Janata Dal.

In sum, the following tentative remarks can be made about the post-Ayodhya developments.

The Hindus whose level of consciousness of Hindu identity grew following the Ayodhya developments are no more firm in their support to the BJP and (many of them are not firm) in construction of the temple. The Hindu communalists, however, have not yet shown any sign of dilution in their communal consciousness. The survival of two types of consciousness among Hindus and stability of the social base of the BJP will depend on how the future political processes will unfold themselves.

Notes

1. Regarding this Mahendra Singh Tikait said "for the first time the Hindus and the Muslims got divided in the villages. And it has been because of the temple issue." Interview: Mahendra Singh Tikait, 14 September 1991.
2. This fieldwork was preceded by a visit to Jalalpur and Khanauda on the eve of election in May 1991. We held dialogues with 83 respondents from these three villages covering almost all agrarian classes belonging to the Jats, Brahmans, Gujars, Sainis, artisans and service castes and Muslims (19 respondents: Jats and lower castes).
3. See *The Time of India*, 3 October 1990.
4. Bukhari, in fact, clarified that his exhortation to the Muslims to vote

for the Janata Dal was not a religious decree (fatwa). Rather it was an appeal. See, *The Time of India*, 4 May 1991.

5. The following discussion is based on the interviews of Kude Singh Saini, 7 September 1991, Jalalpur; Kripal Singh Saini, 7 September 1991, Jalalpur; and Deep Chand Saini, 8 Setember 1991, Lawar. All three of them hail from the middle peasant families and are medical practitioners. They are some of the "intellectuals of Saini society". They played significant roles in the Saini Panchayats held at Lawar town on the eve of general elections of 1984, 1989 and 1991, which took decision to support the BJP.
6. Interviews: Kripal Singh Saini, 7 September 1991.
7. It is not factually correct. Ram Singh, a Saini, was given ticket by the Congress (I) for Roorkee assembly constituency of Saharanpur district in 1980 and 1985 elections.
8. Out of ten "intellectuals of Saini society", who are prominent among others, two are teachers, one is member of the management board of an inter-college; two are doctors, registered medical practitioners - one of them is ex-pradhan of his village, ex-district Minister (*Bhutpurva Jila Mantri*) BJP, Meerut district and ex-block Chairman (Purva Block Adhyaksha, Lawar-Mawana block). One is an advocate, one is member of the Town Area, Lawar, and two are pradhans of their respective villages. Most of them belong to the middle peasant families. Based on interview: Kude Singh Saini, 7 September 1991.
9. See Chapter VI, p.134.
10. See also Chapter V, p. 118, fn.88.
11. Interview: Tej Pal Singh, 19 May 1991.
12. Based on information of Dr. G.R. Malik who held discussion with the farmers of his village immediately after their release from jails, Nagla Shekhu, Meerut district. Interview: Tej Pal Singh 19 May 1991 and field work.
13. See Anita Katyal, "Tikait May Extend Support to BJP", *The Times of India*, 17 May 1991.
14. See *Sunday Observer*, 22 September 1991.
15. See Anita Katyal, *op. cit*. One of them, Sudhir Kumar Balyan became the co-operative minister of UP. Even the BJP candidate for Muzaffarnagar Lok Sabha seat, Naresh Kumar Balyan, belongs to Tikait's khap. Tikait told us that the BJP leaders had approached him on the eve of 1991 election for the BKU's support. But he kept quiet on the question if he put the condition to field the candidates recommended by him. Interview: Mahendara Singh Tikait, 14 September 1991.
16. Though Tikait denied that the BKU supported BJP, he conceded that the Muslim farmers got alienated from it. Interview: Mahendra Singh

Tikait, 14 September 1991. See also *The Sunday Observer*, 22 September 1991.

17. See Chapter VI, pp.100-101.
18. See Chapter V, pp.113-14, fn.55.
19. An example of this was a conflict which took place in Baraut town of Meerut. See Arun Sinha, "Peasant-Merchant Conflict", *Economic and Political Weekly*, Vol. XIII, No. 47, 25 November 1978.
20. For a discussion on the procurement policy, see R.I Duncan, *Levels, The Communication of Programmes and Factional Strategies in Indian Politics with Special Reference to the Bharatiya Kranti Dal and Republican Party of India in Uttar Pradesh and Aligarh District*, Ph.d. Thesis, University of Sussex, 1979, Chapter IV.
21. Based on Interview: Shanti Tyagi, 18 January 1992.
22. The ones wearing pant-shirts were described as the representatives of urbanites and traders. Personal observation at the rally of Meerut.
23. Almost immediately after the election Niloha and Dhaulri incidents occurred. These were two separate incidents/cases which had almost similar nature. The former occurred in Niloha village (during the last week of June and first two weeks of July 1991) of Meerut district and the latter in Dhaulri village (during the second and third week of July 1991) of Muzaffarnagar district. Some villagers were arrested in Niloha in connection with killing of two constables, and in Dhaulri the BKU supporters killed one constable and kept four others as hostages, who had gone to the village in connection with a controversial case of theft. The BKU led two successive agitations on these incidents. Niloha agitation petered out within three weeks, and in case of the Dhaulri incident an agreement was reached between the BKU and the UP co-operative minister, Sudhir Kumar Balyan. The intransigent attitude of the BJP government in UP about both these incidents annoyed Tikait with the BJP. Based on the fieldwork notes. See also *The Times of India*, 13 and 19 July 1991, and *Janasatta* (Hindi), 18 July 1991.

Bibliography

Ahmad, Z.A., *Ceiling on Agricultural Land,* New Delhi, Communist Party of India Publication, 1972.

Alam, Javeed, "Peasantry, Politics and Historiography: Critique of New Trend in Relations to Marxism", *Social Scientist,* vol. II, No. 2, February 1983.

———, *Domination and Dissent : Peasants and Politics,* Calcutta, Mandira, 1985.

Alavi, Hamza, "Peasants and Primordial Revolution" in Ghough, Kathleen and Sharma, Hari P. (ed.), *Imperialism and Revolution in South Asia,* New York, Monthly Review Press, 1978.

Aleav, L., "The Role of Landless Labourers in the North-Western Provinces of India in the Nineteenth Century", *New Indian Studies by Soviet Scholars,* Moscow, 1976.

Araquem da Silva, Ednaldo, "Measuring the incidence of Rural Capitalism : An Analysis of the Survey Data from North-East Brazil", *The Journal of Peasant Studies,* vol. 12, No.1, October 1984.

Baden-Pawell, B.H., *The Indian Village Community,* Delhi, Cosmo Publication, 1971.

———, *The Land Systems of British India,* vol. I, London, Oxford, 1972.

Bardhan, P.K., "The Agrarian Class Formation in India", *The Journal of Peasant Studies,* vol.10, No.1, October 1982.

Baru, Sanjaya, *The Political Economy of Indian Sugar : State Intervention and Structural Change,* Delhi, Oxford University Press, 1990.

Baruah, Sanjib Kumar, *Getting a Fair Share : Politics and Poor in Rural India*, Ph.D. thesis, Chicago University, 1983.

Basavapunniah, M., "On Contradictions : Antagonistic and Non-Antagonistic", *Social Scientist,* vol.11, 9 September 1983.

Batra, Surendra Mohan, *The Place of Livestock in the Social and Economic System of a Village in Haryana,* Ph.D. thesis, University of Delhi, 1981.

Baxter, Craig, "The Rise and Fall of the Bharatiya Kranti Dal", in Weiner, Myron and Osgoodfield, John (ed.), *Electoral Politics in Indian States : Party System and Cleavages,* Vol. IV, New Delhi, Manohar Book Service, 1975.

———, *District Voting Trends in India : A Research Tool,* New York, Columbia University Press, 1969.

Beteille, Andre, *Caste, Class and Power : Changing Patterns of Stratification in a Tanjore Village,* London, University of California Press, 1969.

——— *Studies in Agrarian Social Structure,* Delhi, Oxford University Press, 1974.

———, and Madan, T.N. (ed.), *Encounter and Experience : Personal Account of Field World,* New Delhi, Vikas, 1975.

Bhalla, G.S., "Transfer of Technology and Agricultural Development in India", *Economic and Political Weekly,* vol. XIV, No. 51, December 22-29, 1971.

———, *Changing Agrarian Structure in India : A Study of Green Revolution in Haryana,* Meerut, Meenakshi Prakashan, 1974.

Bhambhri, C.P., "Ideology and Political Parties in India", *Economic and Political Weekly,* vol. III, No. 16, April 20, 1968.

Bharati, Maharaj Singh, *Ganna Chini : Samasya Aur Samadhan* (Hindi), Lucknow, New Janata Press, n.d.

Blair, H.W., "Rising Kulaks and Backward Classes in Bihar : Social Changes in the late 70s", *Economic and Political Weekly,* vol. XIV, No.2, January 2, 1980.

Bliss, C.J. and Stern, N.H., *Palanpur : The Economy of an Indian Village,* Delhi, Oxford University Press, 1982.

Brass, P.R., *Factional Politics in an Indian State : The Congress Party in Uttar Pradesh,* Bombay, Oxford University Press, 1966.

Brass, P.R., *Language, Religion and Politics in North India,* Delhi, Vikas, 1974.

———, *Caste, Faction and Party in Indian Politics : Faction and Party,* vol. I, Delhi, Chanakya Publications, 1984.

———, *Caste, Faction and Party in Indian Politics : Election Studies,* vol. II, Delhi, Chanakya Publications, 1985.

———, "Introduction", "Institutional Factor of Technology : Land Grant Model and the Agricultural University at Pant Nagar", in Anderson Robert S., *et al.,* (ed.), *Science, Politics and Agrarian Revolution in Asia,* Boulder, Westview Press, 1982.

Breman, Jan, *Patronage and Exploitation : Changing Agrarian Relations in South India, Gujarat,* New Delhi, Manohar, 1979.

———, *Of Peasants, Immigrants and Paupers : Rural Labour Circulation and Capitalist Production in West India,* Delhi, Oxford University Press, 1971.

Brown, D.D., *Agricultural Development in India's Districts,* Cambridge, Harvard University Press, 1971.

Byres, T.J., "The Dialectic of India's Green Revolution", *South Asian Review,* Vol. 5, No. 2, January 1972.

———, "Political Economy of Technology Innovation in Indian Agriculture", in Anderson, Robert S., *et al.* (ed.), *Science, Political and Agrarian Revolution in Asia,* Boulder, Westview Press, 1982.

———, "Charan Singh, 1902-1987 : An Assessment", *The Journal of Peasant Studies,* No.2, January 1988.

Chauhan, B.R., *et al.* (compiled), *Doctoral Researches on Meerut Region* (Bibliography), published on behalf of the Library, Meerut University, Meerut, N.D.

Chayanov, A.V., *The Theory of Peasant Economy,* ed. and introduced by Thorner, Daniel, *et al.,* Homewood, Illinois, 1966.

Dasgupta, Biplab, "India's Green Revolution", *Economic and Political Weekly,* Annual Nos. 6-8, February 1977.

Dhanagre, D.N., "An Apolitist Populism", *Seminar*, December 1988.

Desai, D.K., "Intensive Agriculture District Programme : An Analysis of Results", *Economic and Political Weekly,* vol. IV, No. 26, June 28, 1969.

Druggett, Michel, "Marx on Peasants", *The Journal of Peasant Studies,* Vol. 2, No. 2, January 1975.

Duncan, R.I., "Party Politics and the North Indian Peasantry : The

Rise of the Bharatiya Kranti Dal in Uttar Pradesh", *The Journal of Peasant Studies,* Vol. 16, No.1, October 1988.

———, *Levels, The Communication of Programmes and Factional Strategies in Indian Politics with Special Reference to the Bharatiya Kranti Dal and Republican Party of India in Uttar Pradesh and Aligarh District,* Ph.D. thesis, University of Sussex, 1979.

Dutta, Ratna and Joshi, P.C. (ed.), *Studies in Asian Social Development,* Bombay, McGraw Hill, 1971.

Ennew, Judith, Hirst, Paul and Tribe, Keith, "Peasantry as an Economic Category", *The Journal of Peasant Studies,* Vol. 4, No. 4, July 1977.

Etinne, Gilbert, *Studies in Indian Agriculture : The Art of Possible,* Berkeley University Press, 1968.

———, *India's Changing Rural Scene : 1963-1979,* Delhi, Oxford University Press, 1968.

"Farmer Power", *Seminar,* December 1988.

Frankel, Francine R., *India's Political Economy, 1947-1977 : The Gradual Revolution,* Princeton, Princeton University Press, 1978.

———, and Rao, M.S.A. (ed.), *Dominance and State Power in India : Decline of a Social Order,* Vol. I, Delhi, Oxford University Press, 1989.

Frykenberg, R.E. (ed.), *Land Control and Social Struture in Indian History,* Madison, Madison University Press, 1969.

Garg, J.S., and Singh, T.R., "An Inquiry into the Pattern of Unemployment and Level of Earning of Landless Agricultural Labourers in Western UP", in Pandey, S.M. (ed.), *Rural Labour in India : Problems and Policy Perspectives,* Delhi, Shri Ram Centre for Industrial Relations, 1976.

Gibbons, D.S., *et al., Agricultural Modernization, Poverty and Inequality : The Distributional Impact of Green Revolution in Regions of Malaysia and Indonesia,* Hamsphire, Gower Publ., 1986.

Gopal S. (ed.), *Anatomy of a Confrontation : The Babri Masjid-Ramjanmabhumi Issue,* New Delhi, Viking, 1991.

Gupta, Dipankar, "Country-Town Nexus and Agrarian Mobilisation of Bharatiya Kisan Union as an Instance", *Economic and Political Weekly,* Vol. XXIII, No. 51, December 17, 1988.

Gupta, S.C., *Agrarian Relations and Early British Rule in India : A Case Study of Ceded and Conquered Provinces, (1801-1833),* Bombay, Asia Publishing House, 1963.

Harrison, Mark, "Chayanov and Marxists", *The Journal of Peasant Studies,* Vol. 7, No. 1, October 1979.

———, "The Peasant Mode of Production in Works of A.V. Chayanov", *The Journal of Peasant Studies,* Vol.4, No. 4, July 1977.

———, "Chayanov and the Economics of Russian Peasantry", *The Journal of Peasant Studies,* Vol. 2, No. 4, July 1975.

Harriss, Barbara, "Social Classes in Dryland Agriculture", in Harriss, Barbara, *et al.,* (ed.), *Exchange Relations and Poverty in Dryland Agriculture,* New Delhi, Concept, 1984.

Harriss, John, *Capitalism and Peasant Farming : Agrarian Structure and Ideology in Northern Tamil Nadu,* Bombay, Oxford University Press, 1982.

Hasan, Zoya, *Dominace and Mobilisation : Rural Politics in Western Uttar Pradesh, 1930-1980,* New Delhi, Sage Publications, 1989.

———, "Power and Mobilization : Patterns of Resilience and Change in Uttar Pradesh Politics", in Frankel, Francine R. and Rao, M.S.A. (ed.), *Dominance and State Power in India : Decline of a Social Order,* Vol.1, Delhi, Oxford University Press, 1989.

———, "Self-Serving Guardians : Formation and Strategy of the Bhartiya Kisan Union", *Economic and Political Weekly,* Special Article, Vol. XXIV, No. 48, December 2, 1989.

Hobsbowm, E.J., "Peasants and Politics", *The Journal of Peasant Studies,* Vol. I, No. 1, October 1973.

Husain, Imtiaz, *Land Revenue Policy in North India : The Ceded and Conquered Provinces, 1801-1803,* Calcutta; New Age Publishing, 1967.

Irfan Habib, *The Agrarian System of Mughal India, (1556-1707),* Bombay, Asia Publishing House, 1963.

Januzzi, F.T., *Agrarian Crises in India : The Case of Bihar,* New Delhi, Orient Longman Ltd., 1974.

Jetley, Surinder, *Impact of Development on Rural Women : A Case Study from Western UP* (Typescript), 1979.

Jha, S.N., *Leadership and Local Politics : A Study of Meerut District in Uttar Pradesh : 1923-1973,* Bombay, Popular, 1979.

Johnson, M.H., *Relations Between Land Settlements and Party Politics in Uttar Pradesh, 1950-1969 - With Special Reference to the Formation of the Bharatiya Kranti Dal,* Ph.D. thesis, University of Sussex, 1975.

Joshi, P.C., "Field Work Experience : Relived and Reconsidered : Agrarian Society in UP", *The Journal of Peasant Studies,* Vol.8, No.4, July 1981.

———, "Land Reform and Agrarian Change in India and Pakistan since 1947", I and II, *The Journal of Peasant Studies,* Vol.1, Nos. 3-4, April and July 1974.

Karbley, Basile, "Chayanov and the Theory of Peasantry as a Specific Type of Economy", in Throner, Daniel, *et al.* (ed.), *A.V. Chayanov: On the Theory of Peasant Economy*, Homewood, Illinois, 1966.

Karmarov, Eric, "Content and Principal Forms of the Evolution of Agrarian Relations in India", in *New Indian Studies by Soviet Scholars,* Moscow, 1976.

Kaushik, Susheela, *Election in India : Its Social Bases,* Calcutta, K.P. Baghchi and Co., 1982.

Kochanak, S.A., *The Congress Party in India : The Dynamics of One Party Democracy,* Princeton, Princeton University, 1968.

Kohli, Atul, *The State and Poverty in India : The Politics of Reform,* Cambridge, Cambridge University Press, 1987.

Kothari, Rajni, "The Congress 'System' in India", *Asian Survey,* Vol. IV, No. 2, December 1964.

Kotovsky, Grigory, *Agrarian Reforms in India,* New Delhi, People's Publishing House, 1964.

Lehman, D. (ed.), *Agrarian Reform and Reformism : Studies of Peru, Chile, China and India,* London, Faber and Faber, 1974.

Lenin, V.I., "Preliminary Draft Thesis on the Agrarian Question", in *Collected Works*, Vol. 31., Moscow, Progress Publishers, 1966.

———, "Philosophical Notebooks", *Collected Works,* Vol. 38, Moscow, Progress Publishers, 1966.

Lewis, Oscar, *Group Dynamics in a North Indian Village : A Study of Faction,* New Delhi, Programme Evaluation Organisation and Planning Commission, 1954.

———, *Village Life in North India,* New York, Vintage Reprint, 1965.

Maheshwari, Trilok Nath, *Social and Economic History of the Meerut District in the Nineteenth Century*, Ph.D. thesis, Meerut University, 1970.

Mann, S.A. and Dickinson, J.M., "Obstacles to the Development of a Capitalist Agriculture", *The Journal of Peasant Studies,* Vol.5, No. 4, July 1978.

Mathur, Y.B., *Rural Development in India,* National Institute of Hyderabad, 1985.

Metcalf, T.R., *Land, Landlords and the British Raj : Northern India in the Nineteenth Century,* Delhi, Oxford University Press, 1979.

———, "Landlords without Land : The UP Zamindars Today", *Pacific Affairs,* Vol. XI, Nos. 1-2, Spring and Summer 1967.

Michiel, Aruna Nayyar, "Agricultural Modernisation and Rural Inequality in the United States and India", in Anderson, Robert S., *et al.,* (ed.), *Science, Politics and Agrarian Revolution in Asia,* Boulder, Westview Press, 1982.

Misra, B.R., *Land Revenue Policy in the United Provinces under British Rule,* Benaras, Nand Kishore and Brothers, 1942.

Mittal, S.K., "The Role of Meerut College in Freedom Struggle of India", *Social Scientist,* Vol. 7, No. 4, November 1978.

Mohamed, Ahmad Hussain, *Urban Politics in India : A Study of Meerut City, 1876-1970,* Ph.D. thesis, Jawaharlal Nehru University, New Delhi, 1984.

Nadkarni, M.V., *Farmers' Movement in India,* New Delhi, Allied Publishers, 1987.

Narain, Iqbal, *et al., Election Studies in India : An Evaluation,* New Delhi, Allied Publishers, 1978.

Nayyar, Rohini, "Wages, Employment and Standard of Living of Agricultural Labourers in Uttar Pradesh", in *Poverty and Landless in Asia,* ILO, 1977.

Neale, W.C., *Economic Change in Rural India : Land Tenure and Land Reform in UP, 1800-1955,* New Haven, Yale University Press, 1962.

———, "Rural Development and Polity in India", *Pacific Affairs,* Vol. 53, No.4, Winter 1980-81.

Newell, Richard S., "Ideology and Realities : Land Redistribution in UP", *Pacific Affairs,* Vol.45, No.2, Summer 1972.

Omvedt, Gail, "New Movement", *Seminar,* December 1988.

———, (ed.), *Land, Caste and Politics in Indian States,* Delhi, Authors Guild Publications, 1962.

Ooman, T.K., *Social Transformation in Rural India : Mobilisation and State Intervention,* New Delhi, Vikas, 1984.

Orenstein, H., *Gaon : Conflict and Cohesion in Indian Village,* Princeton, Princeton University Press, 1965.

Pai, Sudha, *Changing Agrarian Relations in UP : A Study of the North-Eastern Areas,* New Delhi, Inter-India Publications, 1986.

Palmer, N.D., *Elections and Political Development : The South Asian Experience,* Durham, Duke Univeristy Press, 1975.

Patnaik, Utsa, *Agrarian Question and the Development of Capitalism in India,* Delhi, Oxford University Press, 1986.

———, *Peasant Class Differentiation : A Study in Method with Reference to Haryana,* Delhi, Oxford University Press, 1987.

———, "Class Differentiation within the Peasantry : An Approach to the Analysis of Indian Agriculture", *Economic and Political Weekly,* Review of Agriculture, Vol. XI, No. 39, September 25, 1976.

———, "Neo-Populism and Marxism : The Chayanovian View of the Agrarian Question and its Fundamental Fallacy", *The Journal of Peasant Studies,* Vol.6, No.4, July 1979.

———, (ed.), *Agrarian Relations and Accumulation : The 'Mode of Production' Debate in India,* Bombay, Oxford University Press, 1990.

Pradhan, M.C., *The Political System of the Jats in North India,* London, Oxford Univeristy Press, 1966.

Prasad, Pradhan H., "Rising Middle Peasantry in North India", *Economic and Political Weekly,* Vol.XV, Nos. 5-7, February 1980.

———, "Caste and Class in Bihar", *Economic and Political Weekly,* Vol. 14, Nos. 7-8, February 1979.

Proceedings of Kishan Sabha, Sardhana, Meerut, 1950.

Rahman, Atiur, *Peasants and Classes : A Study in Differentiation in Bangladesh,* Delhi, Oxford University Press, 1986.

Reeves, P.D., "The Politics of Order : Anti non-cooperation in the United Provinces, 1921", *Journal of Asian Studies,* February 25, 1966.

———, "Landless and Party Politics in the United Provinces, 1934-37", in Low, D.A. (ed.), *Soundings in Modern Asian History,* Berkley, Univeristy of California Press, 1968.

———, *et al., A Handbook of Election in Uttar Pradesh, 1920-1951,* Delhi, Manohar, 1975.

Retzlaff, R.H., *Village Government in India : A Case Study,* Bombay, Asia Publishing House, 1964.

Rosen, George, *Democracy and Economic Development in India,* Berkley University of California Press, 1967.

Rosselli, John, "Theory and Practice in India : The Background to the Land Settlement of 1833", *Indian Economic and Social History Review,* Vol. VIII, June 1971.

Rudolph, S.H. and Rudolph, L.I., "The Centrist Future of Indian Politics", *Asian Survey,* Vol. 20, No.6, June 1980.

———, *In Pursuit of Lakshmi : The Political Economy of the Indian State,* Hyderabad, Orient Longman, 1987.

———, *Modernity of Tradition : Political Development in India,* Bombay, Orient Longman, 1967.

Rukobo, Andries Matenda, *Land, Class and Dominance in North Western India : Social Structure, Agrarian Relations and Change in a Muzaffarnagar Village, Western Uttar Pradesh,* Jawaharlal Nehru Univeristy, Ph.D. thesis, 1980.

Saith, A., and Tankha, A., "Agrarian Transition and Differention of Peasantry : A Study of a West UP Village", *Econmic and Political Weekly,* Vol.7, No.4, April 11, 1972.

———, "Economic Decision-Making of the Poor Peasant Household", *Economic and Political Weekly,* Vol.7, Nos. 5-7, February 1972.

Saxena, N.C., "Caste and Zamindari Abolition in U.P.", *Mainstream,* Vol.XXIII, No.42, June 15, 1985.

Scott, James, C., *Weapons of the Weak : Everyday Forms of Peasant Resistance,* London, Yale University Press, 1985.

———, and Kerkvliet Tria, Bendit, J. (ed.), "Everyday Forms of Peasant Resistance in South Asia", *The Journal of Peasant Studies,* Special Issue, Vol. 13, No. 12, January 1986.

Shah, Ghanshyam, *Social Movements in India : A Review of the Literature,* New Delhi, Sage Publications, 1990.

Shahnin, Teodor, "The Peasantry as a Political Factor", *Sociological Review,* Vol.14, March 1966.

———, (ed.), *Peasant and Peasant Societies,* Harmondsworth, Penguin, 1971.

Shankar, Kripa, *Concealed Tenancy and its Implications for Equity and Economic Growth : A Study of Uttar Pradesh,* New Delhi, Concept Publishing Company, 1980.

Sharma, Udayan (ed.), *Violence Erupts,* New Delhi, Radhakrishna Prakashan, 1978.

Sharma, D.D., *Jivan Ke Mod* (Hindi), Delhi, 1962.

———, *Private Papers.*

Shrimali, P.D., *Agrarian Change, Agrarian Tensions, Peasant Movements and Organisations in Uttar Pradesh,* Lucknow University, Department of Economics (mimeographed), 1981.

Shrivastava, Saraswati, "Uttar Pradesh : Politics of Neglected Development", in Iqbal Narain (ed.), *State Politics in India,* Meerut, Meenakshi Prakashan, 1976.

Siddiqui, Asiya, *Agrarian Change in a North Indian State : Uttar Pradesh, 1819-1833,* London, Oxford University Press, 1973.

Sinha, Sanjay, "Economics vs. Stigma : Socio-Economic Dynamism of Rural Leather Work in UP", *Economic and Political Weekly,* Vol.21, No.24, June 24, 1986.

Singh, Baljit, *Next Step in Village India : A Study of Land Reforms and Group Dynamics,* Bombay, Asia Publishing House, 1961.

Singh, Charan, *Abolition of Zamindari: Two Alternatives,* Allahabad, Kitabistan, 1947.

———, *How to Abolish Zamindari : Which Alternative system to Adopt,* Allahabad, Superintendent Printing and Stationnery, UP, India, 1947.

———, *Agrarian Revolution In Uttar Pradesh,* Lucknow, Superintendent Printing and Stationery, UP, India, 1958.

———, *Joint Farming X-Rayed : The Problem and its Solution,* Bombay, Bharatiya Vidya Bhavan, 1959.

———, *India's Poverty and its Solution,* Bombay, Asia Publishing House, 1964.

———, *Land Reforms in UP and the Kulaks,* New Delhi, Vikas Publishing House, 1986.

———, *Private Papers.*

Singh, Harpal, *Panchayat Raj in Meerut District,* Ph.D. thesis, Agra University, 1973.

Singh, Jagpal, "Western Uttar Pradesh and Farmers' Movement", *Sancha* (in Hindi), April 1988.

Singh, J.D., "Grim Contest in West UP", *The Times of India,* December 6, 1979.

Singh, Kehar, *Farmers' Movement and Pressure Group Politics,* New Delhi, Deep and Deep Publications, 1990.

Singh, K.K., *Patterns of Caste Tensions : A Study of Intercaste Tensions and Conflicts,* Bombay, Asia Publishing House, 1955.

Singh, Rajendra, "Caste, Land and Power in UP", in Omvedt, Gail (ed.), *Land, Caste and Politics in Indian States,* Delhi, Authors Guild

Publications, 1982.

Sission, Richard, "Peasant Movements and Mobilisation : The Jats of Rajasthan", *Asian Survey,* Vol.9, December 1969.

Smith, R.E.F., "Note on Chayanov and Theory of Economy", *The Journal of Peasant Studies,* Vol.7, No.4, July 1980.

Stokes, Eric, *The English Utilitarians and India,* Delhi, Oxford University Press, 1982.

———, (ed.), *The Peasants and the Raj : Studies in Agrarian Society and Peasant Rebellion in Colonial India,* Delhi, Vikas Publishing House, 1978.

Sundarayya, P., "Class Differentiation within the Peasantry : Results of Rural Surveys in Andhra Pradesh", *Social Scientist,* Vol.5, No.8, March 1977, and No.9, April 1977.

Tai, Hung Chao, *Land Reforms and Politics : A Comparative Analysis,* Barkley, University of California Press, 1974.

The Bharatiya Kisan Union Documents :

———, *The Constitution of the Bharatiya Kisan Union* (in Hindi). Appellant, Bharatiya Kisan Union (Registered), Apolitical, Printer, Janata Printing Press, Shamli.

———, *35 Demandes of the Farmers* (Printed).

———, *The Amendment made by the BKU in 1987 to the Resolution Related to Dowry Passed at Soron Conference in 1950 and 1956* (in Hindi). Courtesy : Ch. Mahendra Singh Tikait, President, The BKU, Uttar Pradesh, n.d.

The Bharatiya Mazdoor Union Documents :

———, *Demand Charter : The Bharatiya Mazdoor Union* (Reg. No.42), Muzaffarnagar, Presented to the District Magistrate, Muzaffarnagar and the Chief Minister, Uttar Pradesh, August 16, 1990.

Thorner, Alice, "Semi-Feudalism or Capitalism? Contemporary Debate on Classes and Modes of Production in India", *Economic and Political Weekly,* Vol. XVII, No. 50, December 4, 11, and 18, 1982.

Thorner, Daniel, "Peasant Economy as a Category in Economic Histroy", in Thorner, Daniel, *et al.,* (ed.), *A.V. Chayanov : On the Theory of Peasant Economy,* Homewood, Illinois, 1966.

———, *The Agrarian Prospect in India,* New Delhi, Allied Publishers, 1976.

Whayton, Clifton R., "The Green Revolution : A Corn Utopia or Pandora's Box", *Foreign Affirs,* Vol.47, No.3, April 1969.

Whitcomb, Elizabeth, *Agrarian Conditions in Northern India : The United Provinces Under British Rule, 1860-1900*, Vol. I, New Delhi, Thomson Press, 1971.

Wills, Ian, "Green Revolution and Agricultural Employment and Income in Western UP", *Economics and Political Weekly*, Vol. VI, No.13, March 27, 1971.

Wolf, R. Eric, "On Peasant Rebellions", in Shanin Teodor (ed.), *Peasants and Peasant Societies*, Harmondsworth, Penguin, 1984.

Zaheer, M. and Gupta, Jaydeo, *The Reorganisation of Government of Uttar Pradesh : A Study of State Administration*, New Delhi, S. Chand & Co., 1970.

OFFICIAL PUBLICATIONS

Atkinson, E.T., *Statistical Descriptive and Historical Account of Meerut District*, Allahabad, North-Western Provinces Government Press, 1876.

———, *Statistical Descriptive and Historical Account of Muzaffarnagar District*, Allahabad, North-Western Provinces Government Press, 1876.

Cenus of India, United Provinces of Agra and Oudh, Vol. XVIII, Part II, 1931; *Meerut District Census Handbook, Uttar Pradesh Census Handbook*, 1951, 1961, 1971 and 1981, Allahabad, Superintendent Printing and Stationery.

Cooke, C.H., *Final Settlement Report of Meerut District*, Allahabad, Superintendent Printing and Stationery, 1940.

Data Collected from Ceiling Section, Collectorate Office of the District Magistrate, Meerut.

District Statistical Handbooks, Meerut (in Hindi), Economics and Statistics Officer, State Planning Institute, Economics and Statistics Division, Lucknow, UP, 1974,1975, 1976, 1977, 1978, 1979, 1980, 1982, 1983 and 1989.

Elliot, M.H., *Report on the Settlement of the District of Meerut : 1935-40*, Publications details not available.

Imperial Gazettes of India, Vol.XVII, New Edition, London, Oxford at Clarendon Press, 1908.

Joshi, E.B. (ed.), *Uttar Pradesh District Gazetteer, Meerut*, Lucknow, Department of Uttar Pradesh District Gazetteers, 1965.

Nevill, H.R., *Meerut - A Gazetteer being vol. IV of Agra and Oudh,*

Lucknow, Government Branch Press, 1922.

Reports of the Election Commission of India, 1952, 1957, 1962, 1967, 1969, 1971, 1980, 1984 and 1985.

Reports of the Sugar Enquiry Commission, The Government of India, 1965.

Report of the United Provinces Provincial Banking Committee, 1929-30, Vol. II, Allahabad, Superintendent Printing and Stationery, 1930.

Singh, K.L., *Historical and Statistical Memoirs : Zila Bulandshahr,* Allahabad, Printed at the North Western Privinces Press, 1874.

Zia-ur-Rub, *Report on the Industrial Survey of the Meerut District of Uttar Pradesh,* Allahabad, Superintendent Printing and Stationery, 1923.

Index